SMALL BUSINESS MANAGEMENT

How to Start *and Stay* in Business

Richard J. Stillman

University of New Orleans

Little, Brown and Company
Boston   Toronto

For my family

Darlene Ellen	Deborah Lingoni	Grace Joseph
Richard Joseph II	Ellen Darlene	Philip Joseph
Kathleen McKinley	Helen Fisher	Shannon Marie
Thomas Slater	Roy Fisher	

Library of Congress Cataloging in Publication Data

Stillman, Richard Joseph
    Small business management.

    Bibliography: p.
    Includes index.
    1. Small business--Management.   2. New business
enterprises--Management.   I. Title.
HD62.7.S83   1982   658'.022   82-4614
ISBN 0-316-81608-6
ISBN 0-316-81609-4 (pbk.)

Copyright © 1983 by Richard J. Stillman

Library of Congress Catalog Card No. 82-4614

ISBN 0-316-81608-6
ISBN 0-316-81609-4   {PBK.}

9   8   7   6   5   4   3   2   1

ALP

Published simultaneously in Canada by Little, Brown & Company (Canada) Limited
Printed in the United States of America

CREDITS: *pp. 19 –21, Exh. 2-2:* From the book *Do It Yourself Contracting to Build Your Own Home,* 2nd
ed., by Richard J. Stillman. © 1981 by Richard J. Stillman. Reprinted by permission of Chilton Book Co.,
Radnor, PA 19087. *p. 58, excerpt:* From Douglas R. Sease, "Schools Again Offer Courses on Production,"
The Wall Street Journal, January 26, 1981. Reprinted by permission of The Wall Street Journal, © Dow Jones
& Company, Inc., 1981. All Rights Reserved. *p. 60, Exh. 4-2:* From the book *Your Personal Finance
Planner* by Richard J. Stillman. © 1981 by Richard J. Stillman. Reprinted by permission of Prentice-Hall,
Inc., Englewood Cliffs, N.J. 07632.

Preface

"I am concerned about the high failure rate of new business ventures. What can I do to have a better chance of success?" This question is asked frequently at the beginning of my management seminar courses. A study of small business failures points up the fact that poor management is the primary reason for such failures. The purpose of this book is to enhance the success rate of entrepreneurs by providing current information on management.

This book takes a fresh approach in discussing all aspects of owning a small business. It is a practical text that points out how management concepts can be used by anyone who desires to start, operate, and finance a business. Emphasis is placed upon how to make wise decisions based on an understanding of the decision-making process; my management model appears in each chapter to assist the reader in understanding this process. The first two chapters explain how the entrepreneur sets goals, understands the functions he or she must perform, locates available resources, and defines areas of responsibility. Succeeding chapters discuss each of these areas of responsibility in detail and the importance of understanding their interrelationship.

This book is concise but covers all important areas pertaining to starting and staying in business. The audience for this text includes two-year colleges offering small business management courses; four-year universities and colleges with open admissions policies; continuing education programs at schools, colleges, and universities — both credit and noncredit courses; and management development seminars. The style, size, and format also make this book well suited for the individual who wishes to start his or her own business.

ACKNOWLEDGMENTS

I would like to thank a number of organizations and their specialists in the field of small business for their assistance: the Small Business Administration, banks, savings and loan associations, insurance companies, real estate firms, and departments of the federal, state, and local governments.

I also want to express special appreciation to my family. My wife, Darlene, contributed valuable administrative assistance. Thomas, a law student at the University of Puget Sound, furnished excellent advice on the legal aspects of the text. Ellen provided an insight to students' small business interests. Richard, our eldest son, an author and a professor at George Mason University, reviewed the manuscript and offered helpful suggestions.

To Helen and Roy Fisher, successful entrepreneurs, I express appreciation for their many years of wise counsel in the business-management area. Their delightful apartment provided an atmosphere for creative writing. Becky Copley has been indispensable as my assistant for the past three years, and without her this book would have been delayed.

I wish to thank my reviewers for their excellent recommendations: Margaret Shearon, M. I. Veiner, Inc., Fort Lauderdale, Florida; Thomas M. Tworoger, Nova University and President, Kenworth Truck of South Florida; and Neil J. Humphreys, Virginia Commonwealth University.

The staff at Little, Brown also deserves a note of appreciation and thanks for their splendid assistance. This recognition goes to Alex Greene, my editor; Dana Norton, the production editor, who went the extra mile; Billie Ingram, who assisted at all stages of production; Victor Curran, who designed the book and coordinated the art program; and Timothy J. Kenslea, who copyedited the manuscript. It is apparent that publication of a good book requires a team effort and I was fortunate to be part of that team.

Finally, in the event that there are errors or shortcomings in this work, the responsibility is mine. Please inform me of needed revisions or modifications for future editions.

Contents

Part II: Areas of Responsibility   37

Chapter 3: Legal Requirements   38

Chapter 4: Production   56

Part III: The Personal Factor — You   153

Chapter 9: Leadership   154

Part I
Overview of Management

Chapter 1
Understanding Your Management Responsibilities

Chapter 2
Functions of a Manager

The first two chapters of this book provide a basic understanding of what management is all about. They tell the person who wants to start or improve a small business what must be done and how it can be done efficiently. Chapter 1 presents a scientific approach to the establishment of a small business, placing you, the reader, in the position of a business manager responsible for all your affairs and decisions. It goes on to chart the parameters of small business, stressing the interrelatedness of the various components of management. For easy reference, all the components of management are summarized in a schematic presentation, Exhibit 1-1 on page 2. An explanation of how to interpret this diagram is provided on pages 3 – 8. In order to emphasize the interrelatedness of these components, all succeeding chapters contain a similar diagram, adapted to illustrate how each component fits into one's overall management responsibilities. Chapter 2 highlights the three functions every business owner must perform in order to succeed: planning, organizing, and controlling. It also provides examples of how small businesses perform these functions.

Chapter 1
Understanding Your Management Responsibilities

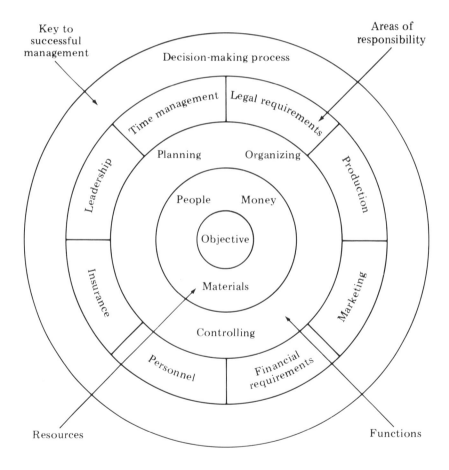

Exhibit 1-1 Stillman's Small Business Management Model: An overview of the five major components of management

> The manager has the task of creating a true whole that is larger than the sum of its parts, a productive entity that turns out more than the sum of the resources put into it.
>
> — Peter F. Drucker

INTRODUCTION

"Lack of managerial know-how is the biggest reason for small business failures." I have heard this comment on numerous occasions from members attending my management seminars. A recent Dun & Bradstreet report highlighted this problem.[1] The exhibit on pages 4–5, reprinted from this report, indicates that over 90 percent of business failures are attributable to inadequate management. The remainder are the result of neglect, fraud, disaster, or unknown factors. An examination of this exhibit points out that poor management is "evidenced by inability to avoid conditions which resulted in inadequate sales, heavy operating expenses, receivables difficulties, inventory difficulties, excessive fixed assets, poor location, competitive weakness, and other apparent causes."[2]

The purpose of this book is to provide managerial information that will be useful to anyone who wants to start a business or improve conditions in an established business. An understanding of management can be an important factor in preventing poor performance. This chapter provides an overview of what management is all about; the succeeding chapters explain in detail the responsibilities of a manager. Let us first look at a definition of management and a model to help explain the material presented in this book.

DEFINITION AND MODEL

What is management? It is the achievement of objectives by the effective use of resources (people, money, and materials). It involves planning, organizing, and controlling by working within a framework of line, staff, and service responsibilities to arrive at sound decisions.

The management model (Exhibit 1-1) will help to explain this definition. In addition, examples will be presented throughout the book to enable you to relate the management model to real-world situations. *Study the model carefully.* It presents a graphic overview of the five major components of management: *objective*; *decision-making process*; *functions*; *resources*; and *areas*

Exhibit 1-2 Causes of 6,619 business failures

	Percent					
	Manu-facturers	Whole-salers	Retailers	Con-struction	Com-mercial services	All
Underlying causes						
Neglect	0.8	0.8	0.7	0.9	1.6	0.9
Fraud	0.8	1.1	0.4	0.3	0.6	0.5
Lack of experience in the line	8.3	9.6	16.2	7.4	9.4	11.9
Lack of managerial experience	13.4	11.2	15.8	18.4	15.4	15.3
Unbalanced experience"	17.6	20.4	18.3	16.6	18.1	18.1
Incompetence	54.6	52.7	42.4	49.7	44.1	46.9
Disaster	0.6	0.2	0.7	0.4	0.6	0.6
Reason unknown	3.9	4.0	5.5	6.3	10.2	5.8
Total	100.0	100.0	100.0	100.0	100.0	100.0
Number of failures	1,013	740	2,889	1,204	773	6,619
Average liabilities per failure	$867,450	$467,257	$269,107	$272.739	$421,321	$401,270
Apparent causes						
Due to						
Bad habits	0.2	0.4	0.2	0.3	0.4	0.3
Poor health	0.4	—	0.2	0.4	0.6	0.3
Marital difficulties	—	0.1	0.1	—	0.3	0.1
Other	0.2	0.3	0.2	0.2	0.3	0.2

On the part of the principals, reflected by						
Misleading na.. ? [a]	—	—	—	—	—	—
False financial statement	0.1	0.3	0.1	0.1	0.1	0.2
Premeditated overbuy	0.1	—	—	0.1	0.4	—
Irregular disposal of assets	0.2	0.3	0.2	0.1	0.6	0.1
Other	0.1	—	—	0.1	—	0.5
Evidenced by inability to avoid conditions which resulted in						
Inadequate sales	57.0[b]	52.7[b]	47.3[b]	59.6[b]	61.2[b]	61.0[b]
Heavy operating expenses	24.3	32.2	31.5	17.0	16.5	36.1
Receivables difficulties	7.7	6.2	13.1	2.4	12.8	13.9
Inventory difficulties	6.7	0.9	1.5	10.6	8.5	5.1
Excessive fixed assets	2.7	3.6	1.5	2.4	0.9	5.4
Poor location	1.5	1.4	0.2	2.8	0.3	0.1
Competitive weakness	21.2	22.4	32.2	19.4	15.9	16.2
Other	1.3	1.3	1.1	1.2	1.6	1.4
Some of these occurrences could have been provided against through insurance						
Fire	0.2	0.1	—	0.3	0.1	0.1
Flood	0.1	0.1	0.1	0.2	—	—
Burglary	0.0	—	—	0.0	—	—
Employees' fraud	0.0	0.1	—	—	—	—
Strike	0.1	—	0.1	—	0.1	0.2
Other	0.2	0.3	0.2	0.2	—	0.3
Percent of total failures	100.0	11.7	18.2	43.6	11.2	15.3

[a] Experience not well rounded in sales, finance, purchasing, and production on the part of the individual in case of a proprietorship, or of two or more partners or officers constituting a management unit.

[b] Because some failures are attributed to a combination of apparent causes, the totals of these columns exceed the totals of the columns for *Underlying Causes*.

Source: Business Failure Record. New York: Dun & Bradstreet, Business Economic Division, 1981, pp. 12–13. Reprinted by permission.

of responsibility. The succeeding chapters refer to the model to emphasize the interrelatedness of all the components of management. This approach will enable you to comprehend the totality of management, and this knowledge of how to run a business will contribute to your success.

OBJECTIVES

Management must establish written goals for its business. This goal-setting exercise enables an organization to direct its efforts toward achieving desired ends. The objectives must be realistic, and should be adopted only after appropriate thought has been given to available resources (people, money, and materials) and to the other components of the management model. The objective should provide answers to the questions of what, when, where, how, and why. If you are a newly established contractor of custom home construction, for example, you may determine that your primary objective is to build elegant homes in prime residential areas, using first-quality subcontractors and materials, and to complete each home within one year at a 15 percent profit margin. (See Exhibit 1-3.)

Establishing a primary objective also means you will need to develop sub-objectives or sub-goals. The more complex the enterprise, the more involved these sub-goals become. You should also develop short-, medium-, and long-term objectives. As the model makes clear, objectives are at the heart of management. All managerial efforts should be concentrated on achieving objectives. It is essential, however, that the various objectives be appropriate, and be modified as conditions change.[3]

RESOURCES

Once you establish your objectives, it will be necessary to determine what resources are required to achieve your goals most efficiently. These resources can be summed up as: people, money, and materials. Any business, to operate effectively, requires qualified people, adequate financing,

Exhibit 1-3   Objective of a builder of custom homes

Question	Primary objective
What	build custom homes
When	within one year
Where	in prime residential areas
How	use first-quality subcontractors and materials
Why	earn 15 percent net profit

and equipment. If you cannot provide adequate resources it will be necessary to modify the primary objective and sub-objectives.

In the home-building field, for example, you might use the three resources as follows: *people* means one full-time individual who has overall responsibility — you, the manager. In addition, you will draw on forty to fifty different subcontractors and suppliers from time to time, as well as the counsel of a lawyer, a banker, an accountant, and knowledgeable people in the home-building industry. *Money* is needed to pay the subcontractors and all other expenses. *Materials* are lumber, roofing, concrete, sheetrock, and a multitude of other supplies. In essence, you process the three inputs of people, money, and materials and the result, the output, is a completed home.

FUNCTIONS

The third circle in the management model refers to the three basic management functions: planning, organizing, and controlling. To effectively accomplish an objective, a manager must be capable of performing these three functions:

1. *Plan* what is going to be done.
2. Implement the plan, using an effective *organization.*
3. Check on what has been accomplished — exercise *control.*

As a home builder you would use a budget to serve as both a *planning* document and a means of *control* (checking) to determine how actual expenditures compare with the estimate. The actual building of the house encompasses the *organizational* or "doing" function. These three functions apply to every type of business activity from the smallest to the largest.

AREAS OF MANAGERIAL RESPONSIBILITY

In addition to establishing objectives, determining available resources, and understanding managerial functions, you must be familiar with the areas of responsibility you will need to work in to accomplish your objectives. Management must decide what line, staff, and service areas are needed to achieve its goals efficiently. A corporation may have its line areas structured to include vice-presidents for production, sales, and finance. In home building, the *line* includes subcontractors like carpenters, plumbers, electricians, and roofers. These people are the "doers" and make up the operational aspect of management.

In addition to the line responsibilities, there is a need for *staff* responsibilities. These are the activities performed by people who help the line people accomplish their various assignments. In major corporations, the staff would consist of such areas as public relations, research and development, personnel, and legal. In a small business, as a newly established home builder, you could perform the vast majority of the staff work yourself: keep the financial records, be the personnel manager, and provide your own research. You might, however, hire a lawyer part-time to do the legal work, and you might rely on a family member or friend for secretarial, clerical, and administrative help.

Service activities include custodial, maintenance, and storage duties. In all organizations it is necessary to perform these services. In our home-building example, this service function may be performed by you the owner or a member of your family. You might sweep up the premises, run errands for the subcontractors, carry refuse to the dump, and perform a multitude of other menial but vital tasks. In contrast, major corporations like General Motors hire thousands of people in this category. The federal government has one huge agency in Washington, D. C. that performs such functions — the General Services Administration.

The type of line, staff, and service activities will vary with the specific organization concerned. But, regardless of size, every business must perform these line, staff, and service duties. Each of these significant areas will be discussed in subsequent chapters.

DECISION-MAKING PROCESS

The final ring (the key to successful management), which is portrayed in Exhibit 1-1, is the decision-making process. In the decision-making process you may draw on all other components of the management model to arrive at sound solutions. In making management decisions, you should keep these questions in mind:

1. What is the objective or problem?
2. Are the necessary facts available to make a sound decision?
3. What are the alternatives?
4. Has the most profitable alternative been selected?

GUIDELINES

During your career as a small business manager you may wish to consider the following guidelines, which are emphasized throughout this book.

○ Time is a valuable commodity; employ it to your advantage. A management approach to any project minimizes the time required to complete it.

○ Be flexible and imaginative. In our dynamic society, have a management strategy attuned to the times — present and future.

○ Make your approach to management a participatory program. Encourage contributions from all members of your organization.

○ Go first class in securing personnel and equipment. The success of an organization rests primarily with its people. Get the best. Similarly, higher priced materials and quality workmanship cost less in the long run — you will have fewer repairs, breakdowns, or delays and a more reliable product or service.

○ Emphasize sound financial management. Heavy borrowing can produce unusual profits, but leverage is a two-edged sword. In times of crisis it can bankrupt a firm.

○ Minimize your costs. Eliminate middlemen wherever possible.

○ Deal only with reputable organizations that have good track records of achievement. There are many reliable firms that have been successful for a long time. Patronize companies that stand behind their work.

○ Pay all company bills by check and in time to take advantage of all available discounts. You can now get an interest-bearing checking account, but keep as little money as possible in your checking account in order to secure higher interest rates from other investments. Still, don't jeopardize your banking relationship by going below any minimum balance that may be required. A friendly banker is very important.

○ Your company should be viewed as a major growth investment. Earnings should be reinvested annually for its further expansion.

○ Your organization must be constantly revitalized to survive and expand. This means frequent exposure to the latest developments. Read pertinent journals. Attend professional meetings and management development programs.

○ Capitalize on the experience of your employees. Use their talents and let them do the things they do best.

○ Do not let the magnitude of a management project frighten you. Look at the various tasks to be accomplished. Then break each task down to its smallest components. From such a perspective each job becomes relatively easy to complete.

○ Make every effort to get along with people. This includes competitors, stockholders, unions, government officials, the media, the public, suppliers, and bank officials. All can be a big help — or a major hindrance.

○ The energy shortage will worsen in the years ahead. Before making an important decision you should have the necessary facts and future projections on energy costs. For example, before constructing a building for your business, you should estimate costs for heating and cooling with gas, electricity, and solar energy.

○ You must weigh inflation carefully in arriving at all significant decisions. For example, in selecting a retirement program for yourself and your employees, you should find out if annual cost-of-living increases comparable to the rise in the Consumer Price Index will be provided.

○ It pays to be in good physical and mental condition. You may be working ten to twelve hours each day, or longer, and the work may be physically demanding. You will also encounter mental stress that requires being tough-minded, as, for example, in negotiations. To cope with these mental and physical challenges, you should have an annual physical examination (more frequent if necessary) and join a gym or health club for regular physical activity.

○ An understanding of the American way of life is a cornerstone of successful management. A democratic environment with a free enterprise system provides a fertile climate for success, and this is the framework within which you will be working. Keep yourself well informed about current political and economic issues and events.

○ Have faith in yourself! Be willing to work your way to success. The American way of life provides the opportunity but you must supply the determination. This determination is expressed well in the following anonymous poem I read as a young man:

It's All in the State of Mind

If you think you are beaten, you are,
If you think you dare not, you don't;
If you like to win, but you think you can't
It's almost a cinch you won't.
If you think you'll lose, you've lost,
For out in the world you find
Success begins with a fellow's will;
It's all in the state of mind.
Full many a race is lost
Ere ever a step is run;
Any many a coward fails
Ere ever his work's begun.
Think big and your deeds will grow,
Think small and you'll fall behind,
Think that you can and you will;
It's all in the state of mind.
If you think you're outclassed, you are;
You've got to think high to rise;
You've got to be sure of yourself before
You can ever win a prize.

Life's battles don't always go
To the stronger or faster man,
But sooner or later the man who wins
Is the fellow who thinks he can.

MANAGERIAL DUTIES

Who is responsible for the management of an organization? It may be the owner or owners of the business, or people who are hired by the owners to be the managers. In either case, their duties include accomplishment of the tasks presented in this chapter:

1. Establishing appropriate objectives.
2. Using resources effectively.
3. Planning, organizing, and controlling.
4. Understanding their areas of responsibility.
5. Finding appropriate solutions to problems by using the decision-making process.
6. Applying the managerial guidelines to various situations.

To fulfill these duties, the manager must be an effective leader. The subject of leadership will be discussed in chapter 9.

THE SMALL BUSINESS ADMINISTRATION

The Small Business Administration (SBA) can be of valuable assistance to you when you are starting your own company or when you require advice while in business.[4] Make full use of this excellent resource.

The Small Business Administration is an independent federal agency created by Congress in 1953 to assist, counsel, and champion the millions of American small businesses. In close coordination with other federal agencies and financial, educational, professional, and trade institutions and associations in the private sector, the SBA provides prospective, new, and established members of the small business community with financial assistance, management training and counseling, and help in getting a fair share of government contracts through more than one hundred offices in all parts of the nation. To provide quick service, the SBA had delegated decision-making authority in the vast majority of its programs to field offices. Take the time, if possible, to visit the office nearest you. SBA representatives can provide much helpful advice at no cost. (See Exhibit 1-4 for a list of their locations.) To find the SBA office in your city, look in the telephone directory under "U. S. Government, Small Business Administration."

The SBA places special emphasis on improving the management ability of small business owners and managers. Its Management and Technical

Exhibit 1-4 Locations of SBA field offices

Agana, GU	Dallas, TX	Los Angeles, CA	Rochester, NY
Albany, NY	Denver, CO	Louisville, KY	St. Louis, MO
Albuquerque, NM	Des Moines, IA	Lubbock, TX	St. Thomas, VI
Anchorage, AK	Detroit, MI	Madison, WI	Sacramento, CA
Atlanta, GA	Eau Claire, WI	Marquette, MI	Salt Lake City, UT
Augusta, ME	Elmira, NY	Marshall, TX	San Antonio, TX
Austin, TX	El Paso, TX	Melville, NY	San Diego, CA
Baltimore, MD	Fairbanks, AK	Memphis, TN	San Francisco, CA
Biloxi, MS	Fargo, ND	Milwaukee, WI	Santa Ana, CA
Birmingham, AL	Fresno, CA	Minneapolis, MN	Seattle, WA
Boise, ID	Greenville, NC	Montpelier, VT	Shreveport, LA
Boston, MA	Harlingen, TX	Nashville, TN	Sioux Falls, SD
Buffalo, NY	Harrisburg, PA	Newark, NJ	Spokane, WA
Camden, NJ	Hartford, CT	New Orleans, LA	Springfield, IL
Casper, WY	Hato Rey, PR	New York, NY	Statesboro, GA
Charleston, WV	Helena, MT	Oakland, CA	Springfield, IL
Charlotte, NC	Holyoke, MA	Oklahoma City, OK	Syracuse, NY
Chicago, IL	Honolulu, HI	Omaha, NE	Tampa, FL
Cincinnati, OH	Houston, TX	Philadelphia, PA	Tucson, AZ
Clarksburg, WV	Indianapolis, IN	Phoenix, AZ	Tulsa, OK
Cleveland, OH	Jackson, MS	Pittsburgh, PA	Washington, DC
Columbia, SC	Jacksonville, FL	Portland, OR	West Palm Beach, FL
Columbus, OH	Kansas City, MO	Providence, RI	Wichita, KS
Concord, NH	Knoxville, TN	Rapid City, SD	Wilkes-Barre, PA
Coral Gables, FL	Las Vegas, NV	Reno, NV	Wilmington, DE
Corpus Christi, TX	Little Rock, AR	Richmond, VA	

Source: U. S. Small Business Administration, *Free Magazine Assistance Publication,* SBA 115A, (Washington, D. C.: U. S. Government Printing Office) April 1980, p. 3.

Assistance Program is extensive and diversified. It includes free individual counseling by retired and active business executives, university students, and other professionals; management courses; and conferences, workshops, and problem clinics. Let's look at the specific management services that are available through local offices.

Counseling

The SBA helps small business owners get individual assistance with management problems, and counsels prospective small business owners who want management information on specific types of business enterprises.

SCORE/ACE and Professional Association Volunteers

In addition to the help provided by SBA management assistance staff, you can obtain management counseling from the members of the Service Corps of Retired Executives/Active Corps of Executives (SCORE/ACE) and numerous national professional associations, all of whom have volunteered to help prospective small business owners and troubled small businesses. The SBA tries to match the need of a specific small business with the expertise of one of its thousands of volunteers. An assigned counselor visits the small business in question and, through careful observation, makes a detailed analysis of the business and its problems. If the problems are complex, the counselor may call on other volunteer experts to help the small business. Finally, a plan is offered to remedy the trouble and assist the business through its critical period.

Small Business Institute (SBI)

Through the Small Business Institute, seniors and graduate students from the nation's leading schools of business provide on-site management counseling to small business owners. The students are guided by a faculty member and an SBA management assistance officer, and they receive academic credit for their participation in the Institute. Although SBI counseling is usually restricted to SBA clients (loan recipients and small firms performing federal contracts), it is available if there are enough student counselors in the program to assist all small business owners who want SBI help.

Call Contracts

The Call Contracts Program provides small business entrepreneurs with management and technical assistance from professional consulting firms under contract with the SBA. The kind of assistance provided ranges from junior and senior accounting to complex engineering.

Courses

Business management courses concerning planning, organizing, and controlling a business, as distinguished from day-to-day operating activities, are cosponsored by the SBA and public and private educational institutions and business associations. The courses are generally held during the evening, and last from six to eight weeks.[5]

Conferences, Workshops, and Clinics

Conferences covering subjects such as working capital, business forecasting, and diversification of markets are held regularly for established businesses. The SBA also conducts pre-business workshops for prospective small business owners, dealing with capital requirements, sources of financing, types of business, business organization, and business site selection. Clinics dealing with the problems of small firms in specific industrial categories are held as needed.

Foreign Trade

The SBA works closely with the U. S. Department of Commerce and other agencies to help generate small business export activity and to furnish information on export opportunities to the small business community.

Remember: the SBA has been established at the taxpayer's expense to help small businesses. You are the taxpayer, so why not take advantage of it? In addition, inquire about other federal agencies that may provide assistance, such as the Farmers' Home Administration (rural businesses), the Department of Energy, the Department of Commerce, the Martime Administration, the Department of Housing and Urban Development and the Export-Import Bank.

FOR MORE INFORMATION

A bibliography is available at the end of the book for those interested in acquiring further information on specific aspects of small business. Most important, you should obtain appropriate publications from the Small Business Administration (SBA). A list of its literature is presented in Appendix A. You might also want to join any associations of individuals or companies involved in your business and subscribe to their magazines, which constantly provide up-to-date information.

SUMMARY

The high rate of small business failure is primarily attributable to lack of managerial know-how. This poor management is apparent in such major problems as lack of money; inadequate sales; excessive operating expenses; receivables and inventory difficulties; poor location; excessive fixed assets; and competitive weakness.

The purpose of this book is to provide managerial guidelines that will be useful to anyone who wants to start a business or improve conditions in an established business. This first chapter provides an overview of what management is all about. The remaining chapters explain in detail the responsibilities of a manager. A model is used in each chapter to help explain this managerial concept.

Management may be defined as the achievement of objectives by effective use of resources. It involves planning, organizing, and controlling by working within a framework of line, staff, and service responsibilities to arrive at sound decisions.

Management must establish goals for its business in order to direct its efforts toward desired ends. Goals should be established only after appropriate thought has been given to available resources and to all other managerial duties. In addition to establishing *objectives* (goals) and marshaling *resources*, a manager must perform three *functions* (planning, organizing, and controlling); understand all *areas of responsibility*; and make sound *decisions*.

It is wise to make full use of organizations that can help you start and stay in business. The Small Business Administration (SBA), for example, can provide valuable assistance. Take time to visit a local SBA office. It also helps to join any associations of people involved in your business and become familiar with their literature.

NOTES

1. *Business Failure Record*, New York: Dun & Bradstreet, Business Economics Division, 1981, pp. 12–13. Inadequate management includes poor cash planning. Without the necessary money a business will fail. (See chapter 6, "Financial Requirements.")

2. *Business Failure Record,* p. 13.

3. The selection of objectives is applicable to all areas of endeavor. For example, it can be applied to your personal finances. Your long-term objective may be to achieve a million dollar retirement nest egg for children and charity after thirty years as a restaurateur. You would also set intermediate goals, however, in order to achieve such an objective. The short-, medium-, and long-term goals would include the amounts you plan to save en route to the million dollars. A sub-goal might go into details of what you expect to achieve from various investments based on dollars generated by the restaurant.

4. You can get an SBA pamphlet entitled *What It Does* from the U. S. Government Printing Office in Washington, D. C.

5. I have been a frequent speaker at such management courses, and response has been favorable from people in attendance.

Chapter 2
Functions of a Manager

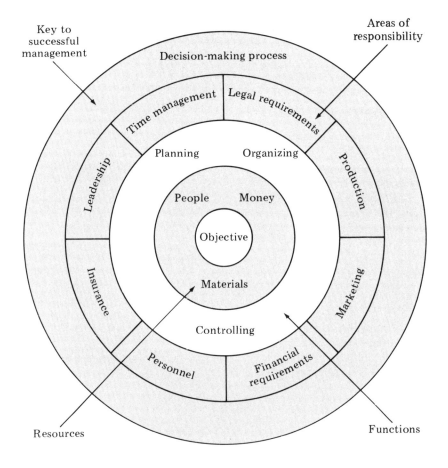

Exhibit 2-1 Stillman's Small Business Management Model: An overview of the five major components of management with emphasis on managerial functions

> It is a bad plan that admits no modification.
>
> — Publilius Syrus

What functions must a small business manager perform successfully? The white area in Exhibit 2-1 indicates that they include planning, organizing, and controlling. The objective is also in white, to show that it must be considered in arriving at all managerial decisions. The shaded portions of Exhibit 2-1 are included to indicate that every other topic in the book is related to this chapter.

The functions of planning, organizing, and controlling must be performed regardless of the firm's size. In starting a business, for example, you must do considerable planning to ensure its success. Once you have determined a plan of action, you will achieve its implementation as the result of an effective organization. You must also establish controls to ensure that the plan is being accomplished correctly. Now let us find out about each of the managerial functions.

PLANNING

Planning may be defined as the formulation of a detailed method before accomplishing something. In developing any plan, you must determine what resources — people, money, and materials — are available to achieve your organization's mission. The planning is accomplished before the doing. Stated another way, competent planning is essential to satisfactory implementation.

In small businesses, the planning function is less complex than in major corporations — but no less important. Lack of adequate planning has doomed many firms to failure. To achieve the best results, a small business manager must understand this significant planning function. Although, for a particular project, planning precedes the other two functions of organizing (doing or operating) and controlling, all three are being carried on simultaneously in any organization. The three functions are a continuous cycle.

What are the advantages for a small business owner or manager in spending time developing a plan before opening the business?

- ○ It reduces the risk of failure by permitting him to consider relevant facts before making decisions.
- ○ It permits the development of goals for the organization, and a determination of the availability of resources to accomplish them.
- ○ It establishes a timetable for putting all the parts of the firm together, so the doors can open as scheduled.

How would you use the planning concept in your small business? We will again consider our residential home builder, but the same principles are applicable to any firm. Adequate planning for the home contractor means determining if this is the correct time to build, reading relevant available literature, speaking with building experts, and observing quality residential construction firsthand. Give serious consideration to location, design, expenditures, time available for the project, and selection of subcontractors and materials. If this planning goes well, the other functions (organizing and controlling) should fall into place.

PERT and Timetable

PERT (Program Evaluation and Review Technique) is a managerial technique that helps you plan each step involved in completing a project. It is a valuable tool that can help you identify and analyze possible problem areas. An analysis of potential difficulties can result in modifications that may reduce the problems or eliminate them altogether.

As a home builder, you might employ PERT for both the planning and building phases (see Exhibit 2-2). You would develop a planning schedule that seemed feasible: a nine-month optimistic schedule and an alternative twelve-month schedule that allows for unplanned incidents. The detailed schedule, much like a budget, provides both a plan and a control technique. You may wish to use a format similar to Exhibit 2-2 in the planning phase of your business, but be sure to design it to meet *your* requirements.

A timetable, listing events in chronological order, can also be of value in checking your progress. Such a timetable should list all major steps in planning to start the company. A model timetable is shown below.

1. Begin planning phase. Discuss techniques to meet needs — PERT, management model, planning steps.
2. Overall objective — complete, at a 15 percent profit margin, a prime-quality residential home within one year.

3. Sub-objectives
   a. Location
      1. Professional residential area
      2. Near good schools
      3. High ground to provide relative safety in the event of floods
      4. Area where property values are rising
   b. Cost — within available resources
   c. Type — designed for popular appeal
4. Complete study of available housing
   a. Read articles.
   b. Obtain ideas from authorities.
   c. Visit sites.
5. Select the desired location from alternatives.
6. Complete down payment on lot.
7. Secure lawyer.
8. Secure funds for lot.
9. Select architect from alternatives.
10. Complete title search.
11. Complete act of sale for lot.
12. Obtain description of materials and necessary plans.
13. Secure estimates for comparison from subcontractors and suppliers.
14. All bids returned from subcontractors.
15. Get plan approved by city and receive permit.
16. Complete itemized budget.
17. Secure home loan.

Exhibit 2-2   PERT chart used during the building phase

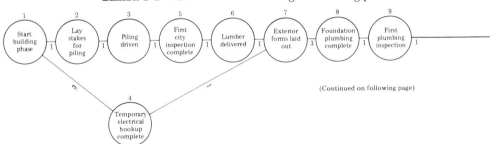

(Continued on following page)

Numbers underlined represent optimistic time for completion of each activity

Sequential numbers for reference only

18. Complete survey of property.

19. Complete planning phase — review.

You will want to tailor your timetable to your own specific goals.

The Plan

Good planning should culminate in a good plan. A vital plan for the home contractor, for example, is an appropriate set of drawings and a description of materials. You hire an architect with a good reputation, one who is a member of the American Institute of Architects (AIA). Your attorney makes sure that the written contract specifies precisely what work the architect will perform for her fee.

Budget

Another essential planning tool is the budget. It itemizes financial resources necessary for a business manager to accomplish a mission. The

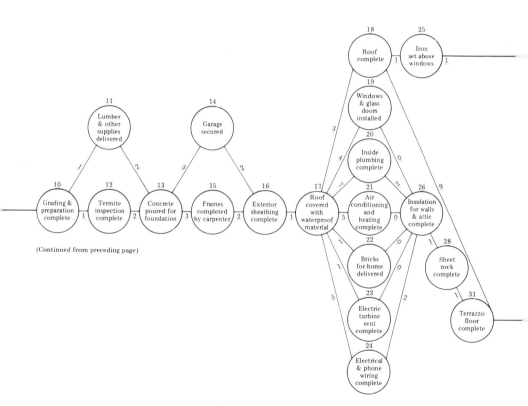

(Continued from preceding page)

format used by the home builder is shown in Exhibit 2-3. You may be able to obtain a form for this purpose from a lending agency. The Small Business Administration can also help. It is essential to itemize every cost you believe will be required to start your business. Remember also to provide an extra reserve for inflation and unexpected events — I recommend 10 percent. The budget, like the PERT, is both a planning and a controlling device. The linkage is apparent when you realize that the plan is no good unless you check (control) to see that it is followed. For more information on the budget and other financial aspects of your business, see chapter 6.

In summarizing this material on planning, I want to re-emphasize its prime importance to the success of any firm in both starting and staying in business. By doing a good job of planning you can reduce risks and make it easier to achieve the company goals. The result of sound planning is a plan that can be implemented. Carrying out the plan can be accomplished with an effective organization.

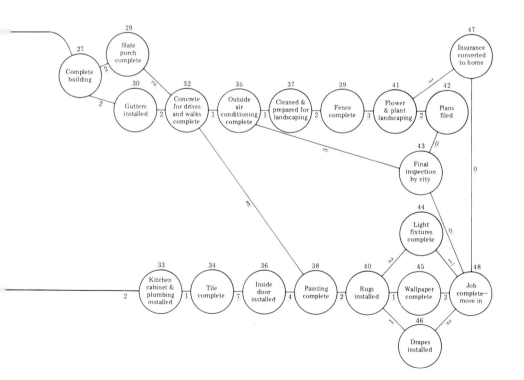

Exhibit 2-3   Budget for the MPMA Construction Company as of January 1, 1983

Item	First estimate	Revised estimate	Actual	Contracted with (name, address, phone, principal to contract)
Preliminary Costs				
Includes such items as lot, taxes, insurance, lawyer's fee, building permit, and survey.				
Foundation				
Piling (#9)	1950.00	1912.00	1912.00	Cadet Pile Drivers, Inc. Hansen Hall Drive 555-3000 Mr. Morgan Cadet
Materials				
Lumber	6579.79	6641.50	6766.14	Mile Run Lumber Company 5164 Hoyne Avenue 555-6111 Mr. Park Mile
Total	xxx	xxx	xxx	

ORGANIZING

The second major function of a small business manager is to organize. Organization may be defined as the administrative structure within which a business performs its duties.

Formal Organization

The structure of a business may be reflected, to a certain degree, in an organizational chart. Exhibit 2-4 is an example of a formal organizational chart for a small, diversified retail service company. It operates a beauty salon, a shoe repair shop, a tailor shop, and a retail outlet. This segmented division delineates major areas of responsibility and points out the hierarchy (superior-subordinate relationships), with the president at the top. Organization must be adapted to the particular type of operation as presently managed. A company may be structured in one of two ways — functional or divisional. The formal organization of the example in Exhibit 2-4 is functional. Related activities of the company are brought together into departments — the tailor shop is one, the beauty salon another, and the retail store a third. In contrast, a divisional breakout could be by geographic region, type of equipment, or type of customer. Small businesses usually find a functional breakout most appropriate.

The organizational structure is not a separate entity that can be consid-

Exhibit 2-4 Organizational chart of XYZ Corporation. Pine Lake, Michigan. June 17. 1983

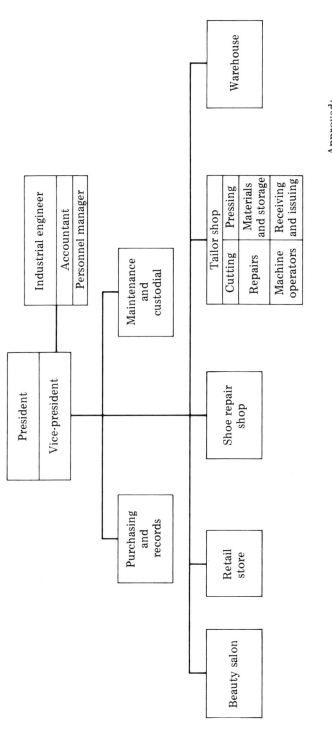

Approved:
Narco Namllits,
President
6/17/83

ered apart from the personnel who provide its staff of life. There can be no inflexible criteria in such areas as line, staff, and service relationships, span of responsibility, or delegation of authority. Due consideration must be given to the people in the company at any one time. A highly active executive staff may require an entirely different organization than a group of older personnel, some of whom may be in semiretirement.

A belief in flexibility, based on individuals presently in control, should be reflected in the composition of any business organization. The organization must be a functional setup. We will discuss this in relation to several management terms.

Span of Responsibility

The span of responsibility for a manager reflects both the number of people reporting to that manager (span of control) and the person in turn to whom the manager reports. The formal structure used in Exhibit 2-4 reflects, for the vice-president, a span of responsibility of eleven (ten people report to him, he reports to the president). In this situation, such a span is effective because of certain factors peculiar to the operation. The supervisors, with two exceptions, are located in a central building. The exceptions are the beauty shop, situated a block away, and the shoe repair shop, next door. The work of this business lends itself to independent action, and the vice-president, at age twenty-nine, is a workaholic. In arriving at the appropriate span of responsibility for your firm, it is essential to weigh such factors as complexity and type of work, degree of homogeneity, distance involved, and the essential ingredient — caliber of people in various positions. In the XYZ Corporation, span of responsibility for a supervisor varies from two to twenty-seven. The fact that the firm is successful under the present set of circumstances in no way implies that the mission could not be accomplished effectively by using other structures with different spans of responsibility. It is desirable, however, to keep supervision to the minimum consistent with efficient operation. As supervisors multiply, management costs increase and communication becomes less effective. Some management texts, in discussing span of responsibility, set certain numbers as the minimum or maximum for effective control, but this is not an area that lends itself to generalization. Management of a particular activity must determine what is desirable after appropriate study, experience, and (if necessary) competent outside advice.

Unity of Command

Good management emphasizes the necessity of placing responsibility on one individual. One person should be responsible for each part of the organization. When this concept is applied, each member of the organization is responsible to only one superior. The net effect is that everyone knows who is the boss and who are the subordinates. This concept of unity has proved to be eminently satisfactory for small businesses,[1] but it requires of management continuing attention and strict adherence to the formal structure.

An interesting problem develops with respect to the concept of unity at that level of organization where it requires two positions to effect the direct change of a command. As portrayed in Exhibit 2-4, the president has a single span of control. The vice-president has ten people reporting to him; and he, in turn, reports to one person. Experience has proved the importance of adhering to this relationship; that is, the president should *not* bypass the vice-president and issue orders directly to the various operations managers, nor should those managers report directly to the president. Such an approach of course enables the president to devote greater time to plans, policies, and important outside activities. Furthermore, it permits the organization to function virtually as effectively with one or the other absent for an extended period. Still, it requires the utmost cooperation so that both parties are thoroughly informed on all important matters.

There is always inherent in such a situation the possibility that the senior may usurp powers of the subordinate, or vice versa. It is absolutely essential that the vice-president recognize that he is not in charge and only *recommends* on matters of policy. This can be achieved if he understands the duties involved, but a truly effective working relationship can be attained as a result of time alone. The principal functions of the president and vice-president in this small diversified business are listed in Exhibit 2-5. It reflects, in general, a division of responsibilities, although I cannot emphasize too strongly that a complete exchange of ideas (effective communication) on any significant action taken or contemplated is essential for best performance.

There is considerable similarity between this type of unity and the executive committee system. Each requires coordination and cooperation for the common good. Perhaps the term "unity of purpose" might be appropriate for the modus operandi of each. The old concept of a master-serf relationship is virtually nonexistent in this country, although there is still a school of thought that adheres to the disciplinary approach. In the purely military arena this can be supported by many examples. In a small business, however, it is sheer folly to expect the best efforts of the group to be elicited by other than a cooperative approach. It is through understanding, tolerance, and mutual respect that greatest progress is achieved. From this approach there evolves a unity of purpose which is a central component of the success of a small business.

Exhibit 2-5 Functional chart of XYZ Corporation, Pine Lake, Michigan, June 17, 1983

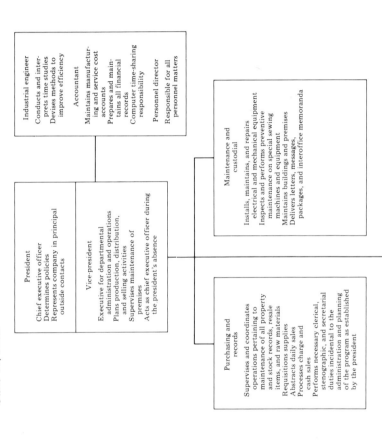

Beauty salon

Provides complete beauty salon services, primarily for local residents

Retail store

Displays and sells merchandise

Takes monthly inventory of stock

Returns articles to vendors for repairs

Plans and coordinates merchandise for store

Accepts special orders for such items as jewelry, luggage, shoes, sporting equipment, cameras, watches, and calling cards

Shoe repair shop

Repairs shoes for local residents

Tailor shop

Superintendent—responsible for all departmental activity

Cutting

Plans, schedules, cuts, and prepares garment parts for sewing

Research and design

Repairs

Alters and repairs uniforms

Machine operators

Manufactures coats, trousers, shirts, jackets, parkas, and gym shorts

Assists in repair work during peak periods

Pressing

Underpresses and finishes all articles manufactured

Materials and storage

Stores and issues raw materials for manufacture and repair of uniforms and shoes

Plans, stores and issues all uniforms

Takes monthly, quarterly, and semiannual inventories

Receiving and issuing

Receives, distributes, and issues garments and shoes requiring repairs

Warehouse

Receives, unpacks, counts, inspects, stores and ships all resale items, raw materials, and machine parts

Takes inventory of stock

Issues stock to various departments

Approved:
Narco Namllits,
President
6/17/83

Line, Staff, and Service Responsibilities

In recent years a variety of views have been forthcoming from scholars and practitioners regarding a delineation of the terms *line, staff,* and *service.* Basically, there does not seem to be a clear-cut distinction among the three areas. In the example in Exhibit 2-4, all three elements are present. The *staff* includes the industrial engineer, the personnel director, and the accountant, who are considered advisors to the operators, or "doers." These individuals report to the vice-president, who directs operations. The *line* duties are accomplished by the tailor shop, the shoe repair shop, the beauty salon, and the retail store. They have direct responsibility for achieving the firm's objectives. Support and guidance come from the industrial engineer, the personnel director, and the accountant. Decisions and orders are not the primary tools of the staff. Counsel, cooperation, and coordination are the techniques most frequently called for. In fact, guidance by an astute industrial engineer may be a supervisor's way of voicing the decision through another person. Thus there is no total compartmentalization of line and staff duties in an organization of limited size.

In addition to *staff* and *line* in Exhibit 2-4, *service* can be illustrated by the maintenance and custodial department. This group performs janitorial work and takes care of machinery and electrical equipment. The supervisor of this department is also used in several staff advisory positions. It may be true that in larger organizations there is less flexibility, but the division among *line, staff,* and *service* is never complete in any work situation.

Decision Making

What is the art of decision making? Chester Bernard said:"The fine art of executive decision consists in not deciding questions that are not now pertinent, in not deciding prematurely, in not making decisions that cannot be made effective, and in not making decisions that others should make."[2] The validity of this definition has been proven time and again. It is of utmost importance for managers to request only what is realistically likely to be accomplished.

An example: Customers at one store had the privilege of placing special orders for merchandise not in stock. When the article arrived, a form letter was sent asking the customer to come in within ten days to pick the item up. These instructions were not being followed in many instances, causing storage, inventory, and cash flow problems. Two courses of corrective action were considered. First, the merchandise might be returned to the supplier or sold to someone else. Every effort had been made to build up goodwill between the customer and the store, however; the store had stressed courtesy and efficient service. A second solution was to require a deposit (or purchase order) and to modify the arrival notice, asking people to stop by the store at the earliest practicable date. Telephone reminders and follow-up notices would also be used. The latter was adopted. It worked. Although the illustration pertains to a minor matter, it points out the value of issuing instructions and making decisions that are most realistic and effective in achieving the desired objectives.

Charts

What are the weaknesses and strengths of charts that may be used by small businesses in portraying their organizations? The structural layout in Exhibit 2-5, for example, reflects only the vertical hierarchy within the organization. As stated earlier in this chapter, charts portray, in some degree, various relationships of authority and responsibility. Exhibit 2-5 does not indicate the relative importance of the five operating departments. One executive receives a substantial salary, has numerous significant functions, and has a sizable staff under his jurisdiction. In contrast, another functional department has only a few people in it, and the management pay scale is correspondingly lower because of the more restricted duties. Nevertheless, these two functional activities are shown as equal. Furthermore, lateral internal communications cannot be presented because of the maze that would be involved. Contacts with all outside activities and with superiors also cannot be realistically shown in a graphic presentation.

Nevertheless, charts do serve a useful purpose in presenting such matters as important functions, positions, and a general understanding of the hierarchy. To be of greatest value, they should be kept current, and *all* personnel should be informed of their purpose. This can be achieved readily by briefing supervisors when modifications are made. In addition, new employees can be given a visual presentation upon reporting to their departments. As in the example of Exhibit 2-5, you should consider the following factors in preparing charts:

○ name of the company
○ its location
○ date
○ title
○ brief description of job or function
○ contents accurate, neat, current, concise
○ layout uniform
○ information authenticated

In numerous very small business firms there is no apparent reason for the preparation and issuance of such formal visual aids. Furthermore, one owner of a successful company (sales exceed $4 million annually) has indicated that publication of an organizational chart would be detrimental to morale because supervisors were under the impression they occupied relatively higher positions than they actually did. The open nature of our society may make some charting helpful, however. Since the grade system, pay scale, and other pertinent data are often available through the grapevine, it may be foolhardy to attempt anything less than a full and frank presentation.

Organizational Guidelines

To summarize the organizational function of the small business manager:

1. Every department within a business should have a clear understanding of what is expected of it. All policy should be evaluated in relation to the mission or objective.

2. Formal organization, to be most effective, should be based on the people who staff the company at the time.

3. Span of responsibility is inherent in the particular work situation. It is axiomatic that for the best fit, the cloth must be cut to the individual pattern. No two environments are alike, so it is not possible to establish a formula for an ideal span. In general, levels of supervision should be kept to the minimum that is consistent with adequate control.

4. Unity of command can be achieved by an unconventional approach. A committee system or coequal relationship may be eminently satisfactory and successful. Furthermore, at the level of organization where more than one supervisory individual is required, there must be an integration of thought, a depth of understanding, and mutual confidence in order to achieve best results.

5. Organizational charts can be useful in portraying a firm's hierarchy as well as the responsibilities of various departments. Full and frank disclosures in all nonclassified areas can be achieved best by using appropriate visual aids with other factual data. Charts should be kept current and held to a minimum necessary to accomplish this purpose. Very small commercial companies normally do not maintain organization, position, or functional charts. There are sound arguments to support their case, including the costs involved, the possibility of unwise disclosures to competitors, and the potential loss of status for some officials.

CONTROLLING

The third significant function of management is control. Control may be defined as the means whereby small business managers or owners are able to determine if they have achieved their goals in accordance with their plans. As stated earlier, there is a significant connection between planning and control. In planning the goals are set. In control, the achievements are measured.

Throughout this book the interrelatedness of all the components of management is stressed. An understanding of this connection or linkage can help the small business owner be successful. This interrelatedness is readily apparent in the control function. The primacy of planning has been discussed earlier in this chapter. The best developed *plan* is meaningless, however, unless it is *implemented* well (through an effective organization) and *checked* (controlled) to see if it is being implemented correctly. If not, changes must be made. A plan must also further the *objectives* of the firm, and draw on the other managerial responsibilities, such as finance, marketing, production, and legal compliance.

In any established enterprise, the functions of planning, organizing, and controlling proceed simultaneously and are a continuous process. These three functions must be accomplished in even the smallest commercial endeavor. The youngster who enters the lawn-mowing business actually considers time, money, and materials in relation to potential customers — that is planning. The operational phase (organization) involves securing and retaining clients, performing the work, collecting the fees, and taking care of the equipment. Finally, the status of income and expenses, the condition of the equipment, and the standard of performance in comparison with competitors must be evaluated. These are achieved through communication, statistical records, and objective analysis — all methods of control.

Thus, to determine the effectiveness of the two major administrative functions of planning and organizing requires the application of certain control techniques. Quantitative and qualitative data permit an insight into the standard of performance and enable the owner or manager to take corrective measures where appropriate. Let us examine control methods that may be used by small businesses. Examples are provided that relate to the two firms mentioned earlier in the chapter, but remember: a manager should use only those control techniques appropriate for the company in question.

Budget

Your budget, as mentioned earlier, can serve as an excellent planning and control document. The first two columns of figures in Exhibit 2-3 indicate the several estimates of what various items cost. The total provides you (in this example the contractor) with an indication of how much money will be required to build the home. This information enables you to talk intelligently with a lending agency.

The estimate, however, does not always coincide with actual costs. In most cases actual cost exceeds the amount planned for in the budget. This era of high inflation has compounded the problem — especially where there are long delays between planning to start a business and actually opening it. Still, if you use your budget effectively as a control device this variation between estimate and actual cost can be minimized. Post the actual price paid for each item promptly. Then check carefully to see if you have exceeded your estimate, and by what amount. You will find the real value of budget control only if you take positive action to correct any problems.

Assume, in the home builder case, that after the foundation work has been completed you find that your budget estimate has been exceeded by 5 percent. The problem is obvious — you spent too much. You must then decide what to do about it. After obtaining the facts, look at alternatives. One solution is to ask the loan agency for more money. A second alternative is to substitute lower-quality materials in the remaining construction to make up the difference. A third possibility is to eliminate something from the building. From the various alternatives you can then proceed to make a sound decision.

PERT

PERT is a splendid planning and control document. If you are using it, you should follow it with care.

Your budget serves as a money control, but PERT permits you to keep a project on schedule. PERT initially enables you to determine how long it will take to complete the job. It also points out the numerous tasks that can be accomplished concurrently to move up the completion date. In the home builder case, if a strike should occur in the cement industry and your schedule shows it is time to lay the driveway, your PERT chart can assist you in selecting a possible alternative task to perform just then. Regardless of how well it is conceived, however, a planning document like PERT cannot foresee all eventualities.

PERT is only as valuable as you make it. If you set it up unrealistically, you are wasting your time.

Supervisors' Meetings

Meetings of company officials[3] should be held as required and should only be as long as is necessary to present the essential information. The purpose of these sessions should be to keep personnel informed of items of basic interest and problems that arise within the organization. They also permit an exchange of ideas between the various supervisors and top management. These meetings provide an excellent control vehicle, because they provide feedback on the status of various projects.[4]

In order to prepare for these weekly sessions properly, the owner of XYZ Corporation (the company that is portrayed in Exhibits 2-4 and 2-5) notes pertinent matters as they come across the desk and forwards them to a secretary. The secretary in turn compiles a summary file that is made available to the president approximately two hours before the conference. This permits appropriate review and consultation so all in attendance can get accurate, up-to-date information.

The first topic of discussion at XYZ meetings is personnel. The personnel manager presents the latest knowledge on this subject, including the number of people currently in the organization, sick leave and annual leave taken, promotions, vacations, and changes in strength as a result of hirings, retirements, resignations, and transfers. The sick-leave situation is portrayed on a large chart. The chart itself acts as a control device because supervisors do not want their areas to show sizable sick-leave figures.

A second major item on the agenda is the weekly status report by the managers of the tailor shop, the shoe repair shop, and the beauty salon. In reporting, these managers use graphic aids that can be seen readily by all present. They review areas of difficulty as well as noteworthy accomplishments, and sometimes corrective action is prescribed by their managers.

To foster interest in these meetings, and to encourage people to speak,[5] every opportunity is taken to have various supervisors relate experiences. As a case in point, after a supervisor returns from a visit to another company he briefs all officials and stresses areas that are of particular value to the organization. Normally, no written report is required.

These meetings are formalized only to the extent necessary to ensure an orderly discussion and to promote effective speaking. All in attendance are always welcome to present their views. When a new technique is being considered, or when a question of company-wide interest has arisen, the discussion is thrown open for general comment. This group participation frequently uncovers valuable new approaches — often suggested by individuals not connected with the problem at first hand.

The supervisory sessions also permit the review of important articles, relevant to the company and its businesses, that appear in such publications as the *Harvard Business Review, Men's Wear, Chain Store Age General Merchandise, Apparel Industry, Small Business,* and *Consumers' Research.*[6]

The secretary in attendance at the conference is responsible for summarizing the information and furnishing a copy of the summary to everyone present within three working days.[7] Supervisors in turn transmit pertinent data to all employees in their areas.

Internal Visits

Things get done best when the boss checks on them. A good method of checking is personal inspection. In a small, centrally located organization, it is relatively easy to observe each phase of the operation several times daily.

You should make every effort to talk with all of the employees, by name, within the course of a few days. You can obtain important information in this way. If you see excellent work being done, make a complimentary comment in front of the group. Those areas requiring corrective action can be quietly brought to the attention of the proper supervisors. Where you uncover a complex problem, make a report on your return to the office and recommend an appropriate course of action. Standards of cleanliness, including appearance of employees, equipment, facilities, and grounds, should be noted during each visit.

This personal scrutiny through constant inspections enables management to know firsthand what is going on in the organization. The value of such visits can be enhanced by their being conducted in a friendly manner. Make corrections, where possible, on the spot and in private to the supervisors concerned. In contrast, give praise in the presence of all within hearing, and if warranted, make it a matter of official record.

Photographs

A camera can be a useful control device. A small one will fit in your pocket, and will enable you to make a permanent record of any potential problem. If there is a question about faulty lumber at the time of delivery, for example, take a picture of it with the delivery truck in the background, or include in the photo the driver who made the delivery. If you are a storekeeper and you intend to open another store, photos of the work on the first can be helpful in going over the step-by-step process. An analysis will enable you to make improvements the next time. Many owners use a camera to support insurance claims (as do many homeowners) by maintaining photos of all equipment.

Communication

It is extremely important to talk with your customers, workers, suppliers, and others in your line of business. The information you receive can be valuable.

When you give instructions, be sure that what you say is clearly understood. One way to find out is to have the person repeat what you said. Keep in mind that customers, workers, and suppliers use different terms and may interpret things differently. If you have any suspicion of misinterpretation or misunderstanding, put your words in writing.[8]

Follow-up Action

Another control measure is positive follow-up action; but take action only to the extent required to get the job done. If a firm, for example, has failed to meet its payments, you may wish to proceed as follows:

1. Call the company and courteously explain the problem. Set a time for it to be corrected.
2. Make a second phone call, firmly explaining that you expect the payment to be made, and set a second deadline.
3. Write a letter stating that you will take legal action if payment is not made within a specified time. Send copies of letters to appropriate parties, such as the Better Business Bureau.
4. Proceed with the necessary legal action. You may find that small-claims court is sufficient to obtain the amount due you. If not, contact your firm's lawyer.

It is wise to take action only for matters of some value. Don't waste your time and energy quibbling over minor amounts to satisfy your ego or your sense of justice. Get on with your business. Once you decide something is important, however, proceed with vigor to gain a fair settlement. In theory, your careful planning and checking should prevent you from having to take drastic steps, but it doesn't always work that way. Occasionally someone in whom you have great trust and confidence will let you down.

SUMMARY

It is essential for a small business to perform well the three management functions of planning, organizing, and controlling. In starting a business, it is first necessary to develop a workable plan. Such a plan must be flexible enough to meet changing conditions — "It is a bad plan that admits no modification." Once you have determined a plan of action, you can achieve implementation through effective organization. Controls must also be established to ensure that the plan is being accomplished correctly.

Planning may be defined as the formulation of a detailed method before accomplishing something. Two planning tools also serve as a means of control. The first is PERT (Program Evaluation and Review Technique). It can help a manager plan each step involved in completing a project. PERT can be useful, for example, in portraying the steps involved in starting a business. It can also assist the owner in finding out about possible problem areas in such a venture. The budget is another essential planning tool. It itemizes the financial resources needed to accomplish an objective or mission.

The second major function of a small business manager is to organize. Organization is the administrative structure within which a business performs its duties. It is often desirable for a business to portray its structure by preparing an organizational chart. This chart reflects the formal hierarchy of a company and the span of responsibility of the managers. A small business's structure, like its plan, should be flexible and should be modified to meet changing conditions.

Controlling is the third essential function a manager must perform. It may be defined as the means whereby small business managers are able to determine if they have achieved their goals in accordance with their plans. A plan is ineffective without adequate controls, so it is necessary to understand the linkage between these two functions. PERT, for example, can spell out a plan for completing a building in nine months, but it is of little value unless you use appropriate controls to check the actual progress. Other controls may be used in addition to PERT and the budget.

Planning, organizing, and controlling are carried on simultaneously in any active business and are a continuous cycle, although for each specific project planning precedes the other two functions of organizing (doing or operating) and controlling.

NOTES

1. Du Pont has for many years used an executive committee system with singular success. It may be possible that a small-scale commercial business could emulate this approach; I know of a well-established partnership that does well under this system of coequals.

2. *The Functions of the Executive*, Cambridge, Mass.: Harvard University Press, 1938, p. 194.

3. In very small businesses it may be desirable, if possible, to hold meetings with all employees in attendance.

4. One successful small business (331 employees) has weekly breakfast meetings at a local hotel that are attended by department heads and key staff personnel. Officials are told at these sessions in what direction the company is actually heading and where it should be going. Interdepartmental disputes may also be resolved at these meetings.

5. At these weekly meetings, each speaker stands in front of the group. A rostrum is available, as are other training aids, including an easel and a pointer.

6. The company subscribes to all the magazines listed and makes them available to the staff.

7. Over the years these memoranda have been appropriately indexed and are an excellent reference resource.

8. All merchandise orders, for example, should be in writing, and a purchase order system should be initiated.

Part II
Areas of
Responsibility

Chapter 3
Legal Requirements

Chapter 4
Production

Chapter 5
Marketing

Chapter 6
Financial Requirements

Chapter 7
Personnel

Chapter 8
Insurance

Part II provides a course of action for starting and staying in business. Each chapter in this section draws on the managerial techniques presented in Part I.

What are the areas of responsibility of a small business manager? They include: legal requirements (chapter 3); production (chapter 4); marketing (chapter 5); finance (chapter 6); personnel (chapter 7); and insurance (chapter 8). A diagram is presented at the beginning of each chapter to emphasize the interrelatedness of all the components of management. It is apparent from such a schematic presentation that a small business manager must understand each of these areas of responsibility in order to be successful. For example: a company can manufacture the best jeans available (chapter 4), but if they are not marketed effectively (chapter 5) the item will not sell and the firm will go under.

Chapter 3
Legal Requirements

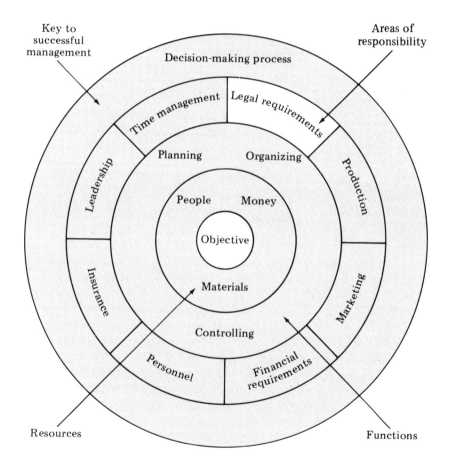

Key to
successful
management

Areas of
responsibility

Decision-making process

Time management

Legal requirements

Leadership

Planning

Organizing

Production

People

Money

Objective

Insurance

Materials

Marketing

Controlling

Personnel

Financial
requirements

Resources

Functions

Exhibit 3-1 Stillman's Small Business Management Model: An overview of the five major components of management with emphasis on legal requirements

> Obedience to the law is demanded as a right, not
> asked as a favor.
>
> — Theodore Roosevelt

What are the legal requirements you must meet to start a firm and then to continue operating it successfully? This chapter will examine types of ownership and the ongoing need for legal services. First we will see how the legal aspects fit into the total approach emphasized throughout the text.

The white area in Exhibit 3-1 indicates the place of legal requirements in our model. The objective is also white to emphasize that it must be considered in arriving at all managerial decisions. It is important to remember that every other topic in this book is related to this chapter.

Here is how this interrelatedness works in the legal affairs of a small business. In determining the need for legal counsel, an owner or manager must decide what responsibilities should be given to the lawyer in order to achieve the goals of the firm. Once selected, the lawyer should become familiar with the company's objectives and assist in their accomplishment. As is apparent from Exhibit 3-1, an attorney should be knowledgeable in the production, marketing, financial, personnel, and insurance aspects of the business. A company's lawyer should also take a leadership role in representing the company and use time, as well as available company resources, wisely to participate in the functions of planning, organizing, and controlling. By taking this total approach, a lawyer can make sound decisions. The following example, which was related to me, illustrates how this managerial concept was used by one small-scale home builder.

> My uncle was a respected lawyer in our community and I hired him four years ago on an annual retainer basis. I had graduated from college in 1977 with a major in management. Each summer, I had worked for a contractor of residential homes. Thanks to my savings from that job and a loan from my dad, I was able to start my own construction firm shortly after receiving my degree. It gave me a great opportunity to apply classroom theories as well as the on-the-job summer experience. My uncle was a big help because of his expertise in the legal aspects of small businesses. He prepared the Articles of Incorporation and prevented many costly pitfalls so I could reach my annual gross profit goal. He gave me solid

legal advice on production (working with subcontractors and suppliers) and marketing (written agreements in regard to my building leases and advertising sources). Resources (people, money, and materials) were always considered prior to taking any legal action. And my uncle worked closely with me on the budget for legal services and other financial matters pertaining to his work. He also provided valuable input in our planning, organizing, and controlling activities. Result: sound decisions in areas such as personnel (abiding by EEOC, etc.), insurance (adequate protection), contracts, permits, zoning, and building code compliance.

LEGAL STRUCTURE

What type of legal structure is appropriate for your company? In establishing a business you must decide what legal form is best suited to meet your needs. There are three principal types of ownership available to the entrepreneur.

Proprietorship

This is the simplest form of legal structure. It establishes the owner with the legal title and exclusive right to the business. What are the advantages and disadvantages of this most popular form of business organization?

Advantages
1. It gives the owner complete control without the need to consider stockholders or partners. This freedom permits the making of prompt decisions. One successful owner put it this way: "What a great feeling to do what I want when I want to do it."
2. It is the easiest form to create and terminate. Therefore, start-up costs are kept to a minimum.
3. All profits accrue to the owner.
4. An individual with minimal outside income normally has a lower tax rate and simpler forms to complete.
5. There is no problem in moving to a partnership or corporate structure if future needs dictate it.
6. You encounter the smallest amount of government interference.

Disadvantages
1. Some or all of the owner's entire personal fortune may be taken away if the company fails and its liabilities exceed its assets. In fact, the owner could even be liable for amounts in excess of his or her personal assets.
2. The ability to expand is often limited by the profit from the business, and this source of funds may be slow during the early years.

3. The owner may feel tied down, unable to get away for long periods. There is no other ownership interest looking out for the firm.
4. The limited-life[1] feature precludes passing the business to a designated heir and complicates its sale when the owner becomes ill or for other reasons desires to sell.

Partnership

The Uniform Partnership Act, adopted by many states, defines partnership as "an association of two or more persons to carry on as co-owners of a business for profit." Though not specifically required by the Act, written articles of partnership are customarily executed.[2] These articles outline the contribution of each of the partners, whether money, material, or managerial, to the business, and generally delineate the roles of the partners in the business relationship. The following are examples of articles typically contained in a partnership agreement:

- Name, purpose, domicile
- Duration of agreement
- Performance by partners
- Character of partners (general or limited, active or silent)
- Contributions by partners (at inception, at later date)
- Authority (of individual partners in conduct of business)
- Separate debts
- Books, records, and method of accounting
- Division of profits and losses
- Draws and/or salaries
- Rights of continuing partner
- Death of a partner (dissolution and winding up)
- Employee management
- Release of debts
- Sale of partnership interests
- Arbitration
- Additions, alterations, or modifications to partnership agreement
- Settlement of disputes
- Required and prohibited acts
- Absence and disability

Some of the characteristics that distinguish a partnership from other forms of business organization are: the limited life of the partnership, unlimited liability of at least one partner, co-ownership of the assets, mutual agency, share in management, and share in partnership profits.

You can have one or more of several kinds of partners:

○ Ostensible partner — active and known as a partner.
○ Active partner — may or may not be ostensible as well.
○ Secret partner — active but not known or held out as a partner.
○ Dormant partner — inactive and not known or held out as a partner.
○ Silent partner (partner by estoppel) — not a true partner in any sense, not being a party to the partnership agreement. He holds himself out as a partner, however, or permits others to make such representation by the use of his name or otherwise. He is therefore liable as if he were a partner to third parties who have given credit to the actual or supposed firm in reliance on the truth of such representation.
○ Subpartner — one who, not being a member of the partnership, contracts with one of the partners to participate in the interest of such partner in the firm's business and profits.
○ Limited or special partner — assuming compliance with the statutory formalities, the limited partner risks only his agreed investment in the business. The limited partner is usually not held liable to the same extent as a general partner so long as he or she does not participate in the management and control of the enterprise or in the conduct of its business.

Like a proprietorship, a partnership has certain definite advantages and disadvantages.

Advantages
1. It permits greater freedom for each owner because one can "mind the store" while the other is away or ill.
2. It provides the opportunity for more capital, as each can provide a share.
3. It enables the several owners to capitalize on the special talents each brings into the business.
4. Tax requirements, as in a proprietorship, are based on personal income tax rates and are often lower than corporate taxes.

Disadvantages
1. All general partners are subject to the entire liabilities of the firm in the event of bankruptcy or going out of business. Furthermore, if partners cannot meet the debts equally, the one with the most personal assets ends up paying off the firm's obligations.
2. A partnership, like a proprietorship, must be terminated on the death or incapacity of one member.

3. Differences may arise because of opposing views in trying to solve problems. If the partners are equal, this could prevent sound decisions and may destroy the firm.
4. The ability to raise funds is not comparable to that in a corporate structure.

Corporation

A corporation is an organizational structure that has been established in accordance with the law and endowed with various rights and responsibilities, including a legal life of its own. Corporate ownership rests with the shareholders, who may or may not manage the corporation. It, too, has advantages and disadvantages.

Advantages
1. Owners' (stockholders') liability is limited to the amount of their investment in the shares of the company. This limited liability is a significant advantage.[3]
2. The corporation has a legal life of its own, so original owners can be replaced with no impact on the continuity of the business. This makes it possible to retain ownership in a family over a number of generations.
3. It may be easier to raise capital because of the corporate structure and the flexibility to buy and sell shares.

Disadvantages
1. The corporation is a more costly and time-consuming entity to establish than a partnership or sole proprietorship.
2. The decision-making process is more complex and cumbersome because the stockholders must be satisfied.

If you incorporate, you may wish to consider the possibility of selecting subchapter S status.[4] The purpose of subchapter S is to permit a small business corporation to elect to have its income taxed to the shareholders as if the corporation were a partnership. One objective of this is to overcome the "double tax" feature of our system of taxation of corporate income (it is taxed once as corporate income, then later as personal income). Another purpose is to permit the shareholders to have the benefit of offsetting business losses incurred by the corporation against their other income.

Among the conditions for electing and maintaining subchapter S status are: that the corporation have ten or fewer shareholders, all of whom are individuals or estates; that there be no nonresident alien shareholders; that there be only one class of outstanding stock; that all shareholders consent to the election; and that a specific portion of the corporation's receipts be derived from active business rather than enumerated passive investments. No limit is placed on the size of the corporation's income or assets.

If your decision is to incorporate, what are the steps involved? Here is the procedure in one state, Washington; it will give you an appreciation of the work involved. The specific requirements will vary somewhat from state to state, so be sure to check carefully in order to comply with all the laws of your state.

- File a request with the secretary of state asking for the appropriate documents to establish a domestic corporation. The secretary of state will submit the documents requested (Initial Report and Certificate of Incorporation) along with a description of the fees and costs involved.
- File an Initial Report with the secretary of state. This report must itemize the following information about the corporation:
  1. Name
  2. Address (county and city) of its registered office
  3. Name and post office addresses of its registered agents
  4. Name and address of its directors (if selected when articles are filed)
  5. Signature of each incorporator or duly authorized agent
- Prepare and submit the Articles of Incorporation (see Exhibit 3-2) to the secretary of state along with the Initial Report. These Articles of Incorporation[5] may include:
  1. A list of the people who desire to organize the corporation and who appear before the notary public
  2. The name of the corporation
  3. Its objectives and purposes
  4. Its duration
  5. Its location
  6. The names of the incorporators
  7. The names of the officers
  8. The names of the directors, or a stipulation of the manner of their election
  9. Any conditions regarding the sale and other transfer of stock
  10. A procedure for amendment of the Articles
  11. Signatures of incorporators, witnesses, and notary public
- Obtain a Certificate of Incorporation from the secretary of state. A certificate will be sent by the secretary of state to the corporation informing it that the Initial Report and Articles of Incorporation have been filed and recorded. It will also give the date the corporate existence began and indicate that all fees and incorporation taxes have been paid.

Exhibit 3-2   Sample Articles of Incorporation for a small business, state of Washington

Articles of Incorporation United States of America
of T & D Photo Equipment, Inc. State of Washington
County of Pierce

Be it known that on this 23rd day of June, 1983, before me, J. C. Scher, a notary public, duly appointed, commissioned, sworn, and qualified in and for the city of Tacoma, county of Pierce, state of Washington, therein presently residing, the following subscribers personally came and appeared: Roy Fisher, Helen Fisher, and Shannon Marie, all domiciled in the state of Washington, and all of full legal age of majority, who declare to me, notary, in the presence of the undersigned competent witnesses, that availing themselves of the provisions of the Washington Business Corporation Law (Title III, Chapter 6, Washington Revised Statutes of 1979), they do hereby organize themselves, their successors and assigns into a corporation in pursuance of said law, under and in accordance with the following articles of incorporation:

Article I

Name
The name of the corporation is: T & D Photo Equipment, Inc.

Article II

Objects and Purposes
The objects and purposes of the corporation are to establish a retail store for the purpose of selling photographic equipment and to engage in any other lawful activity for which corporations may be formed under the Business Corporation Law of Washington. It will be subject to all the laws, taxes, and regulations, of the state, county, and city where it is located.

Article III

Duration
The duration of this corporation shall be in perpetuity, or such maximum period as may be authorized by the laws of the state of Washington.

Article IV

Location
The location and post office address of its registered representative is 121 Richton Avenue, Tacoma, Washington.

Exhibit 3-2 Continued

Article V

Incorporators

The full names and post office addresses of its incorporators are:

Roy Fisher
1526 Edison Avenue
Tacoma, Washington

Helen Fisher
1526 Edison Avenue
Tacoma, Washington

Shannon Marie
3045 North Bay Road
Tacoma, Washington

Article VI

Authorized Capital

The corporation is authorized to issue 1500 shares of common stock with a par value of $10 per share.

Article VII

Officers

The names, post office addresses, and shareholdings of the first officers of the corporation are as follows:

Roy Fisher, President (500 shares)
1526 Edison Avenue
Tacoma, Washington

Helen Fisher, Vice-president (500 shares)
1526 Edison Avenue
Tacoma, Washington

Shannon Marie, Secretary-treasurer (500 shares)
3045 North Bay Road
Tacoma, Washington

Article VIII

Directors

A. Unless and until otherwise provided in the bylaws of this corporation, all corporate powers shall be vested in and exercised by a Board of Directors consisting of three members.

B. The Board of Directors shall have authority to make and alter bylaws subject to the powers of the shareholders to change or repeal the bylaws so made.

Exhibit 3-2 Continued

C. The Board of Directors shall further have authority to exercise all such other powers and to do all such other lawful acts and things which this corporation or its shareholders might do, unless prohibited from doing so by applicable laws, or by the Articles of Incorporation, or by the bylaws of the corporation.

D. A general meeting of the shareholders for the election of directors shall be held annually at the registered office of the corporation or at other places designated by the Board of Directors. The meeting will take place each year on the 20th of February beginning with the year 1983.

E. The Directors shall hold office for one year or until their successors have been duly elected and qualified.

Article IX

Sale and other transfer of stock

No stockholder in this corporation, or his successor, shall have the right to transfer his shares unless the stock shall have been first offered for sale, at a fair market price, to the corporation, and, if the corporation shall refuse to accept the offer, to each of the other shareholders of this corporation.

Article X

Amendments

These articles shall be amended or the corporation may be dissolved in the manner provided by law.

Thus, done and signed in my office in the county of Pierce, state of Washington, on the day, month and year set forth above in the presence of the undersigned competent witnesses, and me, notary, after due reading of the whole.

Witnesses   Incorporators

_____   _____
Becky Boe   Roy Fisher

_____   _____
John Boe   Helen Fisher

                                                     _____
                                                     Shannon Marie

_____
Notary Public

In addition to Articles of Incorporation, a company requires other legal documents. Legal requirements vary from state to state, so be sure to comply with the laws, rules, and regulations of your locality and state as well as those of the federal government. I have used forms from the state of Louisiana.

- *Occupational license.* An application must be submitted to the state in order to receive an occupational license (Exhibit 3-3). In the Louisiana example it is obtained from the Department of Revenue and Taxation. Your company will be assigned a tax number and issued a certificate indicating that the appropriate fee has been paid for conducting the business.
- *Sales tax certificate.* A sales tax certificate is needed from the Department of Revenue and Taxation to guarantee that the appropriate sales taxes are filed and remitted in accordance with the sales and use tax statutes. You can apply for a sales tax certificate with the same form used to obtain an occupational license (Exhibit 3-3).
- *Withholding income tax.* In this case, a business that employs one or more persons at or above a specified minimum salary must register for withholding tax. Once again, the form shown in Exhibit 3-3 will serve the purpose.
- *Corporation franchise tax.* The state of Louisiana requires businesses that incorporate to file a corporation franchise tax initial return (Exhibit 3-4). A tax of ten dollars, along with the completed form, must be submitted to the Department of Revenue and Taxation.
- *Workers' Compensation.* Through Workers' Compensation, a business makes appropriate annual payments so that any employee injured on the job will receive specified payments while out of work. In Louisiana a company must go to a private insurance firm to obtain this protection.
- *Employment Security Law (unemployment insurance).* A Louisiana firm must file a status report with the Louisiana Department of Labor in order to secure an unemployment insurance account number. In this example, a coverage certificate will be issued by the Louisiana Department of Labor, Office of Employment Security, indicating that the corporation has appropriate coverage in the event an employee is laid off or dismissed. The state requires a business to post a notice that states: "Your employer is subject to the Louisiana Employment Security Law and is required to post this notice in a conspicuous place. As a Subject Employer he has contributed to the Louisiana Trust Fund from which benefits are paid. No amount of contributions to the Trust Fund is deductible from your earnings."

Exhibit 3-3 Sample application for occupational license, sales tax certificate, and withholding income tax, state of Louisiana

---

CR-1

STATE OF LOUISIANA
**DEPARTMENT OF
REVENUE AND TAXATION**
P. O. BOX 201
BATON ROUGE, LA 70821

FOR OFFICE USE ONLY

1. Date of Application

Month	Day	Year

APPLICATION FOR AND/OR REQUEST FOR
(Check one or more squares)

FOR OFFICE USE ONLY

FOR OFFICE USE ONLY

2. A. ☐ Sales Tax Certificate
   B. ☐ Withholding Income Tax
   C. ☐ Occupational License Tax _____
   ☐ New Business
   ☐ Renewal _____
   Previous Year License No.

C.R.N.

3. Class _____
   (OLT)
4. SIC _____
   (Sales)

5. Federal Employer ID Number ☐ None

6. LA Sales Tax Number ☐ None

7. LA W/H Number ☐ None

8. A. Taxpayer Name

B. Area Code-Phone Number

C. Trade Name

D. Mail Address

E. City, State, Zip Code

F. Location-Street, City, State, Zip Code

G. Parish Location

9. Type of Organization   A. ☐ Individual   B. ☐ Partnership   C. ☐ Corporation   D. ☐ Governmental   E. ☐ Non-Profit   F. ☐ Other

10. If corporation or partnership Name, Title, Soc. Sec. No., Resident Address and Phone of Officers or Partners.

Name	Title	SSN
Resident Address		Phone-
Name	Title	SSN
Resident Address		Phone-
Name	Title	SSN
Resident Address		Phone-

11. If Sole Owner (individual) Name

SSN

Resident Address

Phone-

12. Ending Month of Accounting (Fiscal Year)

13. Number of Employees Earning $275/Month or More and Paid **FROM THIS** Location (8-F Above)

14. Location of Accounting Records Are Maintained-Check One as Noted in
Item 8 (If other, show other street, ☐ D ☐ F ☐ address, city & state)

15. If Corporation, State of Incorporation

16. Reason for Applying
   A. ☐ Started New Business   C. ☐ Other (specify) _____
   B. ☐ Purchased Going Business—Name of previous Owner

17. Date Business Started/ Acquired at **THIS LOCATION**

Month	Day	Year

18. First Date Wages Paid at **THIS LOCATION**

Month	Day	Year

19. **Excluding** This One How Many Other Business Locations Do You Have in Louisiana?

20. Nature of Business

Description of Sales or Activity

If applying for Occupational License complete Schedule A (reverse side). If transferring License complete only Line 32 on reverse side.

I affirm that the information given on this application and attached schedules is true and correct

Signature of Applicant

Title

Signature of Preparer If different from above

Exhibit 3-3 Continued

OCCUPATIONAL LICENSE SCHEDULE "A"

Please review the instructions for this schedule very carefully. If you have any questions dial Toll-free from within the state 1-800-272-9855. If you are in the Baton Rouge area or out-of-state dial 504-925-7318.

Refer to instructions to determine base and rate (fee) to be used in lines 21 thru 31.

Class of License being applied for_____

License Year_____Open Date for This License _____

COMPLETE ONLY **ONE** OF **21** THRU **25**

21. BUSINESS OPENED DURING THE PREVIOUS CALENDAR YEAR ☐

Gross sales for remainder of calendar year ▶ $ _____
Less: Deductions (describe) _____
▶ $_____ equals ▶ $_____ which divided by number of days in operation ▶ _____ days equal $ _____ which multiplied by 365 amounts to a taxable sales of ▶ $_____

22. BUSINESS OPENED LESS THAN 30 DAYS ☐

Tax due will be the minimum of applicable rate table

23. BUSINESS OPENED MORE THAN 30 DAYS ☐

Gross sales for first 30 days ▶ $ _____
Less: Deductions (describe) _____
▶ $_____ equals ▶ $_____ which multiplied by number of months, or major fraction thereof, remaining in year, _____ months amounts to a taxable sales of ▶ $_____

24. BUSINESS OPENED BETWEEN DECEMBER 2 AND DECEMBER 31 ☐

Gross receipts for remainder of calendar year ▶ $_____

25. BUSINESS OPENED ON OR PRIOR TO JANUARY 1 OF THE PREVIOUS YEAR ☐

Gross sales ▶ $_____
Less: Deductions (describe) _____
▶ $_____ equals taxable gross of ▶ $_____

26. LICENSE FEE RATE DUE BASED ON TABLE _____ $ _____

27. To be used by those occupations paying fee based on units, indicate numbers of seats, spaces, pool tables, etc.

Item	Number	Fee	Total For This Item
Total			$ _____

28. Amount of tax due (Lines 26 & 27) $ _____

29. Interest $ _____

30. Penalty $ _____

31. Total Amount Due   Remit This Amount ▶ $ _____

32. License Number(s) being transferred_____
(License(s) must be attached and signed on back side by licensee in order that the transfer may be made)

Exhibit 3-4 Corporation franchise tax, initial return form, state of Louisiana

CFT—4
R-6479

STATE OF LOUISIANA

CORPORATION

FRANCHISE TAX

INITIAL RETURN

LOUISIANA REVENUE ACCOUNT NUMBER

Name

Street Number or P. O. Box

City & State

FEDERAL EMPLOYER IDENTIFICATION NUMBER

This Return Must be Filed With The Department of Revenue and Taxation—P. O. Box 201, Baton Rouge, Louisiana 70821.

Period covered _____ through _____
Date charter filed with the Secretary of State or Date of Louisiana Qualification or other taxing incidence.   Date of Close of First Accounting Period

NOTE: If your books are kept on a calendar year basis, the period covered must end on the last day of December. If a fiscal year basis is used, the period must end on the last day of any other month and may not exceed 12 months.

NAME AND ADDRESS OF FORMER OWNER, IF THIS CORPORATION IS SUCCESSOR TO AN EXISTING BUSINESS

INCORPORATED IN STATE OF   DATE INCORPORATED

DATE BEGAN BUSINESS IN LOUISIANA   NATURE OF BUSINESS OPERATION

PRINCIPAL PLACE OF BUSINESS

PRINCIPAL LOUISIANA OFFICE LOCATION   PARISHES IN WHICH PROPERTY IS LOCATED

Every corporation subject to the tax must file an initial return on Form CFT—4 and pay a tax of $10.00. This return is due on or before the fifteenth day of the fourth month following the month in which the tax accrues. For a domestic corporation, the tax accrues on the date shown on the charter issued by the Secretary of State. For a foreign corporation, the tax accrues on the date it exercises its charter in Louisiana, is authorized to do or actually does business in Louisiana, or uses any part of its capital or plant in Louisiana. As an example, the tax of ABC accrued on March 21, 1978; its initial return and payment of $10.00 tax would be due on or before July 15, 1978, no matter what accounting year is adopted. Where a calendar year is adopted, the initial return covers the period from March 21, 1978, through December 31, 1978; the next return (covering the calendar year 1979) would be due on or before May 15, 1979 and must be made on Form ICFT 620. If a fiscal year ending June 30, 1978 were adopted, the initial return would cover the period from March 21, 1978, through June 30, 1978, the next return (covering the fiscal year ending June 30, 1979) would be due on or before November 15, 1978, and must be made on Form ICFT 620. Delinquent returns and payments must include applicable penalty and interest.

Corporation franchise tax for domestic corporations continues to accrue, regardless of whether any assets are owned or any business operations are conducted, until a "Certificate of Dissolution" is issued by the Louisiana Secretary of State.

Corporation franchise tax for foreign corporations continues to accrue as long as the corporation exercises its charter, does business, or owns or uses any part of its capital or plant in Louisiana and, in the case of a qualified corporation, until a "Certificate of Withdrawal" is issued by the Louisiana Secretary of State.

1. Franchise Tax . . . . $ _ _ _ _ _ _ _ 10.00
2. Penalty—If Report is Delinquent (5% per each 30 days or fraction thereof not to exceed 25% of Line 1). . . _ _ _ _ _ _ _ _ _ _ _
3. Interest (12% per annum from due date to date of payment) . . . .
4. Total Amount Due (Make remittance payable to Department of Revenue and Taxation) . . . . $

VERIFICATION AND SIGNATURES

I declare under the penalties for filing false reports that this return (including any accompanying schedules and statements) has been examined by me and to the best of my knowledge and belief is a true, correct and complete return. If the return is prepared by a person other than the taxpayer, his declaration is based on all the information relating to the matters required to be reported in the return of which he has knowledge.

_____   _____   _____
(Signature of Officer) (Title)   (Signature of Officer) (Title)   (Date)

_____   _____   _____
(Date)   (Individual or Firm Signature)   (Address)

LEGAL COUNSEL

A business, regardless of size, will need ongoing legal advice. It is clear that a qualified lawyer is necessary in starting a business.[6] There will also be legal problems that arise as a result of business activity. A small business may need to call on the services of a lawyer only infrequently. In this case, payment is made as the services are rendered. Another option is for a lawyer to be on a retainer. For a yearly amount, the lawyer will be available as required. Some small businesses may find it most economical to have a lawyer on the full-time staff. Then, too, some corporations have as a founding officer a lawyer whose services can be used in legal matters.

How to Select a Qualified Lawyer

It is important to obtain a suitable lawyer to meet the initial needs of your firm. How do you go about it? There are many actions that can help.

- Check with business friends or associates who have employed a lawyer in helping them start their businesses.
- Ask bankers, lawyers, the city attorney's office, and other professionals about lawyers who specialize in small business.
- Check with the local or nearby Small Business Administration field office for advice.
- Call the local or nearby American Bar Association for their recommendations.
- Contact a law school in the vicinity. They may have qualified full-time professors who do this kind of work, or perhaps there are adjunct faculty members who have a full-time practice specializing in small business.
- Before making a decision, talk with several lawyers who seem to meet your needs. Find out where they went to school, how long they have been in business, and what their interest is in doing this work. Be sure to determine a fee for their services.
- Legal-services lawyers may be available for minority-owned businesses. Their assistance would be very inexpensive.

A similar approach to that outlined above could be used in obtaining the continuing services of a lawyer. It is important to find a person who works well with you. A fellow runner at the YMCA told me, "I found some of the best help for my small business based on daily contacts at the health center. My lawyer, accountant, architect, insurance agent, and tax consultant all became close friends as a result of working out together. After all, what better way to know someone than by conversations over the years while running three to six miles?"

BINDING ARBITRATION

Binding arbitration can save costly legal fees for defending a firm from nuisance suits. A small business should join the American Arbitration Association and have binding arbitration clauses written into all contracts. In binding arbitration, a neutral person is selected by the parties to a dispute or appointed by statutory authority. The arbitrator conducts a hearing and makes a determination in order to settle the controversy. His decision is binding on both parties.

SUMMARY

A business owner has three choices in deciding what type of legal structure is best for a new firm. A *proprietorship* is the simplest way to get started and is the most common. It is relatively easy to change. The other two forms are *partnership* and *corporation*. The beauty of a corporate structure is its continuing life and limited liability. You may find the subchapter S corporate form best for your company; it permits shareholders to have their income taxed as if the corporation were a partnership, and it may result in sizable tax savings.

Before starting a business you must weigh carefully the advantages and disadvantages of each type of legal entity. Then you can decide what is best for you at the time.

Other legal requirements in starting a business may include getting an occupational license and a sales tax certificate, and arranging for Workers' Compensation, and unemployment insurance.

There is no substitute for a qualified lawyer to help you start a business and continue it successfully. The business owner today is confronted with myriad rules, regulations, and laws of local, state, and federal governments. Violations can be very costly. A qualified lawyer can be helpful in avoiding legal pitfalls, and can be of assistance when you do become involved in legal action. Accordingly, take your time and make a thorough search before selecting the lawyer to work with your firm.

NOTES

1. Limited life in proprietorship means business exists only as long as the owner lives or wishes to stay in business.

2. Source for the material on partnership is the SBA pamphlet MA 231, *Selecting the Legal Structure for Your Firm*, by Antonio M. Olmi, Washington, D. C.: U. S. Government Printing Office, pp. 4 – 6.

3. In a purely legal sense, incorporation means that in most situations the owners cannot be held personally liable for the firm's obligations. From a practical

standpoint, however, when money is borrowed the owners and their spouses may have to sign the debt instruments.

4. Internal Revenue Code 1371–1379.

5. Forms for Articles of Incorporation will vary, and you must decide what is appropriate in accordance with the laws of your state and local government.

6. Take time to select a lawyer to meet your needs. In securing legal guidance to start a business, it is desirable either to get a reliable fee estimate or to be charged a flat rate up front.

Chapter 4
Production

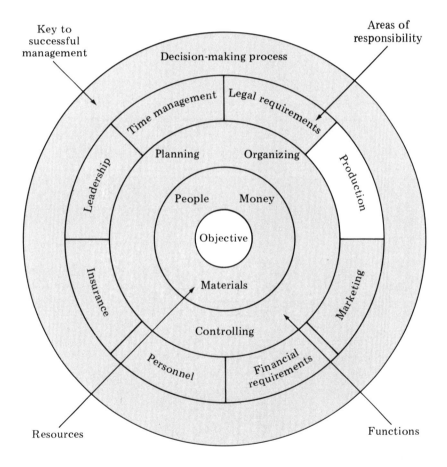

Exhibit 4-1 Stillman's Small Business Management Model: An overview of the five major components of management with emphasis on production

> The key to productivity is fine tuning
> management goals to perceive customer
> demands and worker needs — at a profit.
>
> — George Joseph

What production responsibilities must be met to start and then continue operating a successful small business? This chapter will examine the process of producing goods and services for sale. Topics presented include acquisition of skills, management of manufacturing, management of inventory, store design, and break-even analysis. Let us first see how production fits into the total managerial approach emphasized throughout the text. The white area in Exhibit 4-1 represents production matters. The objective is white to point up that it must be considered in arriving at all managerial decisions.

THE PRODUCTION PROBLEM

Production may be defined as the creation of goods and services that satisfy human wants. In the long run the quality of a product has to be sufficiently high for the firm to survive. From the turn of this century until recently, the productive capability of the United States has been the envy of the world. Our output of products like cars, cameras, television sets, and radios far surpassed foreign competitors. We mass-produced quality items at reasonable prices. Small businesses started by the likes of Thomas Edison, Henry Ford, and Harvey Firestone became giant corporations. Many small firms continue to provide vital material to major companies and to the public. Unfortunately, at the present time some other nations have surpassed the United States in the quality and economy of some of their manufactured products. The automobile industry is a prime example: first Germany successfully exported their small cars, and then by 1980 Japan had become the world's number one car manufacturing nation. The automobile is only one example. As consumers, we have only to look at the labels of origin on any recent purchases.

What is the problem? Why did the United States lose its industrial lead in so many areas? One of the factors was lack of flexibility in product design.

This is apparent in the following account of a 1966 conversation with one car manufacturer:

> In this era of the energy crisis and concern over pollution, there may be greater pressure in the future on manufacturers of luxury automobiles to reduce their size. In Europe, the most expensive cars are considerably smaller than comparably priced vehicles built in the United States. This trend to smaller vehicles may influence your decision because of the reduced resale value in the event the largest cars are no longer manufactured.
>
> This question of size recalls a conversation in 1966 between my wife and the president of a major automobile company. We had recently returned from living in Europe for three years.
>
> *Wife:* Why don't you build a small car like the Europeans? We found them to be so practical and economical.
>
> *President:* Look, we make our largest profit per car on our biggest and most expensive vehicles. From an economic standpoint, it would be foolish to make a small car. We don't intend to do so.[1]

Not enough first-rate minds have been going into manufacturing, and not enough courses in it have been offered in our business schools. A 1981 *Wall Street Journal* article made the following points:

> Manufacturing began to lose its position in business schools in the early 1960s. The main reason was the view that there wasn't much more to be learned about manufacturing. At the time, the nation had the world's most modern, well-equipped industrial base, and the computer was still in its infancy.
>
> Students, too, shunned manufacturing then. That was the time when you were supposed to be helping society by doing countercultural things, recalls Harvard Business School Prof. Robert Hayes. "One of the least countercultural things you could do was go into a dirty factory and make people work harder."[2]

What can be done about this production problem? Professor Martin Starr of Columbia University offered a solution:

> What the country needs is a trained cadre of managers who can go into factories, analyze what's wrong, and then take steps to correct it. Engineers can't do that because they don't have the management and finance background, and finance specialists can't do it because they lack the technical knowledge. Only by producing managers who can apply a broad knowledge of business and technical processes to manufacturing problems will U. S. industry regain its competitive edge, he says.[3]

All businesses, from the smallest to the largest, need to keep the quality of their products and services up if they are to survive in the increasingly competitive years ahead. We shall examine approaches that small business owners can take to cope with their production responsibilities.

ACQUISITION OF SKILLS

First, and perhaps foremost, all owners and managers can improve their knowledge of production. Many colleges and universities offer excellent courses in production and operations management. In some places you can audit courses even if you do not have the required academic credentials. Contact the dean of a business school for further information. If time or location does not permit you to attend a class, you can obtain excellent literature on production at local libraries. Read especially what foreign nations like Japan are doing in this field. Another excellent source is the nearest Small Business Administration office. You can obtain sound advice from officials, and SBA publications provide an abundance of good reading. (See Appendix A.)

Management programs and seminars are put on by commercial firms, universities, and professional groups. It should be easy to select a program that pertains to small businesses, or to your business in particular.

If your firm is large enough you should consider hiring a top graduate from one of the better business schools who has majored in production and operations management. Smaller businesses that cannot afford a full-time expert can still obtain sound manufacturing advice by retaining the services of a respected management consulting firm. Ask the SBA for assistance or advice on who might be available in your area. Local university faculties often have members with knowledge about the technical aspects of manufacturing who can be brought in to consult.

Although a firm may have a production manager or part-time consultant the owner should still be familiar with the production process. The remainder of this chapter will discuss production concepts of interest to small manufacturers or retail outlets.

The production process is depicted graphically in Exhibit 4-2. It starts with inputs of information and various resources. The resources in turn must be processed by the organization, and the output is an achievement of the productivity goals. Exhibit 4-2 uses a money management model to illustrate this total approach, concept. A small firm could modify this model to suit its needs. *Inputs* might be people, money, and materials. The *processing* for, say, a uniform manufacturer would be accomplished through the various plant activities (see the section of chapter 2 that refers to organization, pp. 22 – 30). The output would be finished uniforms that met company standards and customer needs (see George Joseph's comment in this chapter's epigraph). Stated another way, an organization takes available re-

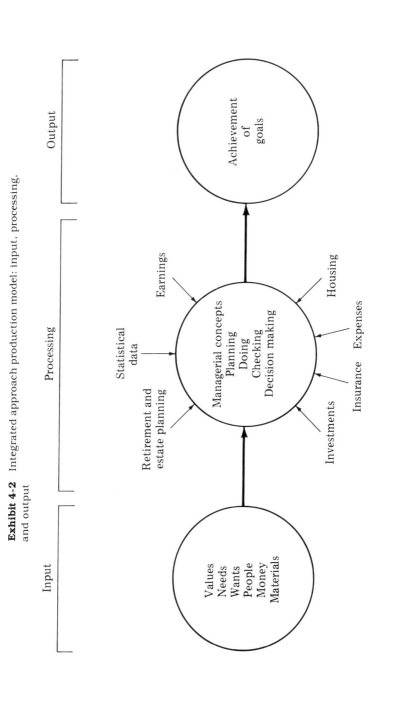

Exhibit 4-2 Integrated approach production model: input, processing, and output

Input

Processing

Output

Values
Needs
Wants
People
Money
Materials

Retirement and
estate planning

Statistical
data

Earnings

Managerial concepts
Planning
Doing
Checking
Decision making

Housing

Insurance   Expenses

Investments

Achievement
of
goals

sources and transforms them into salable products. What is required to do this successfully?

MANAGEMENT OF MANUFACTURING

Every company has a formula for business success, even though it may not be explicitly stated. These formulas, also called competitive strategies, are a combination of the way a company chooses its markets, approaches those markets, and handles its finances to achieve the objectives of the managers and owners.[4]

A sensible way to review manufacturing is to examine the critical ingredients of a company's formula for success. This should allow you to determine the performance criteria your manufacturing must meet to make the formula work. This is not always an easy task, however, because there are many factors that influence manufacturing. A partial list would include:

- ○ Investment — capital investment in plant, facilities, and inventories.
- ○ Unit cost — the cost of each item produced, measured on the basis of direct labor, materials, and overhead.
- ○ Quality — the dependable expectation that shipped product meets adequate design specifications and customer needs.
- ○ Delivery — the average amount of time that elapses between the receipt of an order and shipment of the product.
- ○ Delivery reliability — the percentage of the time that an order is shipped to a customer on the date promised.
- ○ New product capability — the number of new products that plant management and engineering can introduce in a year, and the length of time required to gear up for production of these new products.
- ○ Break-even point — the dollar sales at which income just covers the fixed overhead and direct costs of production.

Establish a sound basis for evaluating manufacturing decisions, after giving some thought to the formula for success, so that you can make the correct trade-offs in these areas. A qualified production manager should be able to identify alternative manufacturing methods, and to apply the appropriate techniques in deciding on the trade-offs involved. If you cannot afford a manufacturing expert, contact the SBA and obtain their advice and literature on the subject.

MANAGEMENT OF INVENTORY

What is inventory and why is effective management of it so important to a business?[5] Inventory may be defined as stocks of anything that is essential to operate a business. These stocks represent a large portion of the business investment, and must be well managed to maximize profits. In fact, many small businesses cannot absorb the losses that can arise from poor management of inventory. Unless inventories are controlled, they are unreliable, inefficient, and costly. Managers usually lean toward keeping inventory levels on the high side, yet this greater investment, given a constant amount of profit, yields a low return. This is one of the contradictory demands made on the manager of inventory. Others include:

○ Maintain a good assortment of products — but not too many.
○ Increase inventory turnover — but only at a good profit.
○ Keep stocks low — but not too low.
○ Make volume purchases to get lower prices — but don't overbuy.
○ Get rid of obsolete items — but not before their replacements have taken hold in the market.

Successful inventory management involves attempting to balance the costs of inventory with the benefits of inventory. Many small business owners fail to appreciate the true costs of carrying inventory, which include not only the direct costs of storage, insurance, taxes, and the like, but also the cost of money tied up in inventory. They often do not realize that small reductions in inventory investment may result in large changes in the company's total cash position. For example, one reward of improved inventory management may be an increase in working capital without having to borrow money.

Computing the Inventory Turnover Rate

Inventory turnover rate is important because it permits comparison with your inventory and the average rate of the industry. In some business, for example, turnover is rapid where in others it is much slower. Grocery stores, for example, have a faster turnover rate than furniture stores. You can determine turnover rate by determining how long it takes you to sell your merchandise within a year's period. If you can turn it over four times a year twice, you can carry half as much merchandise. Therefore, this is an important factor to analyze. The Inventory turnover ratio can be expressed as follows:

$$\frac{\text{Cost of goods sold}}{\text{Merchandise inventory}}$$

One simple, commonly used measure of performance is the inventory turnover rate. This rate gives a rough guideline by which managers can set goals and measure performance, but you must realize that the turnover rate varies with the kind of inventory, the type of business, and the way the ratio is calculated (whether on sales or cost of goods sold). For example, the inventory turnover rates for manufacturers of paperboard containers range annually from 4.5 to 21.0; even then they are all calculated on cost of goods sold.

Rates such as these are published periodically by trade associations and professional organizations. They can be useful in setting guidelines for your own company, but they must be evaluated with care.

Manual Recordkeeping Methods

At a very basic level, inventory records maintained by a business provide the information that is needed to make decisions about inventory management. But the determination of the number and kind of records to be maintained, as well as the type of control system to be used, depends on the type and size of inventory. In many small businesses where visual control is used, records may be needed only for slow-moving or expensive items, if at all. But in a larger organization where many items from various suppliers are involved, more formal inventory records such as card files are appropriate. Whatever types of records you maintain, the accuracy and discipline of the recording system is critical.

It is important to remember that many opportunities for improved efficiency and cost reduction are not realized simply because records are insufficient or inaccurate. Most of the various techniques for improved inventory management depend on reasonably accurate inventory data.

Many smaller manufacturers, wholesalers, and retailers with relatively few items in inventory use manual inventory control systems. They use card records, inventory tags, and accounting data to capture the information necessary to establish economical order quantities, order points, and other guidelines for effective inventory control. As the number of items and suppliers and the general importance of inventory increases, however, it is often desirable to consider use of a computerized system for inventory control.

Using Computers in Inventory Management

Today the use of computer systems to control inventory is far more feasible for the small business than ever before, because of the widespread existence of computer service companies (listed in the Yellow Pages of many telephone directories) and the decreasing cost of small computers. Often the justification of a computer-based system is easier because a company's accounting and billing procedures can also be handled on the computer.

Most computer manufacturers offer free written information on inventory management systems available for use with their computers. In addition, computer service companies often have material available describing the use of their computer software, such as programs for inventory management. These companies are a good source of general descriptions of inventory management techniques, as well as a help with specific inventory management problems.

Before selecting a computer or any software, find out what successful competitors are using. Visit at least three firms that are currently using the system. If the computer package is expensive, you may want to lease. Do not lease for more than three years; by then a new generation of computers will have come along and made the existing equipment obsolete.

Whether you use a manual or a computerized inventory management system, the important thing to remember is that inventory management involves two separate but closely related elements. The first is knowing what and how much to order, when to order, and what price to pay; the second is making sure that the items, once brought into inventory, are used properly to produce a profit.

If you decide that a computer is appropriate for your firm, be sure to use it wherever you can in your business. It can provide essential information that can enable a manager or owner to make wise decisions.

STORE PLANNING AND DESIGN

A well-designed store enhances merchandising, which is the reason for the store's existence. Store planning and design[6] can cover a wide scope of activities, ranging from redoing a storefront or rearranging fixtures to opening a completely new store. Important issues in store planning and design include the location of the store, customer circulation pattern, mode of displaying the merchandise, availability of appropriate space, use of light and color, and compliance with relevant building and retailing codes. Cost is always an important and often the decisive consideration. Flexibility can also be a major issue where the accommodation of new products, display requirements, or adaptation to seasonal changes is critical.

You can obtain store planning and design assistance from store planning and design firms, manufacturers of store fixtures who offer a design service, and interior design and architectural firms. Services may include space and traffic pattern recommendations, fixture design or selection, and lighting, color, and material selection.

The design can begin with a determination of customer and staff requirements, merchandise to be displayed, desired appearance, cost considerations, and future growth needs. Based on this information, the designer may develop a set of preliminary proposals for your review. These proposals may take various forms, but quick sketches are often used to communicate the preliminary concepts, with the final proposals being carried into floor plans, elevations, and related detailed drawings and specifications.

Sometimes models and color samples are also employed to illustrate the proposals. Firms vary somewhat in their procedures, but this is a fairly typical approach. As a store-owner, you will want to consider the way a firm charges for its services (flat fee, hourly rate, or area rate), and you will want to see examples (in photographs or site visits) of prior work the firm has done.

You should consider the physical environment of the store an integral part of its operation and a potentially important factor in its success. Thus planning and design can make a significant contribution to the achievement of the desired goals of the store.

BREAK-EVEN ANALYSIS

Break-even analysis (also referred to as cost-volume profit analysis) provides a small manufacturer with information on what sales volume is necessary to cover costs. Consider the H & R Radiator Corporation as an example of how break-even analysis may be used. Assume that H & R must decide whether to produce a new radiator created by the research and development staff. First, marketing must estimate the number of units that will be sold, then production determines how many radiators must be manufactured to make it a worthwhile investment. This requires a determination of all fixed[7] and variable[8] costs. The H & R Corporation must produce the new radiators at a price that will make it a profitable venture. Too few will drive the unit cost, and thus the price, up; too many will tie up inventory resources. Marketing informs management that it can sell 30,000 units the first year. Production can then proceed with its break-even analysis, as one factor in determining the feasibility of the project. The new radiator can be sold to distributors at $50.00 per unit. Fixed costs are estimated at $500,000 and variable expenses come to $30.00 for each radiator.

You can arrive at the break-even point by using the following formula:

$$\text{Break-even point (BEP)} = \frac{\text{Total fixed costs}}{\text{Selling price} - \text{variable costs}}$$

$$\text{BEP} = \frac{\$500,000}{\$50 - \$30} = \frac{\$500,000}{\$20} = 25,000 \text{ radiators}$$

The break-even concept can be portrayed as shown in Exhibit 4-3. The H & R Corporation covers all its costs if sales total 25,000 radiators. Every radiator sold beyond this number provides a $20.00 profit for the firm. This profit figure is obtained by subtracting the variable cost ($30.00) from the selling price ($50.00). Therefore, the estimated 30,000 sales in the first year will produce a profit of $100,000 (5,000 × $20.00). An analysis of the

Exhibit 4-3 Break-even analysis of the H & R Radiator Corporation

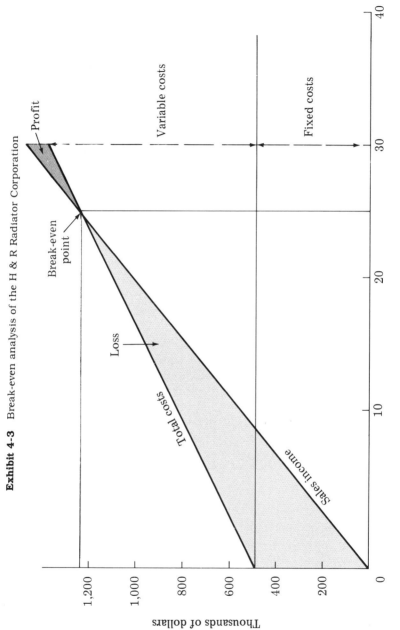

break-even data will assist management in deciding to press ahead with the new radiator in view of the first-year profit projection. In contrast, if a substantial loss were indicated, the H & R owner might scrap the project.

Break-even analysis can assist an owner in making a rough estimate of gain or loss based on sales volume. A graph like Exhibit 4-3 can be used to test modifications in cost and selling price. But break-even analysis is not without its weaknesses. Its simplistic approach does not lend itself to precise estimates. Fixed costs, for example, are shown remaining the same over marked variations in quantity. This is not necessarily true. In the radiator case, for example, as volume increases a firm can expect more machinery failures. If it increases substantially, they might need a new plant altogether. This type of analysis also does not look at cash flow considerations (see chapter 6). Management could not go into production of the new radiator without adequate funds available to pay for the raw materials, labor, and other expenses. As a consequence, break-even analysis should only be used as one factor in arriving at production decisions.

SUMMARY

Production may be defined as the creation of goods and services that satisfy human wants. In the long run, the quality of a product has to be sufficiently high for a firm to survive. In recent years there has been a slippage in the quality and economy of certain products manufactured in the United States. One of the contributing factors has been lack of flexibility in product design. The automobile industry is a prime example.

It is important for a small business to meet changing wants of its customers. A neighborhood bakery, for instance, made all its own products. It produced the same merchandise for over twenty years, but in this time the ethnic makeup of the neighborhood changed markedly. Sales fell until the owner hired a specialist who pointed out the need to meet the desires of the current shoppers. A change in product mix, coupled with effective advertising, resulted in new high profits.

Small business owners have excellent opportunities to improve their knowledge of production. Many schools offer excellent evening courses on this subject. The SBA, trade associations, and local libraries can provide excellent literature. Special seminars are offered by various organizations and schools.

Although a firm can have a production manager or part-time consultant, it is still desirable for the owner to be familiar with the manufacturing process. This process may be represented as a three-part operation. First, there is the input of resources (people, money, materials); second, the processing of the resources by the organization; and third, the output of the finished product. Stated another way, the primary production responsibility of an owner is to make effective use of resources (inputs) within an efficient organizational structure (processing) so that quality finished goods or services may be sold at a fair profit.

In manufacturing, factors to be considered include: unit cost, quality, delivery, delivery reliability, investment, new product capability, and break-even point. The determination of break-even points provides a firm with information on what sales volume is necessary to cover costs and make a reasonable profit.

Two other production aspects are inventory management and store design. Inventory management requires reliable and efficient controlling of all stock essential to operating a business. Managers usually lean toward keeping inventory levels on the high side, yet this greater investment yields a low return. This is one of the contradictory demands made on the manager. Store design can consist of rearranging fixtures to opening a completely new store. Important issues include its location, demographics, display, and use of color and light.

NOTES

1. Stillman, Richard J., *Guide to Personal Finance: A Lifetime Program of Money Management*, 2nd ed., Englewood Cliffs, N. J.: Prentice-Hall, 1975, pp. 115–116.

2. Sease, Douglas R., "Schools Again Offer Courses on Production," *The Wall Street Journal*, January 26, 1981, p. 25.

3. As paraphrased by Sease, p. 25.

4. This section is based on the SBA Small Business Bibliographies pamphlet no. 88, *Manufacturing Management*, by Jeffery Miller, Washington, D. C.: U. S. Government Printing Office, 1979.

5. This section is based on the SBA Small Business Bibliographies pamphlet no. 75, *Inventory Management*, by Edward W. Davis and D. Clay Whybark, Washington, D. C.: U. S. Government Printing Office, 1979.

6. This section is based on the SBA Small Business Bibliographies pamphlet no. 79, *Small Store Planning and Design*, by Robert B. Bartholomew, Washington, D. C.: U. S. Government Printing Office, 1979.

7. Fixed costs are expenses that remain constant regardless of the number of radiators produced. This would include items such as building, rent, owner's salary, certain taxes, and insurance.

8. Variable costs are those expenses directly related to the number of radiators produced — wages of assembly-line workers, electrical cords, iron, and other raw materials. These are usually constant per unit, hence, the greater the volume, the higher the total of variable costs.

Chapter 5
Marketing

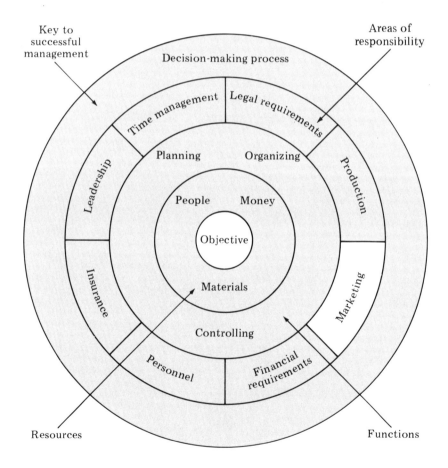

Exhibit 5-1 Stillman's Small Business Management Model: An overview of the five major components of management with emphasis on marketing

> The organization must learn to think of itself not as producing goods or services, but as *buying customers*, as doing the things that will make people *want* to do business with it.
>
> — Theodore Levitt

What are the marketing requirements to start a small business and then to continue operating it successfully? This chapter will examine ways to determine the feasibility of opening a firm. Other marketing considerations that will be presented include advertising, public relations, and pricing.

How does the marketing responsibility fit into the total managerial approach emphasized throughout this book? The white area in Exhibit 5-1 represents the area of marketing requirements. The objective is white to point up that it must be considered in arriving at all managerial decisions.

The interrelatedness of production to all managerial activities can be illustrated as follows: the H & R Company has developed a new electric steam radiator. The effective *marketing* of the radiator is essential to its success. However, *production* (chapter 4) has to be of high quality to ensure continued sales. *Legal* aspects (chapter 3), such as possible lawsuits, should also be weighed. *Insurance* (chapter 8), *financing* (chapter 6), and *personnel* requirements (chapter 7) must be reviewed and modified if necessary. Effective *leadership* (chapter 9) and the judicious use of *time* (chapter 10) are also important factors in the marketing of the radiator. To arrive at sound decisions, the owner or manager must develop an effective marketing *plan* for the radiator, *implement* the plan, and use an effective *control* system. The wise use of limited resources — people, money, and materials — is also essential to the product's success.

MARKET FEASIBILITY STUDY

Before starting a business, you must determine the best place to locate. If a company does not have enough customers to buy the product or service, it cannot succeed. A study of market potential is very important in selecting the right site. This entails careful planning before making a decision. One approach is to develop a questionnaire and conduct a random sampling of potential customers in the target area to determine the demand. Personal observation of where successful competitors are located can also be useful.

Other valuable tools in deciding where to locate are data from the U. S. Bureau of the Census. The bureau prepares excellent reports that provide detailed information on localities with 50,000 or more residents. General characteristics of the population are presented, including race, age, sex, country of origin, years of schooling, occupation, income, value of housing, and rental costs.

How can you apply census data in deciding on an appropriate place to start a business — in this example, a retail store?

Site Analysis

Every store has a trading area — a geographic region from which it draws its potential customers. Data for trading areas, regardless of size, can generally be assembled by combining a number of census tract tables. These may be the best single source of information. If you are going to make a complete store location analysis, however, you should supplement it with other material. [1]

Unlike a manufacturing operation, which can ship its products elsewhere, the potential business of a retail store is limited to its trading area. The primary area can range from a few blocks, for a small neighborhood store, to a thirty-five-mile radius for a store located in a large shopping center. Keep in mind that the radius may shrink in the years ahead with rising energy costs and the potential interruption of fuel supplies.

Your primary concern as the prospective owner of a single store will be factors that have direct bearing on your store's trading area. Far too many small retailers select a store site by chance: the most common reason given is "noticed vacancy." The high turnover rate would be considerably lower if retailers analyzed in advance the trading area's population and housing characteristics, the nature and quality of the competition, local traffic, and the accessibility of the site. Another important variable to be aware of is total consumer purchasing power and your store's expected share of this total. Every location analysis must be custom-made, focussing on the particular line of retailing. Answers to questions like the following can be found in census reports:

- How many persons or families are there in the trading area? How has this changed over time?
- Where do they work?
- How many young or old people are there? How many children? How many teenagers?
- How many families with small children or with teenagers?
- How many one-person households? How many small or large families?
- What is the average income of the families? Of the individuals?
- What do they do for a living?

o Is the area an older, established one, or one where most residents are newcomers?
o How many families own their homes? How many rent?
o What are the values of the homes? What are the monthly rents?
o What is the age and quality of the homes?
o Do the homes have air conditioning? Other appliances?
o How many of the families own automobiles? How many own two or more?

A number of other considerations will have varying importance in your choice of a retail location, depending on the nature of your business. The following list of questions, while not exhaustive, may help you decide on a retail location:

o How much retail, office, storage, or workroom space do you need?
o Is parking space available and adequate?
o Are special lighting, heating, cooling, or other installations required?
o Is the store easily accessible?
o Is the area served by public transportation?
o Will advertising and travel expenses be much higher if you select a relatively remote location?
o Can the area be a source of employees?
o Is there adequate fire and police protection?
o Will sanitation or utility supply be a problem?
o Is external lighting in the area adequate to attract evening shoppers and make them feel safe?
o Are customer rest rooms available?
o Does the store have awnings or decks to provide shelter during bad weather?
o Will crime insurance be prohibitively expensive?
o Will pickup and delivery service be provided?
o What are the risks of fire or riot damage?
o Is the site heavily dependent on seasonal business?
o Is it convenient to where you live?
o Do the desired customers live nearby?
o Is the population density of the area sufficient?
o Can an effective security system be installed to minimize the possibility of material and personal losses?
o Does the area have a strong merchants' association?

Obtaining data about the characteristics of possible locations is of critical importance. Before making a final decision, determine if similar businesses are located nearby. Other successful firms indicate that the location is a good one. They can also be a factor in bringing customers into your store. After all, if people are already in the vicinity, they are likely to want to comparison shop. Capitalize on your proximity to other businesses by using appropriate advertising, including announced specials and sales. There will be more about advertising later in this chapter.

U. S. Bureau of the Census Publications

Where can you get U. S. Bureau of the Census material on location and other valuable marketing data? Bureau of the Census publications are available for reference at many libraries. They can also be used or purchased at U. S. Department of Commerce district offices, which are located in forty-three major cities. Some seven hundred "cooperative offices" run by local chambers of commerce also offer Bureau of the Census leaflets and other informative printed matter. Nearly all of the publications can be purchased from the Superintendent of Documents, U. S. Government Printing Office, Washington, D. C. 20402, but some publications can only be obtained from the Bureau of the Census. For an order form listing tract and block reports, write to the Publications Distribution Section, U. S. Bureau of the Census, Social and Economic Statistics Administration, Washington, D. C. 20233.

Business Suitability Study

In your market research, you should also do a self-analysis to see if the location and the work are appropriate for you as the potential owner. Before opening a business, consider what areas of the company are likely to grow and what areas appeal to your personality. After all, work can be an enjoyable experience if you do what you like where you want to do it. Exhibit 5-2 provides a rating scale to assist in making a decision on location. In addition to doing the community research, analyze the potential satisfaction you would derive from various businesses. You can use Exhibit 5-3 for this purpose.

Merchants' Associations

Most first-time business owners do not appreciate how effective a strong merchants' association can be in promoting and maintaining business in a given area. The presence of an effective merchants' association can strengthen a business and save it money through group advertising programs, group insurance, and collective security and maintenance measures.[2]

A strong merchants' association can accomplish far more than an individual store-owner. Some associations have induced city planners to add highway exits near their shopping centers. Others have lobbied for and received funds from cities to remodel their shopping centers, including extension of parking lots, refacing of buildings, and installation of better light-

Exhibit 5-2   Site analysis worksheet

	A	B	C	D
Community				
Growth potential				
Friends				
Demand for product				
Government contracts				
Capable work force available				
Adequate suppliers				
Money sources				
Transportation				
Competition				
Total				

```
1 — Outstanding
2 — Good
3 — Fair
4 — Poor
```

Rapidly growing cities include Las Vegas, Nevada; Austin, Texas; Tucson, Arizona; Fort Lauderdale, Florida; Houston, Texas; Phoenix, Arizona; Oxnard, California; Tacoma, Washington; San Diego, California; Anaheim, California; Salt Lake City, Utah; Tulsa, Oklahoma; Portland, Oregon; Seattle, Washington; Oklahoma City, Oklahoma; Tampa, West Palm Beach, Florida; Baton Rouge, Louisiana; Riverside, California; and Orlando, Florida. This worksheet is applicable to any locality.

ing. Let's face it — politicians are sensitive to blocs of potential votes and sources of potential campaign contributions.

Merchants' associations can be particularly effective in promoting stores by using common themes or scheduling special events during holiday seasons. The collective draw from these promotions is usually several times what a single retailer could have mustered.

How can you determine if the retail location you are considering has the benefit of an effective merchants' association? Ask other store-owners in the area. You will also want to determine:

○ Membership of the association
○ Officers
○ Frequency of meetings
○ Yearly dues
○ Accomplishments of the last year

Exhibit 5-3 Business suitability study — Self-analysis worksheet

	Business A	Business B	Business C
How well does the business meet my values and goals in life?			
Will I enjoy what I will be doing and be willing to put in twelve hours or more a day doing it?			
Will the anticipated yearly income meet my needs?			
What about other benefits that appeal to me such as security; car; travel; education; insurance; medical and dental protection?			
What are the growth and merger possibilities?			
Will the business permit me to reach my full potential?			
How are the working conditions?			
Is it convenient to my residence?			
How secure a retirement program can I establish?			
Other considerations:			
Total			

```
1 — Outstanding
2 — Good
3 — Fair
4 — Poor
```

What if there is no merchants' association? It is generally (though not always) true that a shopping area or center with no merchants' association, or with an ineffective one, is on the decline. You will probably see excessive litter or debris in the area, vacant stores, a parking lot in need of repair, and other symptoms. Avoid locations that show these warning signs. On-site investigations are essential if you are to avoid selecting the wrong area.

MARKET RESEARCH ASSISTANCE

Where can a potential owner get help in market research? To start, the best bet is the nearest Small Business Administration field office. The SBA can provide excellent advice on location and how to go about making a feasibility study. They will also provide pamphlets. These services of the SBA are free. Many market research firms will, for a fee, make the necessary studies for a potential owner. The Yellow Pages in New Orleans, for example, lists twenty such businesses under the heading "Market Research & Analysis." Notations after company names include: "Professional Interviewing — Specialized Research Skills" and "Feasibilities — Surveys — Forecasts." The right firm can provide valuable assistance, but it is essential that you select a company that can do the best job for you. Check with the SBA and the Better Business Bureau before making a decision. Also ask if the firm has done such research recently for similar new businesses. Get the names and then call these people to find out if they were satisfied. Be sure to get a written contract that specifies precisely what is to be done and how much it will cost.

Contact nearby universities to determine if faculty members do feasibility studies. Talk to the chairman of the marketing department or the dean of the business school. Again it is essential to determine the capabilities of the person before making a commitment. Be sure to firm up the fee and have a written agreement. It is also possible that a professor may have a marketing class take on such a project, or a graduate student undertake it for credit. It never hurts to ask school officials about these possibilities.

ADVERTISING

You can have the best product or service in the world, but without an effective advertising program your firm is doomed to failure. Advertising is an important part of the total marketing package that must be geared to achieving the firm's objectives.

In determining what advertising media are most suitable, you will find that costs are a significant factor. How can you reach the biggest possible market for a product or service with the lowest possible expenditure?

Look at Exhibit 5-4, a checklist that indicates available media. There are many choices, and it is important to select those most suitable to the needs of your company. It also pays to take full advantage of all free sources, such as window displays and bulletin boards. In starting a business, use Exhibit 5-4 to list initial advertising costs — estimated and actual. It is important to estimate yearly advertising expenses, and to check that actual costs stay within the estimate.

Exhibit 5-4   Advertising media and cost worksheet

Medium	Initial cost		Annual cost	
	Estimate	Actual	Estimate	Actual
Television				
Radio				
Newspapers				
Direct mail				
Magazines				
Trade journals				
Store displays				
Package displays				
Billboards				
Handbills				
Creative art				
Advertisement on subways and buses				
Specialty				
Free sources				
Personal appearances on TV and radio				
Human interest stories for newspaper				
Bulletin boards				
Total				

Advertising Cost Ratio

To keep from overspending, you may want to use a ratio as a basis for deciding how much to spend for advertising. This ratio can be expressed as follows:

$$\frac{\text{Advertising expenditures}}{\text{Net sales}} = \text{Advertising cost ratio}$$

Let us assume that it will require advertising expenditures of $1,000 to achieve net monthly sales of $80,000. The computation would be as follows:

$$\frac{1,000}{80,000} = .0125 = 1.25\%$$

If sales exceed this $80,000 amount, you can apply the ratio (1.25 percent) and have a larger budget available for advertising. This larger amount may also allow you to modify the media mix of your advertising. Filling out the checklist in Exhibit 5-4 again can help you achieve the best return on advertising dollars.

Advertising Guidelines

You should observe the following points in developing an appropriate advertising program for a small business.

- Develop a program to meet your firm's objectives.
- Stay within a predetermined budget.
- Capitalize on free advertising.
- Obtain a formal contract for all advertising and spell out precisely what is desired — misunderstandings can be expensive.
- Use your own creative ideas in developing copy for newspapers, radio, TV, and other media. After all, no one knows the product or service better than the owner.
- White space sells. Do not try to put too much information in an ad.
- Seek qualified assistance whenever necessary. The SBA, business friends, and nearby universities can be helpful.
- A first-quality advertising agency may be appropriate for some small businesses. Check costs carefully and determine if it is a wise investment of your resources.
- Make yourself newsworthy. Get on radio and TV talk shows. Donate to charitable organizations and be a sponsor of special fund-raisers. Have contests and giveaways that gain free publicity.

PUBLIC RELATIONS

I have had the pleasure of speaking to the Deep South Bakery Association on several occasions. To prepare myself for these presentations, I visited a number of bakeries in my hometown. As a result of these visits, I came to know some of the owners quite well. The most impressive public relations program I observed was managed by a gentleman who had been in the bakery business for over forty years. His view of public relations was, "Look, I have a good product and I want people to know about it. Advertising can be expensive, but the costs of good publicity are negligible." Public relations, in essence, is letting the public — customers, employees, suppliers, creditors, friends, and financial institutions — know about the fine products or services your firm provides. My baker friend's successful public relations techniques included:

- Creating a unique neon sign for his store. It read "Mr. Wedding Cake," and it had his picture on it.

- ○ Printing his packaging materials with the motif from the neon sign.
- ○ Offering to attend important weddings and personally cut the cake. He was delighted when the papers covered the affair and included his picture with the bride and groom in the cake-cutting ceremony.
- ○ Providing the local media with interesting pictures and stories about his business.
- ○ Participating in the activities of local community associations and clubs.
- ○ Greeting his customers personally and by name.

"Mr. Wedding Cake" had an excellent public relations program. Every small business owner should have techniques that communicate effectively the quality of his products or services. Do not hesitate to prepare stories and photos for the media. Your employees can also help spread the word by emulating the boss's pride in the company. You may want to let people and groups visit your shop or plant. Brief tours of bakeries, restaurants, and other small businesses allow an owner to explain and show off quality work. Take advantage also of speaking opportunities at various functions where you can talk about your company. Even an introduction alone is beneficial — "It is my pleasure to introduce Joan Smith, president of XYZ Corporation."

PRICING AND DISTRIBUTION

Price may be defined as what a firm charges for a product or service. The problem facing management is to set the right price so that people will buy in the quantities necessary to meet the firm's objectives. Steps to take in establishing the right price include:

- ○ Determining the firm's costs, both direct and indirect, and adding an appropriate profit margin.
- ○ Finding out what the competition is charging.
- ○ Determining what competitive edge your firm's product or service has over other companies.
- ○ Assessing the impact of future inflation.
- ○ Maintaining flexibility in pricing to meet rapidly changing economic conditions.

In starting a business, it is important to have competitive prices. It is also desirable to be innovative. This may require setting different prices over a period of time. With accurate records of sales, you can determine the desirability of being above or below the average for the industry or market area. One small retail business's slogan was, "We undersell." Its pricing experience was that profits were greater on higher volume at smaller profit margins per item. Others may find that catering to the carriage trade at higher-than-average markups can be more profitable. But conditions can change rapidly, so it is essential to have a flexible pricing policy.

SUMMARY

It is important to complete appropriate market research before starting a business. The selection of a good location is an essential part of this research. The U. S. Bureau of the Census can provide excellent information on the characteristics of a particular locality. You should also consider such factors as the growth potential of various communities, the success rate of similar businesses, and your own suitability to the business.

If you have neither the time nor the training to do market research, get assistance from experts in the field. The SBA, universities, and private firms are the ones to contact for this help.

A firm can have the best product or service in the world, but without an effective sales force and advertising program it is doomed to failure. Effective advertising must influence people to buy the specific item. Many media are available for advertising, and it is important to select those most suitable to the needs of your company.

A good public relations program can be an effective and economical means of communicating the high quality of your firm. In essence, public relations is letting the public — customers, employees, suppliers, creditors, friends, and financial institutions — know about your firm.

Price may be defined as what a firm charges for a product or service. Steps to take in establishing the right price include: determining costs; finding out what the competition is charging; determining the impact of inflation; exploring possible competitive advantages of the firm's product or service; and maintaining flexibility to meet changing economic conditions.

NOTES

1. This section is based on the SBA Small Marketers' Aid publication no. 154, *Using Census Data to Select a Store Site*, by Louis H. Vorzimer, Washington, D. C.: U. S. Government Printing Office, 1979, pp. 2 – 11.

2. This section is based on the SBA Small Marketer's Aid publication no. 168, "Little Things Mean a Lot," by Jeffery P. Davidson, Washington, D. C.: U. S. Government Printing Office, 1979, p. 3.

Chapter 6
Financial Requirements

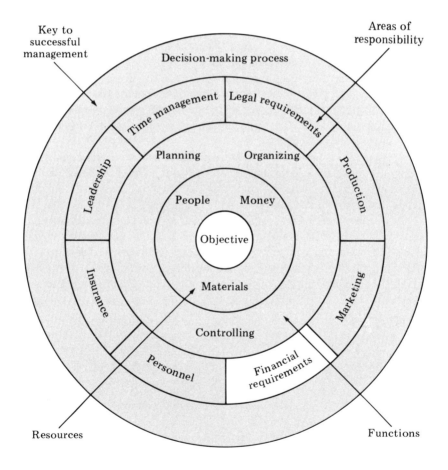

Key to successful management

Areas of responsibility

Decision-making process

Time management

Legal requirements

Planning

Organizing

Leadership

Production

People

Money

Objective

Insurance

Materials

Marketing

Controlling

Personnel

Financial requirements

Resources

Functions

Exhibit 6-1 Stillman's Small Business Management Model: An overview of the five major components of management with emphasis on financial requirements

> Business, you know, may bring money, but
> friendship hardly ever does.
>
> — Jane Austen

What are your financial responsibilities in starting a firm and then continuing to operate it successfully? This chapter will examine sources of capital, borrowing costs, cash flow, financial statements, analysis of financial records, and income tax requirements. Let us first see how the financial aspects of management fit into the total managerial approach emphasized throughout this text. The white area in Exhibit 6-1 represents financial matters. The objective is also white to emphasize that it must be considered in arriving at all managerial decisions.

SOURCES OF CAPITAL

Lack of money is an important cause of business failures. It is therefore essential to understand the sources of capital and the cost of borrowing money. Where can you raise the money needed to start your business, or secure additional funds once you are in operation? We shall discuss a number of sources.

Your Resources

Invest your own funds in your business. [1] If your firm is a success, the return on your investment will normally be higher than the interest or dividends available through other investments. A sizable investment of your own capital also gives you a greater chance of receiving loans from lending institutions. By putting up much of your own money you are saying that you believe in your company's success. You are also making it less risky for the lender: in case of bankruptcy, you as the owner would be the last to receive any of the liquidated assets. [2]

Friends and Relatives

You may be able to obtain some money at low or no interest from a relative or a friend. Perhaps that rich aunt will make a loan at a nominal rate. Personal sources can be especially helpful if you have no business experience and run into difficulty securing money elsewhere. A word of caution: this type of borrowing can turn friends into enemies. It is extremely important to pay back such loans on time and in full.

The Small Business Administration

For the small business that needs money and cannot borrow it on reasonable terms from conventional lenders, the Small Business Administration offers a broad range of loan programs.[3] The agency may either participate with a bank or other lender in making a loan, or guarantee up to 90 percent of a loan that a bank or other lender agrees to make. If the bank or other lender cannot provide funds by either of these methods, the SBA can consider lending the entire amount as a direct government loan. The demand for direct loans traditionally exceeds the SBA's supply of direct loan monies, however, so most of the SBA's loans are made in cooperation with banks. SBA loans may be used for business construction, expansion, or conversion; the purchase of machinery, equipment, facilities, supplies, or materials; or working capital.

Types of SBA loans are as follows:

○ *Regular Business Loans.* Under Section 7(a) of the Small Business Act, as amended, the SBA is authorized to make regular business loans to small firms on a direct, participatory, or guaranteed basis.

○ *Economic Opportunity Loans.* The agency grants Economic Opportunity Loans to help persons who are socially or economically disadvantaged[4] start and maintain their own businesses.

○ *Local Development Company Loans.* Local Development Companies are groups of local citizens organized to improve their area's economy by assisting small businesses. Such companies may apply for SBA loans to buy land, build new factories or shopping centers, acquire machinery and equipment, or expand or convert existing facilities — provided that the project will assist at least one small business. Local Development Companies themselves must provide a reasonable share of the cost of the project, usually at least 20 percent of the total amount.

○ *State Development Company Loans.* State Development Companies must be organized by a specific act of a state legislature to assist the statewide growth and development of business, including small business. They may apply for SBA State Development Company Loans, the monies from which are then used to supply small businesses within the state with long-term loans and equity capital.

○ *Pool Loans.* Pool loans are made to corporations formed and capitalized by groups of small businesses. They may be used for the purchase of raw materials, equipment, inventory, or supplies to do research and development or to establish research and development facilities.

○ *Revolving Line of Credit Guarantees.* A small firm that cannot set a line of credit from a bank to fulfill construction or other contracts may apply to the SBA for a Revolving Line of Credit Guarantee. The agency can guarantee the credit extended by the bank for up to 18 months.

○ *Displaced Business Loans.* Small firms that suffer substantial economic injury when they are displaced by federally aided renewal or other construction projects are eligible to apply for SBA Displaced Business Loans to help them relocate or re-establish their business. Reasonable upgrading of the business while it is being re-established is permitted.

○ *Handicapped Assistance Loans.* Small business owners who are physically handicapped, and public and private nonprofit organizations that employ and operate in the interests of physically handicapped persons, are eligible for Handicapped Assistance Loans.

○ *Physical Damage Natural Disaster Recovery Loans.* When the president, or the administrator of the SBA, declares a place a disaster area after a natural disaster such as a hurricane, a tornado, a flood, or an earthquake, or after a widespread fire or other catastrophe, homeowners, renters, and the owners of small and large businesses within the disaster area may apply to the SBA for Disaster Recovery Loans to repair or to replace their damaged or destroyed property.

○ *Economic Injury Natural Disaster Loans.* When the president, the secretary of agriculture, or the administrator of the SBA declares a place a disaster area after a natural disaster, owners of small businesses that have suffered economic losses as a result of the disaster may apply to the SBA for Economic Injury Natural Disaster Loans. These loans provide working capital and funds to pay financial obligations that the owners could have met if the disaster had not occurred.

○ *Product Disaster Loans.* The SBA makes Product Disaster Loans to small firms that suffer substantial economic injury when they cannot process or market a product for human consumption because of disease or toxicity resulting from either natural or undetermined causes.

○ *Base Closing Economic Injury Loans.* Base Closing Economic Injury Loans are made to small firms that have suffered, or will suffer, substantial economic injury as a result of the closing of a major federal military installation or a severe reduction in the scope of operations and size of a major military installation. These loans can be used to help a small firm continue in business at its existing location, re-establish its business, purchase a new business, or establish a new business.

○ *Strategic Arms Economic Injury Loans.* The SBA is authorized to make Strategic Arms Economic Injury Loans to assist, or to refinance the existing indebtedness of, any small business directly or indirectly affected by a significant reduction in the scope or amount of federal support for any project as a result of any international agreement limiting the development of strategic arms or the installation of strategic arms facilities.

○ *Emergency Energy Shortage Loans.* Emergency Energy Shortage Loans were authorized by amendments made to the Small Business Act in August 1974. They may be made to small businesses that are suffering economic injury as a result of shortages of fuel, electrical energy, or energy-producing resources, or as a result of shortages of raw or processed materials caused by shortages of energy.

○ *Regulatory Economic Injury Loans.* Small firms that must make changes in their equipment, facilities, or operations because of new federal laws and regulations are eligible for SBA Regulatory Economic Injury Loans, if the agency determines that the concerns are likely to suffer substantial economic injury without such loans. Examples of federal regulations and laws that have required major changes in small firms are: the Federal Coal Mine Safety Act of 1969, the Egg Products Act, the Wholesome Poultry Products Act, the Wholesome Meat Products Act of 1967, the Occupational Safety and Health Act of 1970, the Clean Air Act of 1970, and the Federal Water Pollution Control Act of 1974.

○ *Small Business Investment Companies [SBICs].* Another way SBA helps finance small firms is through privately owned and operated Small Business Investment Companies (SBICs). SBICs are licensed, regulated, and in certain cases financed by the agency. They supply venture capital and long-term financing to small firms for expansion and modernization. Some SBICs also provide management assistance to small businesses.

○ *301(d) Small Business Investment Companies [301(d) SBIC's].* In cooperation with the U. S. Department of Commerce, the SBA has instituted a specialized application of the SBIC principle in the licensing of 301(d) Small Business Investment Companies, formerly called Minority Enterprise SBICs. The 301(d) SBICs are dedicated to assisting small businesses owned and managed by socially or economically disadvantaged persons. Such disadvantage may arise from cultural, social, or chronic economic circumstances or background, or from other causes. This category often includes, but is not restricted to, black Americans, American Indians, Hispanic-Americans, oriental Americans, Eskimos, and Aleuts. Vietnam-era service in the armed forces may be a contributing factor in establishing social or economic disadvantage. 301(d) SBICs are owned and operated by established industrial or financial concerns and community, private, or public investors who combine money and management resources to assist disadvantaged entrepreneurs.

Most small independent businesses are eligible for SBA loans. The exceptions are speculative firms, newspapers, radio and television stations, other media companies, and — normally — businesses engaged in gambling. Under the Disaster Loan Recovery Program, owners of small *and* large businesses are eligible to apply for SBA Disaster Loan Assistance. The SBA defines a small business as one that is independently owned and operated, is not dominant in its field, and meets the criteria stated in Exhibit 6-2.

The SBA is also committed to making it possible for small and emerging contractors who, for whatever reasons, find bonding otherwise unavailable, to issue bonds. The agency is authorized to guarantee to a qualified surety up to 90 percent of the losses incurred under bid, payment, or performance bonds issued to contractors on contracts valued up to $1 million. The contracts may be for construction, supplies, or services provided by either a prime contractor or a subcontractor, for government or nongovernment work.

Life Insurance Policies

Life insurance policies with cash surrender values[5] are a good source of money because the interest rate is reasonable. You can borrow most of the policy's cash surrender value, which is usually about 6 percent. The Veterans Administration, for example, permits you to borrow up to 94 percent on government life insurance. The loan statement in their policy reads as follows:

> At any time after the expiration of the first policy year, and before default in payment in any subsequent premium, and upon execution of the loan agreement satisfactory to the Administrator of Veterans' Affairs, the United States will lend to the Insured on the sole security of this policy, any amount which shall not exceed ninety-four per centum of the cash value and any indebtedness shall be deducted from the amount advanced on such loan. The loan shall bear interest at the rate not to exceed six per centum per annum, payable annually, and at any time before default in payment of premium the loan may be repaid in full or in amounts of five dollars or any multiple thereof. Failure to pay either the amount of the loan or the interest thereon shall not void this policy unless the total indebtedness shall equal or exceed the cash value thereof. When the amount of indebtedness equals or exceeds the cash value, this policy shall cease and become void.

You should understand the conditions outlined in the policy before taking out the loan. You buy life insurance for its protection. If you borrow money on it, do not be forced into having the policy voided. You must also keep in mind that if you should die during the time you have borrowed on your policy, the money due your beneficiary will be reduced by the amount of your indebtedness.

Exhibit 6-2   Eligibility criteria for SBA loans

Type of business	Annual receipts not exceeding
Service	$2 – $8 million"
Retail	$2 – $7½ million"
Wholesale	$9½ – $22 million"
General construction	$9½ million"
Special trade construction	$5 million
Farming and related activities	$275,000
	Average number of employees
Manufacturing	250 – 1,500"

" Varies by industry — check with a local SBA field office for further details.

Some insurance companies do not specify any information on loans in the policy itself. If this is the case with your policy, write to your company or contact its local agent to get details on its loan policy. One company, for example, permits its policyholders to borrow up to 100 percent of the cash value of their insurance as computed on the last preceding anniversary of the date they purchased the policy.

In addition to the low interest rate, borrowing on life insurance is also relatively simple to do. All some companies require is your signature on copies of a one-page loan agreement and certificate of assignment that indicates the exact amount you want to borrow. This type of borrowing is much easier than the other loans that will be discussed later in this chapter.

Credit Unions

Give credit unions careful consideration as a source of loans. You must be a member to be eligible to borrow from a credit union. The main advantage of borrowing from a credit union is that the total cost of your loan is often lower than it would be at other lending institutions. One credit union stresses that interest is its only finance charge, with no services or credit reports added on to raise the total cost. This credit union also pays the premiums for credit life insurance, and does not impose a finance charge on any amount you have already repaid. It also lets you pay ahead of schedule without having any penalty imposed.

In their loan applications, credit unions ask for considerably more detail than you would have to supply if you borrowed on your life insurance, but less than is required by other lending agencies.

Commercial Banks

Reputable commercial banks are a good source of loans. Their interest rates are more reasonable than those of small loan companies. They do, however, require a stronger financial position. These banks usually offer two types of loans. The first is the unsecured loan, in which you obtain the money on your signature alone. The unsecured loan costs more than the second type, the secured loan, which requires you to put up collateral. This collateral may be in the form of bonds, stocks, a savings account, or property. If the loan is made for starting a business, the business itself would normally serve as the collateral. If you fail to meet your loan obligation, the lending agency may force your firm into bankruptcy in order to recover the amount due. The remainder, if any, would be distributed among other creditors or returned to you.

If you borrow money against a savings account, you can usually get it at 2 percent above what the bank pays its savers in interest. In 1982, for example, a New Orleans bank paid 5¼ percent on its savings accounts and permitted its savers to borrow up to the amount of their savings at 7¼ percent. In contrast, those with no such accounts are charged two and one-half times that amount.

But why keep your money in a bank at 5¼ percent and pay 7¼ percent to borrow it? Withdraw your savings to start your business or provide additional working capital. By using your savings, you cut the costs. You will also save the considerable time and effort that would be spent in filling out loan applications and financial statements.

Let me re-emphasize the importance of having a friendly relationship with your banker. Commercial banks may not want to lend you money unless you agree to maintain appropriate deposits with them. Treat your banker like a very good customer. One entrepreneur put it this way: "Don't buy him lunch — buy him dinner."

Savings and Loan Associations

Savings and loan associations make collateral loans like those made by commercial banks. If you want to buy your building, for example, or subcontract it yourself, a savings and loan association is a good loan source. They will also make signature loans against the amount of money you have in a share account. The differential might amount to about 2 percent. If your passbook account is paying you 5¾ percent, for example, the association might charge you 7¾ percent. In contrast, if you have no savings account with the association, charges on secured loans have recently been as high as 18 percent.

Personal Loan Companies

Small loan companies charge the highest legally authorized rate of interest. This is an expensive way to get financing. In every sizable community in the United States there are small loan companies actively seeking your business. These firms make large profits because they may charge from 24 to 42 percent interest, with the exact rate regulated by the individual states. On occasion, some finance companies may be less expensive and more reliable than certain banks. A finance company may specialize in a particular industry, such as heavy trucking.

INTEREST COSTS

Determine the cost of borrowing money and get the best possible loan to suit your business needs. The best interest rate can be determined easily. It is also essential, however, to do business with a reliable, reputable company.

The Truth-in-Lending Law requires every lending firm to list its yearly charges as a percentage. In loan shopping, you may want to use the form shown in Exhibit 6-3 to make a list of your options.

Exhibit 6-3 Loan cost worksheet

Firm	Annual finance charges	Other expenses	Total cost	Name of organization (person to contact, address, phone)
A				
B				
C				

If you want to check on the annual percentage charged by the lending agency, you can use the following formula:

$$\frac{2\,AB}{C\,(D + 1)} = E$$

where:

A = total finance charge in dollars

B = number of payment periods in one year (use 12 if monthly payments, 52 if weekly, regardless of the months or weeks specified in the loan agreement)

C = dollar amount of the loan

D = actual number of payments to be made
E = annual finance charge, as a percentage

Let us now apply the formula. Assume you obtain a $30,000 loan and agree to repay the lending agency $34,200 in 24 monthly payments. Using the formula above, you get 13.44 percent as the annual finance charge.

$$\frac{2 \times 4,200 \times 12}{30,000\ (24 + 1)} = \frac{100,800}{750,000} = .1344 = 13.44\%$$

Remember that when you are quoted an add-on rate of interest, it can be misleading. If a loan officer states, "There's a 20 percent add-on," for example, this does not mean that you will be paying $6,000 on a one-year loan of $30,000. The vast majority of personal loans are paid off in installments.[6] This requires the borrower to pay back the money in equal amounts during the life of the loan, so on a one-year loan, you are in possession of only six-twelfths of the principal ($15,000) at the end of six months. To determine the rate you are actually paying in interest, use the formula above, applying it on a $30,000 loan repayable monthly over one year at a cost of $6,000.

$$\frac{2 \times 6,000 \times 12}{30,000\ (12 + 1)} = \frac{144,000}{390,000} = .3692 = 36.92\%$$

Tables are available that calculate this interest. Ask your lending agency to let you see them. These tables often include interest costs for life, accident, and health insurance. Lending agencies like to sell these extras because it means added profit. The life insurance also protects the lender in the event of your death or the failure of your firm.

The Impact of Inflation and Taxes

In an era of very high interest rates, such as the double-digit rates of 1979 to 1981, a new business having to borrow large sums may be at a competitive disadvantage with older firms who obtained funds at much lower costs. Inflation and taxes can reduce your borrowing costs, however, and they should be taken into consideration. The annual erosion in the purchasing power of the dollar can be expected to continue. There are, however, two unknowns: the percentage increase and the specific items whose costs will rise. Let us assume that a business that could be bought for $100,000 last year has risen to $105,000 twelve months later. In this case, your dollar power has been reduced by nearly 5 percent (the increase of $105,000 over $100,000). If you had borrowed the $100,000 last year to buy the business, you could pay the money back with cheaper dollars.

Assume that your $100,000 loan could be obtained at 12 percent, with the entire interest and principal to be paid at the end of the twelfth month. In such a case the impact of inflation would in theory result in your paying only about 7 percent interest ([$112,000 − $105,000] ÷ 100,000). Your actual interest savings will depend on the rate of inflation affecting your particular purchase. It could be zero for the business in question.

The second point to consider is the possible income tax advantage of borrowing. Assume that you are a proprietorship and in the 50 percent tax bracket. The federal government permits you, in using the long form (Form 1040), to deduct interest charges from taxable income. Using the example above, it would enable you to save $6,000 of the $12,000 interest charge.

Amortized Loans

In contrast to the easily computed borrowing costs on term loans[7] described above, the amortized loan is complex to determine and requires the use of amortization tables. The amortized loan calls for equal monthly payments that include both interest and principal during the life of the loan. Thus there is no huge principal payment to be made at the end of the loan period.

Assume that you decide to buy or subcontract[8] your own building and need to borrow $100,000 for thirty years at 12 percent. A recapitulation of these costs (see Exhibit 6-4) indicates that interest amounts to over $269,000 and the grand total exceeds $369,000. See Appendix C for details on the monthly payments required over a thirty-year period. Exhibit 6-5 permits you to determine interest and principal costs on mortgage rates varying from 10 to 14 percent, and makes it clear that even a half-percent differential can save you a lot of money over thirty years. It pays to shop around for the best loan available.

Whenever possible, try to get a fixed rate loan, unless interest rates are unreasonably high. Be familiar with the concept of present value. You want your loan to be for as long a term as possible, with as long an amortization schedule as possible. You want to pay back the loan with as low a monthly payment as you can negotiate. Perhaps you can convince the lender to collect interest only during the first year. Stay away from demand notes: they are an absolute no-no. Long-term debt is where it's at.

Loan Eligibility

Whether you receive a loan, and at what rate, depends on your past record. What factors determine whether you will pay a fair price for using a lending agency's money? One senior bank official informed me that bank officers examine the loan application and the firm's financial statements with care. They give special consideration to the following points:

○ *Past employment.* They pay particular attention to your number of years on the job and salary. They also study your past positions. The bank wants to be sure that you have been successful, so they can predict that your new firm will earn enough money to make payments.

○ *Indebtedness.* They take a hard look at your list of creditors, unpaid balances, and monthly payments. The bank also looks at your response

Exhibit 6-4 Recapitulation — Annual payments on a $100,000 loan at 12 percent over a thirty-year period

Yearly payment	Interest paid	Principal paid	Total payment (interest + principal)
1	$ 11,981	$ 367	$ 12,348
2	11,934	414	12,348
3	11,881	467	12,348
4	11,823	525	12,348
5	11,754	594	12,348
6	11,680	668	12,348
7	11,595	753	12,348
8	11,499	849	12,348
9	11,393	955	12,348
10	11,271	1,077	12,348
11	11,130	1,218	12,348
12	10,981	1,367	12,348
13	10,806	1,542	12,348
14	10,611	1,737	12,348
15	10,392	1,956	12,348
16	10,143	2,205	12,348
17	9,863	2,485	12,348
18	9,549	2,799	12,348
19	9,193	3,155	12,348
20	8,790	3,558	12,348
21	8,343	4,005	12,348
22	7,834	4,514	12,348
23	7,262	5,086	12,348
24	6,617	5,731	12,348
25	5,890	6,458	12,348
26	5,071	7,277	12,348
27	4,148	8,200	12,348
28	3,107	9,241	12,348
29	1,935	10,413	12,348
30	618	10,384	11,002
Totals	$269,094	$100,000	$369,094

Exhibit 6-5 Monthly payments, principal and interest, on loans ($40,000 to $150,000) over thirty years

Amount of mortgage	Percent									
	10	10½	11	11½	12	12½	13	13½	14
$ 40,000	$ 351	$ 366	$ 381	$ 396	$ 412	$ 427	$ 442	$ 458	$ 474
50,000	439	457	476	495	514	534	553	573	592
60,000	527	549	571	594	617	640	664	687	711
70,000	614	640	667	693	720	747	774	802	829
80,000	702	732	762	792	823	854	885	916	948
90,000	790	823	857	891	926	961	996	1031	1066
100,000	878	915	952	990	1029	1067	1106	1145	1185
110,000	966	1006	1048	1090	1132	1175	1218	1261	1304
120,000	1054	1098	1143	1189	1235	1282	1328	1375	1422
130,000	1141	1189	1238	1288	1338	1388	1439	1490	1541
140,000	1229	1281	1334	1387	1441	1495	1550	1604	1659
150,000	1317	1372	1430	1486	1543	1602	1661	1719	1778

to an important question: Have you been in bankruptcy or had any judgments, garnishments, or other legal proceedings against you?

o *Home ownership.* If you own your own home and made a reasonable down payment, that indicates responsibility. Renters who have lived in one place for a long time are also looked on with favor.

o *Net worth.* They review the financial statement to see that assets clearly exceed liabilities. Savings accounts, stocks, bonds, and other liquid assets are helpful. It is a good idea to have an account with the lender from whom you want to borrow money.

o *Other considerations.* The size of your family is taken into account; a large family requires a healthy income. Prompt payment of suppliers, credit card accounts, charge accounts, and other creditors is a favorable factor.

o *Credit bureau check.* Before the bank grants any loan, the bank official emphasized, you must be checked out by a credit bureau. This bank is currently granting credit only to those with a high credit rating.

o *Personal investment of funds in the business.* The amount of your own money you plan to put into the firm is a very important factor. One bank manager said: "It lets us know the owner's belief in the potential of the company — the greater the amount, the better we like it."

o *Ratios.* A variety of financial ratios (either projected or actual) are available in analyzing your balance sheet in comparison to other firms. For example, find out what the financial ratios should be in your industry and compare it to your own. It may be the first item your banker will examine.

FINANCIAL TOOLS

You won't succeed at your business unless you can raise enough money to get started. Once you have enough money to begin operations, you must use it wisely to stay in business. Two important financial tools will help you — cash flow projection and operating plan forecast.

Cash Flow Projection

Cash flow may be defined as the amount of money available to a firm at any given time. You can determine it by subtracting cash outlays for operating expenses from cash income. Another way to determine cash flow is to compute the net profit and add the dollars set aside for depreciation. A business must have a satisfactory cash flow to survive. For this reason, a new business should make a monthly cash flow projection.[9] A cash flow projection is a forecast of the cash funds[10] a business anticipates receiving, on the one hand, and disbursing, on the other hand, throughout a given span of time, and the anticipated cash position at specific times during the period projected. The purpose of preparing a cash flow projection is to predict deficiencies or surpluses in cash. If deficiencies are revealed in the cash flow, financial plans must be altered either to provide more cash (by, for example, securing more equity capital or loans, or increasing selling prices of products), or to reduce expenditures, including inventory, or to allow fewer credit sales until you reach a proper cash flow balance. If surpluses of cash are revealed, it might indicate excessive borrowing or idle money that you could put to work. The objective is to develop a plan that, if followed, will provide a well-managed cash flow.

The Small Business Administration has prepared an excellent form entitled *Monthly Cash Flow Projection* (see Exhibit 6-6). Get this form from the SBA and use it to project cash flow in starting your business. If you examine Exhibit 6-6 you will see that by using this format you can estimate your total cash receipts for the first year of operation as well as your total cash payout. You need to have cash on hand if your firm is to survive. The SBA form also has excellent guidelines, including instructions for filling out all the information on the monthly cash flow projection table and for making an appropriate analysis. The importance for the business owner or manager of making this analysis cannot be emphasized too strongly. The SBA puts it this way:

1. The cash position at the end of each month should be adequate to meet the cash requirements for the following month. If too little cash, then additional cash will have to be injected or cash paid out must be reduced. If there is too much cash on hand, this money is not working for your business.
2. The cash flow projection, the profit and loss projection, the break-even analysis, and good cost control information are tools which, if used properly, will be useful in making decisions that can increase profits to ensure success.
3. The projection becomes more useful when the estimated information can be compared with actual information as it develops. It is important to follow through and complete the actual columns as the information becomes available. Utilize the cash flow projection to assist in setting new goals and planning operations for more profit. Furthermore, you should daily review your cash position as well as projected sources and use of funds. Plan ahead so you only borrow money as required.

Operating Plan Forecast

In addition to preparing the cash flow statement, the small business owner should prepare an operating plan forecast (profit and loss projection).[11] What is the value of such a forecast? An operating plan forecast can yield many benefits to the small business owner or manager. First, the forecast is a valuable planning tool. Second, when the planning phase has been completed, the forecast becomes a key management tool in controlling the business operations to achieve the planned objectives. Let us see how the operating plan forecast can be useful as both a planning document and a controlling tool.

First, its use as a planning tool: the forecast enables the owner or manager to preview the profit or loss that can be expected each month and for the business year, based on reasonable predictions of monthly sales, costs, and expenses. By having a preview of future operations, the owner or manager can compare the year's expected profit or loss in advance with the profit goals established for the business. If the results forecasted are not satisfactory, there is time to identify what must be done to correct the situation.

How can the forecast serve as a control tool? A completed forecast enables the owner or manager to compare the figures on actual performance, as they become known, with the targets projected for that month. When the results are out of line, you can take steps to correct them. By being able to see quickly where the trouble is, you will lose less time and money in getting back on the track toward your overall profit goals.

Exhibit 6-7 shows the forecasting form developed by the Small Business Administration to assist you in listing the desired information. As you can see, the operating plan forecast lists monthly revenues from sales as well as cost of sales in order to arrive at your gross profit. To determine net profit, subtract from gross profit such expenses as salary, payroll, outside services, supplies, repairs and maintenance, advertising, car, accounting and legal, rent, telephone, utilities, insurance, taxes, interest, depreciation, and any other miscellaneous expenses. Exhibit 6-7 provides two columns for your computations — estimate and actual. Analyze your estimate with care against what you actually spent. By making such an analysis, you can see where you may be spending too much or too little and make appropriate modifications promptly.

You can perform another helpful analysis by using the percentage column in Exhibit 6-7. This percentage gives you an opportunity to compare costs, etc., over a period of time. It promptly signals, for example, any sharp rise in cost for a particular item such as payroll.

Balance Sheet and Statement of Income

Two essential financial records for a business to maintain are a balance sheet and a statement of income. A balance sheet is an accounting statement listing the amount and type of assets, the liabilities, and the net worth of an organization at a particular time. The statement of income is an accounting record of income, expenses, and net income for a specified time. A new business should prepare a balance sheet during the planning phase to estimate

Exhibit 6-6   Cash flow projection worksheet

MONTHLY CASH

INSTRUCTIONS ON REVERSE SIDE

NAME OF BUSINESS		ADDRESS					OWNER					

	Pre-Start-up Position		1		2		3		4		5	
YEAR MONTH	Estimate	Actual	Estimate	Actual	Estimate	Actual	Estimate	Actual	Estimate	Actual	Estimate	Actual
1. CASH ON HAND (Beginning of month)												
2. CASH RECEIPTS (a) Cash Sales												
(b) Collections from Credit Accounts												
(c) Loan or Other Cash injection (Specify)												
3. TOTAL CASH RECEIPTS (2a+2b+2c=3)												
4. TOTAL CASH AVAILABLE (Before cash out) (1+3)												
5. CASH PAID OUT (a) Purchases (Merchandise)												
(b) Gross Wages (Excludes withdrawals)												
(c) Payroll Expenses (Taxes, etc.)												
(d) Outside Services												
(e) Supplies (Office and operating)												
(f) Repairs and Maintenance												
(g) Advertising												
(h) Car, Delivery, and Travel												
(i) Accounting and Legal												
(j) Rent												
(k) Telephone												
(l) Utilities												
(m) Insurance												
(n) Taxes (Real estate, etc.)												
(o) Interest												
(p) Other Expenses (Specify each)												
(q) Miscellaneous (Unspecified)												
(r) Subtotal												
(s) Loan Principal Payment												
(t) Capital Purchases (Specify)												
(u) Other Start-up Costs												
(v) Reserve and/or Excrow (Specify)												
(w) Owner's Withdrawal												
6. TOTAL CASH PAID OUT (Total 5a thru 5w)												
7. CASH POSITION (End of month) (4 minus 6)												
ESSENTIAL OPERATING DATA (Non-cash flow information) A. Sales Volume (Dollars)												
B. Accounts Receivable (End of month)												
C. Bad Debt (End of month)												
D. Inventory on Hand (End of month)												
E. Accounts Payable (End of month)												
F. Depreciation												

SBA FORM 1100 (8-75) REF: SOP 60 10 1

Exhibit 6-6   Continued

FLOW PROJECTION

TYPE OF BUSINESS				PREPARED BY				DATE		

6		7		8		9		10		11		12		TOTAL		
														Columns 1–12		
Estimate	Actual	Estimate	Actual	Estimate	Actual	Estimate	Actual	Estimate	Actual	Estimate	Actual	Estimate	Actual	Estimate	Actual	
																1.
																2. (a)
																(b)
																(c)
																3.
																4.
																5. (a)
																(b)
																(c)
																(d)
																(e)
																(f)
																(g)
																(h)
																(i)
																(j)
																(k)
																(l)
																(m)
																(n)
																(o)
																(p)
																(q)
																(r)
																(s)
																(t)
																(u)
																(v)
																(w)
																6.
																7.
																A.
																B.
																C.
																D.
																E.
																F.

Exhibit 6-7   Operating plan forecast

OPERATING PLAN FORECAST (Profit and Loss Projection)												
		Month 1			Month 2			Month 3			Month 4
Revenue (sales)	Ind %	Estimate	Actual	%	Estimate	Actual	%	Estimate	Actual	%	Estimate
Total Revenue (sales)											
Cost of Sales											
Total Cost of Sales											
Gross Profit											
Expenses											
Salary expense: Sales people office and other											
Payroll Expenses (taxes, etc.)											
Outside Services											
Supplies (office and operating)											
Repairs and Maintenance											
Advertising											
Car, Delivery and Travel											
Accounting and Legal											
Rent											
Telephone											
Utilities											
Insurance											
Taxes (real estate, etc)											
Interest											
Depreciation											
Other Expenses (specify each)											
Miscellaneous (unspecified)											
Total Expenses											
Net Profit											

SBA FORM 1099 (8-75) REF: SOP 60 10 1

Exhibit 6-7 Continued

						Name of Business										
		Month 5			Month 6			Month 7			Month 8			Month 9	
Actual	%	Estimate	Actual	%	Estimate	Actual	%	Estimate	Actual	%	Estimate	Actual	%	Estimate

Exhibit 6-7 Continued

Form Approved
OMB No. 100–R 0084

					For Period Ending									
		Month 10			Month 11			Month 12			Totals			
Actual	%	Estimate	Actual	%	Estimate	Actual	%	Estimate	Actual	%	Estimate	%	Actual	%

its financial condition at the time it opens for business. Such a record will give an estimate of what the company will own and owe, and its net worth (assets minus liabilities). You should also prepare an estimate of income and expenses for the first year of business at this time. Such an estimate can help you decide on the feasibility of your venture and make modifications to ensure profitability. These records will also be necessary when you discuss loan prospects with a lending institution. You must also prepare a balance sheet and statement of income every year. Exhibit 6-8 is an example of a balance sheet and Exhibit 6-9 of a statement of income used by a hypothetical small business. Another helpful tool in achieving your company's objectives is a three-year financial plan, a long-term projection of income and expenses.

FEDERAL INCOME TAX

A major obstacle to acquiring a sizable fortune from your business is the heavy federal income tax burden. *Avoid* taxes whenever possible, but do not *evade* them. There is a prison of difference between the two. Pay what is legally due — but not a penny more.

The type of ownership you select for your business will determine what federal income tax form you use. If you are a sole proprietorship, you must use Form 1040, Schedule C, *Profit or (Loss) from Business or Profession.* An examination of Schedule C (see Exhibit 6-10) indicates that this two-page document should not be difficult to prepare if you have kept good records. In part I you report income from all business sources and in part II you make deductions for all the costs of doing business. The deduction of costs from income gives you your annual net profit or net loss. There are also three schedules on the reverse side of the page dealing with expense account information, cost of goods sold, and depreciation. Use the schedules appropriate for your business. Keep in mind that the gain or loss shown on Schedule C is included with your other personal income on Form 1040. If your nonbusiness income is small, proprietorship could mean the smallest expenditure of your tax dollars. This would be especially true in the early years, when profits might be low.

If you are involved in a partnership, you must use Form 1065, *U. S. Partnership Return of Income* (Exhibit 6-11), to report the income, deductions, credits, gains, and losses from your operations. Every partnership engaged in a trade or business, or having income from sources within the United States, must file Form 1065. A partnership must file even if its principal place of business is outside the United States or if all its members are nonresident aliens. A resident partnership must file Form 1065 by the fifteenth day of the fourth month following the close of its tax year. A foreign partnership whose partners are nonresident aliens must file its return by the fifteenth day of the sixth month following the close of its tax year. Form 1065 is more complicated than Schedule C. The services of a qualified tax accountant can be very helpful in keeping partnership records and assisting your firm in filing this return.

As the profits from your business increase, you may find it reasonable to change from a proprietorship or a partnership to a corporate structure. You can determine this by computing your federal income taxes using both the corporate and the individual forms. (Taxes should be only one factor in arriving at your decision. See chapter 3, "Legal Requirements," for further details.)

Form 1120, *U. S. Corporation Income Tax Return* (Exhibit 6-12), is used to report income, gains, losses, deductions, and credits of domestic corporations. In general, a corporation must file Form 1120 by the fifteenth day of the third month after the end of the tax year. A new corporation filing a short-period return must file by the fifteenth day of the third month after the short period ends. A corporation that has dissolved must generally file by the fifteenth day of the third month after the date it dissolved.

OTHER INCOME TAXES

In addition to federal income tax payments, other income taxes may be required. Check with your state, county, and community to be sure that you meet their tax requirements. In planning where to locate or incorporate your business, you should determine the tax costs of each location. Some communities eagerly seek out certain businesses and make special tax inducements or concessions.

SUMMARY

Adequate funding is essential to starting any business. You should invest your own savings in your company. This can be an important factor in securing a loan, because your willingness to risk your own capital indicates to the lending agency your belief in the business. Potential loan sources are family, friends, life insurance policies, credit unions, commercial banks, savings and loan associations, and personal loan companies. The best source of financial assistance may be the Small Business Administration. [12] It provides a broad range of loan programs. I strongly recommend you talk about money needs with a local SBA field office representative before making a decision on what loan is best for you.

Before starting your own business you should get your personal financial house in order. To be a strong candidate for a loan, it helps to have a

Exhibit 6-8 MPMA Hypothetical Manufacturing Company
Balance Sheet as of December 31, 1983

ASSETS

Current assets
Cash		$ 11,412	
Time deposits		100,000	
Accounts receivable	267,750		
(Less reserve for bad debts)	(28,199)		
Inventories		239,551	
Raw materials	406,281		
Finished goods	42,989		
		449,270	
Prepaid insurance and			
expenses		32,949	
Total current assets			$ 833,182

Fixed assets
Land	29,600		
Buildings	687,228		
Improvements	35,192		
Dies, jigs, and tools	177,757		
Machinery and equipment	291,104		
Furniture and fixtures	84,607		
Transportation equipment	40,462		
Total fixed assets			$1,345,950
Patents, at cost			$ 48,715

Other assets
Claims for refund of income			
taxes paid		14,936	
Goodwill		91,934	
Total other assets			$ 106,870
Total assets			$2,347,717

Exhibit 6-8   Continued

LIABILITIES

Current liabilities
Notes payable	$ 10,500	
Installments due on bond indebtedness	14,100	
Accounts payable and accrued expenses	81,853	
Customer's credit balances	3,659	
Taxes payable		
Federal income tax	49,975	
State income tax	5,298	
Federal excise tax	1,445	
Federal and state payroll taxes	5,472	
Employee's income tax withheld	6,978	
Total current liabilities		$ 179,280

Other liabilities
Notes payable	21,000	
Bonds payable and accrued interest	120,850	
Total other liabilities		$ 141,850

Total liabilities		$ 321,130

Net worth
Capital stock — common, par value		
$10.00 per share. Authorized and		
issued, 10,000 shares	100,000	
Earned surplus		
Balance as of January 1, 1983	1,615,729	
Net income — January 1, 1983 to		
December 31, 1983	310,858	

Total net worth		$2,026,587
Total liabilities and net worth		$2,347,717

Exhibit 6-9 MPMA Hypothetical Manufacturing Corporation,
statement of income for the year ended December 31, 1983

Sales		
Heating pads	$632,105	
Vaporizers	410,621	
Sterilizers	325,942	
Plastic containers	243,979	
Thermostats	122,138	
Total sales		$1,734,785
Cost of Goods Sold		871,842
Gross profit on sales		862,943
Selling, general, and administrative expenses		
Executive salaries — officers	85,876	
Administrative salaries — other	18,843	
Commissions	87,313	
Advertising	79,469	
Shipping and wrapping supplies	11,391	
Freight and cartage — out	60,154	
Shipping and receiving labor	7,783	
Office salaries	19,214	
Postage and office supplies	14,474	
Auto and travel expense	10,986	
Depreciation	11,811	
Telephone and telegraph	16,210	
Interest	17,839	
Professional fees	20,905	
Sales promotion and entertainment	4,124	
Sundry general expenses	1,353	
Bad debts	13,290	
Total selling, general, and administrative expenses		480,783
Operating income		382,160
Other income		10,150
Income before taxes		392,310
Income taxes		81,452
Net Income		$ 310,858

Exhibit 6-10 Federal income tax form Schedule C, used for sole proprietorship

---

SCHEDULE C	**Profit or (Loss) From Business or Profession**	OMB. No. 1545-0074
(Form 1040)	(Sole Proprietorship)	**1981**
Department of the Treasury	Partnerships, Joint Ventures, etc., Must File Form 1065.	08
Internal Revenue Service (O)	▶ Attach to Form 1040 or Form 1041. ▶ See Instructions for Schedule C (Form 1040).	

Name of proprietor	Social security number of proprietor

A Main business activity (see Instructions) ▶ _____ ; product ▶ _____

B Business name ▶ _____

C Employer identification number

D Business address (number and street) ▶ _____
City, State and ZIP Code ▶ _____

E Accounting method: (1) ☐ Cash (2) ☐ Accrual (3) ☐ Other (specify) ▶ _____

F Method(s) used to value closing inventory:
(1) ☐ Cost (2) ☐ Lower of cost or market (3) ☐ Other (if other, attach explanation)

	Yes	No
G Was there any major change in determining quantities, costs, or valuations between opening and closing inventory? . . If "Yes," attach explanation.		

H Did you deduct expenses for an office in your home? . . . .

Part I Income

1 a Gross receipts or sales	1a		
b Returns and allowances	1b		
c Balance (subtract line 1b from line 1a)	1c	
2 Cost of goods sold and/or operations (Schedule C-1, line 8)	2	
3 Gross profit (subtract line 2 from line 1c)	3	
4 a Windfall Profit Tax Credit or Refund received in 1981 (see Instructions)	4a	
b Other income (attach schedule)	4b	
5 Total income (add lines 3, 4a, and 4b) . . . . ▶	5	

Part II Deductions

6 Advertising		**29 a** Wages . .	
7 Amortization		**b** Jobs credit	
8 Bad debts from sales or services .		**c** WIN credit	
9 Bank service charges		**d** Total credits	
10 Car and truck expenses		**e** Subtract line 29d from 29a .	
11 Commissions		**30** Windfall Profit Tax withheld in	
12 Depletion		1981	
13 Depreciation (see Instructions) .		**31** Other expenses (specify):	
14 Dues and publications		**a** _____	
15 Employee benefit programs . .		**b** _____	
16 Freight (not included on Schedule C-1) .		**c** _____	
17 Insurance		**d** _____	
18 Interest on business indebtedness .		**e** _____	
19 Laundry and cleaning		**f** _____	
20 Legal and professional services .		**g** _____	
21 Office supplies and postage . . .		**h** _____	
22 Pension and profit-sharing plans .		**i** _____	
23 Rent on business property . . .		**j** _____	
24 Repairs		**k** _____	
25 Supplies (not included on Schedule C-1) .		**l** _____	
26 Taxes (do not include Windfall		**m** _____	
Profit Tax, see line 30)		**n** _____	
27 Travel and entertainment . . .		**o** _____	
28 Utilities and telephone		**p** _____	

32 Total deductions (add amounts in columns for lines 6 through 31p) . . . . ▶	32	
33 Net profit or (loss) (subtract line 32 from line 5). If a profit, enter on Form 1040, line 11, and on Schedule SE, Part II, line 5a (or Form 1041, line 6). If a loss, go on to line 34	33	

34 If you have a loss, do you have amounts for which you are not "at risk" in this business (see Instructions)? . . ☐ **Yes** ☐ **No**
If you checked "No," enter the loss on Form 1040, line 11, and on Schedule SE, Part II, line 5a (or Form 1041, line 6).

For Paperwork Reduction Act Notice, see Form 1040 Instructions.

Exhibit 6-10 Continued

Schedule C (Form 1040) 1981   Page **2**

SCHEDULE C–1.—Cost of Goods Sold and/or Operations (See Schedule C Instructions for Part I, line 2)

1 Inventory at beginning of year (if different from last year's closing inventory, attach explanation) .	**1**	
2 a Purchases	**2a**	
b Cost of items withdrawn for personal use	**2b**	
c Balance (subtract line 2b from line 2a)	**2c**	
3 Cost of labor (do not include salary paid to yourself)	**3**	
4 Materials and supplies	**4**	
5 Other costs (attach schedule)	**5**	
6 Add lines 1, 2c, and 3 through 5	**6**	
7 Inventory at end of year	**7**	
8 Cost of goods sold and/or operations (subtract line 7 from line 6). Enter here and on Part I, line 2 . ▶	**8**	

SCHEDULE C–2.—Depreciation (See Schedule C Instructions for line 13)

Complete Schedule C–2 if you claim depreciation ONLY for assets placed in service before January 1, 1981. If you need more space, use Form 4562. If you claim a deduction for any assets placed in service after December 31, 1980, use Form 4562 to figure your total deduction for all assets; do NOT complete Schedule C–2.

Description of property (a)	Date acquired (b)	Cost or other basis (c)	Depreciation allowed or allowable in prior years (d)	Method of computing depreciation (e)	Life or rate (f)	Depreciation for this year (g)
1 Depreciation (see Instructions):						
2 Totals			**2**			
3 Depreciation claimed in Schedule C–1			**3**			
4 Balance (subtract line 3 from line 2). Enter here and on Part II, line 13 . . . . ▶			**4**			

SCHEDULE C–3.—Expense Account Information (See Schedule C Instructions for Schedule C–3)

Enter information for yourself and your five highest paid employees. In determining the five highest paid employees, add expense account allowances to the salaries and wages. However, you don't have to provide the information for any employee for whom the combined amount is less than $50,000, or for yourself if your expense account allowance plus line 33, page 1, is less than $50,000.

Name (a)	Expense account (b)	Salaries and wages (c)
Owner		
1		
2		
3		
4		
5		

Did you claim a deduction for expenses connected with:	Yes	No
A Entertainment facility (boat, resort, ranch, etc.)?		
B Living accommodations (except employees on business)?		
C Conventions or meetings you or your employees attended outside the North American area? (see Instructions) . . .		
D Employees' families at conventions or meetings?		
If "Yes," were any of these conventions or meetings outside the North American area?		
E Vacations for employees or their families not reported on Form W–2?		

Exhibit 6-11 Federal income tax form 1065, used for a partnership

Form **1065**	**U.S. Partnership Return of Income**	OMB No. 1545–0099
Department of the Treasury Internal Revenue Service	For calendar year 1981, or fiscal year beginning _____, 1981, and ending _____, 19 ____.	**1981**

A Principal business activity (see page 12 of Instructions)	Use IRS label. Other- wise, please print or type.	Name	D Employer identification no.
B Principal product or service (see page 12 of Instructions)		Number and street	E Date business started
C Business code number (see page 12 of Instructions)		City or town, State, and ZIP code	F Enter total assets from Sched- ule L, line 13, column (D). $

G Check method of accounting: **(1)** ☐ Cash **(2)** ☐ Accrual **(3)** ☐ Other (attach explanation)

H Check applicable boxes: **(1)** ☐ Final return **(2)** ☐ Change in address.

IMPORTANT—Fill in all applicable lines and schedules. If you need more space, see page 2 of the Instructions. Enter any items specially allocated to the partners on Schedule K, line 17, and not on the numbered lines on this page or in Schedules A through I.

Income

1a	Gross receipts or sales $_____ 1b Minus returns and allowances $_____ Balance ▶	1c	
2	Cost of goods sold and/or operations (Schedule A, line 34)	2	
3	Gross profit (subtract line 2 from line 1c)	3	
4	Ordinary income (loss) from other partnerships and fiduciaries (attach statement)	4	
5	Nonqualifying dividends.	5	
6	Nonqualifying interest	6	
7	Net income (loss) from rents (Schedule H, line 2)	7	
8	Net income (loss) from royalties (attach schedule)	8	
9	Net farm profit (loss) (attach Schedule F (Form 1040))	9	
10	Net gain (loss) (Form 4797, line 11)	10	
11	Other income (attach schedule)	11	
12	**TOTAL** income (loss) (combine lines 3 through 11)	12	

Deductions

13a	Salaries and wages (other than to partners) $_____ 13b Minus jobs credit $_____ Balance ▶	13c	
14	Guaranteed payments to partners (see page 4 of Instructions)	14	
15	Rent	15	
16	Interest **(Caution—see page 4 of Instructions)**	16	
17	Taxes	17	
18	Bad debts (see page 5 of Instructions)	18	
19	Repairs	19	
20	Depreciation from Form 4562 (attach Form 4562) $_____, less depreciation claimed in Schedules A and H and elsewhere on return $_____, Balance ▶	20	
21	Amortization (attach schedule)	21	
22	Depletion (other than oil and gas, attach schedule—see page 5 of Instructions)	22	
23a	Retirement plans, etc. (see page 5 of Instructions)	23a	
23b	Employee benefit programs (see page 5 of Instructions)	23b	
24	Other deductions (attach schedule)	24	
25	**TOTAL** deductions (add lines 13c through 24)	25	
26	Ordinary income (loss) (subtract line 25 from line 12)	26	

Schedule A—COST OF GOODS SOLD AND/OR OPERATIONS (See Page 6 of Instructions)

27	Inventory at beginning of year (if different from last year's closing inventory, attach explanation) .	27	
28a	Purchases $_____ 28b Minus cost of items withdrawn for personal use $_____ Balance ▶	28c	
29	Cost of labor	29	
30	Materials and supplies	30	
31	Other costs (attach schedule)	31	
32	Total (add lines 27 through 31)	32	
33	Inventory at end of year	33	
34	Cost of goods sold (subtract line 33 from line 32). Enter here and on line 2, above	34	

Please **Sign** **Here**	Under penalties of perjury, I declare that I have examined this return, including accompanying schedules and statements, and to the best of my knowledge and belief it is true, correct, and complete. Declaration of preparer (other than taxpayer) is based on all information of which preparer has any knowledge.		
	▶ Signature of general partner	▶ Date	

Paid **Preparer's** **Use Only**	Preparer's signature ▶	Date	Check if self-em- ployed ▶ ☐	Preparer's social security no.
	Firm's name (or yours, if self-employed) and address ▶		E.I. No. ▶	
			ZIP code ▶	

For Paperwork Reduction Act Notice, see page 1 of Form 1065 Instructions

Exhibit 6-11 Continued

Form 1065 (1981)	Schedule A *(Continued)*	Page **2**

35 a Check all methods used for valuing closing inventory: *(i)* ☐ Cost
(ii) ☐ Lower of cost or market as described in regulations section
1.471–4 (see page 6 of Instructions) *(iii)* ☐ Writedown of "subnormal" goods as described in regulations section 1.471–2(c) (see page
6 of Instructions).

	Yes	No
b Did you use any other method of inventory valuation not described in line 35a? . . . . If "Yes," specify methods used and attach explanation . .		

c Check if the LIFO method was adopted this tax year for any goods. (If checked, attach Form 970) . . . . ☐

d If you are engaged in manufacturing, did you value your inventory using the full absorption method (regulations section 1.471–11)? . . . .

e Was there any substantial change in determining quantities, cost, or valuations between opening and closing inventory? If "Yes," attach explanation.

	Yes	No

Schedule D—CAPITAL GAINS AND LOSSES (See Page 6 of Instructions)

Part I Short-term Capital Gains and Losses—Assets Held One Year or Less

a. Kind of property and description (Example, 100 shares of "Z" Co.)	b. Date acquired (mo., day, yr.)	c. Date sold (mo., day, yr.)	d. Gross sales price minus expenses of sale	e. Cost or other basis	f. Gain (loss) for the year (d minus e)	g. Gain (loss) after 6/9/81
1a						

1b Short-term capital gain from installment sales from Form 6252, line 19 or 27 . . . . .
2 Partnership's share of net short-term gain (loss), including specially allocated items, from other partnerships and from fiduciaries . . . .
3 Net short-term gain (loss) from lines 1a, 1b, and 2. Enter here and on Schedule K (Form 1065), line 5 . . . .

Part II Long-term Capital Gains and Losses—Assets Held More Than One Year

4a						

4b Long-term capital gain from installment sales from Form 6252, line 19 or 27 . . . . .
5 Partnership's share of net long-term gain (loss), including specially allocated items, from other partnerships and from fiduciaries . . . .
6 Capital gain distributions . . . .
7 Net long-term gain (loss) from lines 4a, 4b, 5, and 6. Enter here and on Schedule K (Form 1065), line 6 . . . .

Schedule H—INCOME FROM RENTS (See Page 4 of Instructions) If you need more space, attach schedule.

a. Kind and location of property	b. Amount of rent	c. Depreciation (explain on Form 4562)	d. Repairs (attach schedule)	e. Other expenses (attach schedule)

1 Totals . . . .
2 Net income (loss) (subtract total of columns c, d, and e from column b). Enter here and on page 1, line 7 . . .

Schedule I—BAD DEBTS (See Page 5 of Instructions)

a. Year	b. Trade notes and accounts receivable outstanding at end of year	c. Sales on account	Amount added to reserve		f. Amount charged against reserve	g. Reserve for bad debts at end of year
			d. Current year's provision	e. Recoveries		
1976						
1977						
1978						
1979						
1980						
1981						

Exhibit 6-12 Federal income tax form 1120, used for a U. S. corporation

Form **1120**	**U.S. Corporation Income Tax Return**	OMB No. 1545-0123
Department of the Treasury Internal Revenue Service	For calendar year 1981 or other tax year beginning .... , 1981, ending .... , 19 .... ▶For Paperwork Reduction Act Notice, see page 1 of the instructions	**1981**

Check if a— **A.** Consolidated return ☐ **B.** Personal Holding Co. ☐ **C.** Business Code No. (See page 9 of Instructions)	Use IRS label. Other-wise please print or type.	Name	**D.** Employer identification number
		Number and street	**E.** Date incorporated
		City or town, State, and ZIP code	**F.** Total assets (see Specific Instructions) $

Gross Income

1	**(a)** Gross receipts or sales $ .... **(b)** Less returns and allowances $ .... Balance ▶	1(c)	
2	Cost of goods sold (Schedule A) and/or operations (attach schedule)	2	
3	Gross profit (subtract line 2 from line 1(c))	3	
4	Dividends (Schedule C)	4	
5	Interest on obligations of the United States and U.S. instrumentalities	5	
6	Other interest	6	
7	Gross rents	7	
8	Gross royalties	8	
9	**(a)** Capital gain net income (attach separate Schedule D)	9(a)	
	(b) Net gain or (loss) from Form 4797, line 11(a), Part II (attach Form 4797)	9(b)	
10	Other income (see instructions—attach schedule)	10	
11	TOTAL income—Add lines 3 through 10	11	

Deductions

12	Compensation of officers (Schedule E)	12	
13	**(a)** Salaries and wages .... **13(b)** Less WIN and jobs credit(s) .... Balance ▶	13(c)	
14	Repairs (see instructions)	14	
15	Bad debts (Schedule F if reserve method is used)	15	
16	Rents	16	
17	Taxes	17	
18	Interest	18	
19	Contributions (not over 5% of line 30 adjusted per instructions)	19	
20	Amortization (attach schedule)	20	
21	Depreciation from Form 4562 (attach Form 4562) .... , less depreciation claimed in Schedule A and elsewhere on return .... , Balance ▶	21	
22	Depletion	22	
23	Advertising	23	
24	Pension, profit-sharing, etc. plans (see instructions)	24	
25	Employee benefit programs (see instructions)	25	
26	Other deductions (attach schedule)	26	
27	TOTAL deductions—Add lines 12 through 26	27	
28	Taxable income before net operating loss deduction and special deductions (subtract line 27 from line 11)	28	
29	**Less: (a)** Net operating loss deduction (see instructions—attach schedule) . . 29(a)		
	(b) Special deductions (Schedule C) .... 29(b)	29	
30	Taxable income (subtract line 29 from line 28)	30	

Tax

31	TOTAL TAX (Schedule J)	31	
32	**Credits: (a)** Overpayment from 1980 allowed as a credit		
	(b) 1981 estimated tax payments		
	(c) Less refund of 1981 estimated tax applied for on Form 4466 . (........)		
	(d) Tax deposited: Form 7004 .... Form 7005 (attach) .... Total ▶		
	(e) Credit from regulated investment companies (attach Form 2439)		
	(f) Federal tax on special fuels and oils (attach Form 4136 or 4136–T)	32	
33	TAX DUE (subtract line 32 from line 31). See instruction C3 for depositary method of payment . (Check ▶ ☐ if Form 2220 is attached. See instruction D.) ▶ $	33	
34	OVERPAYMENT (subtract line 31 from line 32)	34	
35	Enter amount of line 34 you want: Credited to 1982 estimated tax ▶ .... Refunded ▶	35	

Please Sign Here

Under penalties of perjury, I declare that I have examined this return, including accompanying schedules and statements, and to the best of my knowledge and belief, it is true, correct, and complete. Declaration of preparer (other than taxpayer) is based on all information of which preparer has any knowledge.

▶ _____ Signature of officer _____ Date ▶ _____ Title

Paid Preparer's Use Only

Preparer's signature ▶	Date	Check if self-employed ▶ ☐	Preparer's social security no.
Firm's name (or yours, if self-employed) and address ▶		E.I. No. ▶	
		ZIP code ▶	

Exhibit 6-12 Continued

Form 1120 (1981)   **Schedule A**   Cost of Goods Sold (See Instructions for Schedule A)   Page **2**

1 Inventory at beginning of year . . . . _____
2 Merchandise bought for manufacture or sale . . . . _____
3 Salaries and wages . . . . _____
4 Other costs (attach schedule) . . . . _____
5 Total—Add lines 1 through 4 . . . . _____
6 Inventory at end of year . . . . _____
7 Cost of goods sold—Subtract line 6 from line 5. Enter here and on line 2, page 1 . . . . _____
8 (a) Check all methods used for valuing closing inventory. (i) ☐ Cost (ii) ☐ Lower of cost or market as described in Regulations section 1.471–4 (see instructions) (iii) ☐ Writedown of "subnormal" goods as described in Regulations section 1.471–2(c) (see instructions)

   (b) Did you use any other method of inventory valuation not described above? . . . . ☐ Yes ☐ No

    If "Yes," specify method used and attach explanation ▶ ....
   (c) Check if the LIFO inventory method was adopted this tax year for any goods (If checked, attach Form 970.) . . . . . ☐

   (d) If the LIFO inventory method was used for this tax year, enter percentage (or amounts) of closing inventory computed under LIFO . . . .

   (e) If you are engaged in manufacturing, did you value your inventory using the full absorption method (Regulations section 1.471–11)? . . . . ☐ Yes ☐ No

   (f) Was there any substantial change in determining quantities, cost, or valuations between opening and closing inventory? . . . ☐ Yes ☐ No
    If "Yes," attach explanation.

Schedule C   Dividends and Special Deductions (See instructions for Schedule C)

	(A) Dividends received	(B) %	(C) Special deductions: multiply (A) × (B)
1 Domestic corporations subject to 85% deduction		85	
2 Certain preferred stock of public utilities		59.13	
3 Foreign corporations subject to 85% deduction		85	
4 Wholly-owned foreign subsidiaries subject to 100% deduction (section 245(b)) .		100	
5 Total—Add lines 1 through 4. See instructions for limitation			
6 Affiliated groups subject to the 100% deduction (section 243(a)(3))		100	
7 Other dividends from foreign corporations not included in lines 3 and 4 . .			
8 Income from controlled foreign corporations under subpart F (attach Forms 3646) .			
9 Foreign dividend gross-up (section 78)			
10 DISC or former DISC not included in line 1 (section 246(d))			
11 Other dividends			
12 Deduction for dividends paid on certain preferred stock of public utilities (see instructions)			
13 Total dividends—Add lines 1 through 11. Enter here and on line 4, page 1 ⟶			
14 Total deductions—Add lines 5 through 12. Enter here and on line 29(b), page 1 ⟶			

Schedule E   Compensation of Officers (See instruction for line 12)

1. Name of officer	2. Social security number	3. Time devoted to business	Percent of corporation stock owned 4. Common	5. Preferred	6. Amount of compensation	7. Expense account allowances

Total compensation of officers—Enter here and on line 12, page 1 . . . .

Schedule F   Bad Debts—Reserve Method (See instruction for line 15)

1. Year	2. Trade notes and accounts receivable outstanding at end of year	3. Sales on account	Amount added to reserve 4. Current year's provision	5. Recoveries	6. Amount charged against reserve	7. Reserve for bad debts at end of year
1976						
1977						
1978						
1979						
1980						
1981						

good past employment record, limited or no indebtedness, home ownership, a net worth where assets clearly exceed liabilities, a record of prompt payment of accounts, good credit bureau standing, and a willingness to invest your own funds in the business.

A business manager or owner should become familiar with financial tools that can be helpful in starting and staying in business. These tools include the cash flow projection, the operating plan forecast, financial ratios, and break-even analysis. As a business manager, you must hire a first-class accountant to take care of all financial matters unless your business is very small and you can perform these functions yourself. In addition, you should have yearly certified audits. Such audits can result in lower interest rates and increase the confidence of both suppliers and lending institutions.

NOTES

1. In a partnership there would be more such money available. A corporate structure would also provide more ownership capital.

2. There is a school of thought that holds that a small business owner should invest as little of his own money as possible. This, of course, works better when interest rates are not too high. According to this school of thought, optimal leverage may be defined as having as much debt as your financial sources and suppliers will allow, with your own money available as an adequate reserve.

3. This section is based on the SBA pamphlet, *SBA: What It Does*, Washington, D. C.: U. S. Government Printing Office, 1977, p. 5.

4. The SBA considers all Vietnam-era veterans, for example, to be economically disadvantaged.

5. Cash surrender value is the dollar amount a policyholder would receive from the insurance company on canceling the policy.

6. There is such a thing as a single-payment loan, but lending agencies normally only make them to major corporations.

7. A term loan requires that regular interest payments be made at established times. When the final interest payment is due the total amount — the principal — must also be repaid.

8. For details on subcontracting a building, you may wish to read *Do-It-Yourself Contracting to Build Your Own Home: A Managerial Approach*, 2nd ed., by Richard J. Stillman, Radnor, Pa.: Chilton Book Company, 1981. The book points out how you can save up to twenty-five percent by acting as your own contractor.

9. This cash flow projection material is based on the SBA form no. 110, *Monthly Cash Flow Projection*.

10. Cash funds include cash, checks, and money orders paid out or received.

11. This material is based on the SBA form no. 1099 (3-75) Ref: SOP 60 101, *Operating Plan Forecast (Profit and Loss Projection)*.

12. I use the word "may" because when the SBA grants or guarantees a loan they usually tie up every asset of the owner. Such action makes it difficult to borrow additional funds from another source later.

Chapter 7
Personnel

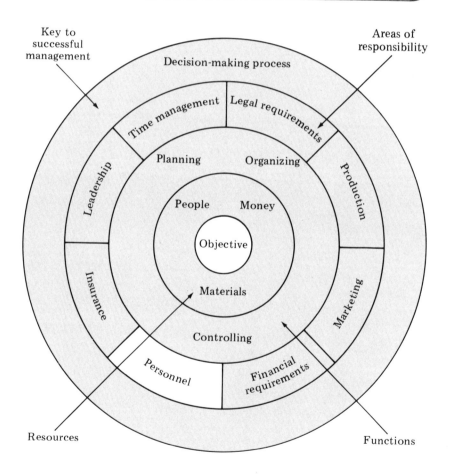

Key to
successful
management

Areas of
responsibility

Decision-making process

Time management

Legal requirements

Planning

Organizing

People

Money

Objective

Leadership

Production

Insurance

Materials

Marketing

Controlling

Personnel

Financial
requirements

Resources

Functions

Exhibit 7-1 Stillman's Small Business Management Model: An overview of the five major components of management with emphasis on personnel

> In order that people may be happy in their work,
> these three things are needed: They must be fit
> for it. They must not do too much of it. And they
> must have a sense of success in it.
>
> — John Ruskin

The appropriate management of human resources is an essential responsibility in all businesses, regardless of size. In fact, the smaller the business, the more important it is to select the right person for the right job. In a four-person company, for example, one bad apple can produce more problems than a similar number in a large corporation. In this chapter we shall examine the selection process and all other aspects of getting and keeping quality employees.

How does the management of human resources fit in with the other duties that small business managers must perform to be successful? Personnel is emphasized (in white) in Exhibit 7-1, as one of eight areas of managerial responsibility. The objective also is emphasized, to show that it must be considered in arriving at all decisions. As stressed throughout this book, it is important to recognize and understand this total and interrelated approach in order to manage a business efficiently. Personnel, for example, must be involved with legal responsibilities, production, marketing, insurance, finance, leadership, and time management. After all, the personnel manager must work with staff and managers in each of these areas to provide the people required to do the work. The personnel manager must also perform the *functions* of planning, organizing, and controlling, using *resources* (people, money, materials) wisely in order to make sound *decisions*.

PERSONNEL DEPARTMENT

Some small businesses may be big enough to require establishing a personnel department, under the direction of a personnel manager. In smaller firms the owner may perform this task as well as other management duties, so anyone who wants to start and stay in business should understand what is included in the field of human resources management (see Exhibit 7-2).

What are personnel responsibilities in a small business? They may in-

Exhibit 7-2 Stillman's Personnel Management Model: An overview of the five components of personnel

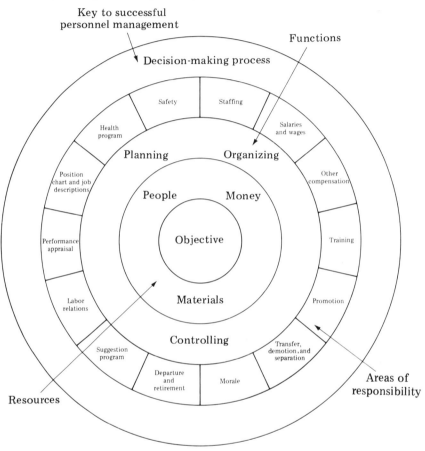

clude staffing; determination of salaries, wages, and other compensation; training; keeping morale high; running a suggestion program; labor relations; preparing job descriptions and conducting performance appraisals; and maintaining safety and health programs. Let us examine each of these human resources responsibilities.

STAFFING

The staffing aspects of personnel management include recruiting, selecting, orienting, transferring, promoting, demoting, and separating staff members. In starting a company, determine how many people will be required to run the business at first and then in the future, as you grow. Your personnel plan must specify the costs involved and the duties of each person. In recruiting, you should develop a big enough list of eligible candidates to make a good selection. Sources may include references from friends, relatives, advertisements, and state and private employment agencies. Keep a record of all candidates who apply. This provides a ready reference when you need new staff members and enables you to review the background of eligible candidates. Exhibit 7-3 may be used as a guide in preparing your own employee information sheet.

Selection

You should select a new staff member from among at least three qualified candidates. Conduct appropriate tests, or have an employment office conduct them. If possible, have applicants for certain positions perform the tasks that will be required of them, so you can note their degree of skill. It may be advisable to conduct a double interview with any finalists in a pleasant environment with few distractions. Make every effort to put the person at ease. The immediate supervisor should confer with the candidate and outline the duties involved. Let the candidate see the place where work will be performed and observe operations. Stress such standards as hours of work, sick leave, and work rules. Attempt to determine whether the candidate is genuinely interested in becoming a member of the company. Only in a satisfactory two-way exchange of information will the applicant be able to determine whether he or she really wants to work for your organization. The owner, or whoever is the supervisor's immediate superior, should then give a personal interview of from five to fifteen minutes. After at least three applicants have been interviewed, hold a meeting to select the best potential employee. Discuss each person frankly, make a decision, and notify the successful candidate or employment office. In the smallest mom-and-pop operations, it may be the husband and wife who do the interviewing.

What do you look for in general? Different situations require different qualities. For a selling position, consider appearance, previous work record (including frequency in changing jobs), poise, personality, interest, background, courtesy, and education. Experience has indicated that for this kind of position too much education and background can be just as unsatisfactory as not enough. Judge all candidates on their individual merits, regardless of sex or age.

Can you spend too much time interviewing? Seldom. Effort expended in selecting the right person for the job may save you the hours of work and the heavy expense of training, firing, and replacing an employee. The double interview also conveys to the candidate the interest of management and the importance placed on securing the best available employee.

Exhibit 7-3   Employee information sheet

Name _____
          Last   First   Middle   Nickname

Date of birth _____

Home address _____

_____
                    City   State   Zip

Telephone number _____

Educational institutions attended	Specialization	Years Completed
_____ (High School)	_____	_____
_____ (College)	_____	_____
_____ (Other)	_____	_____

Names of last three employing firms and the positions you held
(Military or civilian, part-time or full-time. List name of supervisor and
address of company.)

_____

_____

_____

_____

_____

_____

Why do you want to work for this company? (Be specific.)

_____

_____

References (List name, address, and telephone number.)

1. _____

2. _____

3. _____

Orientation

Every effort should be made to make an employee, on first reporting to work, feel accepted, feel like part of the firm. The manager or owner should extend greetings whenever possible. The immediate supervisor should introduce the new employee to fellow workers and review privileges as well as duties and responsibilities. See that a new person understands what is expected in the way of organizational standards. Shortly after the new employee arrives, the personnel manager should conduct an orientation. The following topics are discussed by one manufacturing company at briefings for new employees:

1. Welcome
2. Purpose
   To give a better understanding of our company.
3. Presentation
   Covers the following areas: mission; background data; organization; production schedule; inventory status; cost determination; responsibilities and opportunities.
4. Mission
   Manufacture of hospital uniforms and supplies distributed by wholesalers.
5. History of uniforms manufactured by the company
   Pictures and displays.
6. Organization
   a. Authorized strength
   b. Volume of business
7. Production schedule: Current year
8. Current inventory picture
9. Cost determination
10. Responsibilities and opportunities
    a. Standards — importance of being at work on time.
    b. Suggestion program — financial awards. Company savings exceeded $150,000 last year, and the top employee award amounted to $1,140.
    c. Personnel matters: available insurance; training; performance appraisal; job description; annual leave; sick leave; promotion policy; recreation and health facilities; safety; incentives; parties.
    d. Problems, personal or otherwise: Please feel free to discuss these matters with your supervisor or the personnel manager.
11. Summary
    Suggestions of ways to improve our operation are always welcome.

12. Questions

13. Tour of tailor shop

In an effective orientation, you should point out employee responsibilities as well as convey the notion that management has the employee's interest and welfare at heart. Stress the fact that each member of the organization is important in accomplishing the company's objective.

SALARIES AND WAGES

Fair compensation of all employees is a difficult challenge. Obviously, the greater the responsibility a person has in an organization, the greater should be the pay — other benefits, opportunities, and privileges being equal. When starting a business it is desirable to find out the going rate of pay established by competitors in your community. Contact the nearest Small Business Administration field office for their views. Your pay plan for key employees should be in writing. Any guarantees should have a beginning and an end.

Conversations with my students — virtually all of whom work — and with many people in business have, over the years, convinced me that the primary concern of most people is for an equitable salary. Other nonmonetary benefits do not have the meaning of a fair day's pay for a fair day's work. Pay raises that keep pace with the cost of living are also valued. Most people also expect merit to be rewarded with additional remuneration.

This primacy of pay has been disputed time and again by scholars who list a variety of desires placed ahead of money. They point to the need for recognition, dignity of the individual, social acceptance, and the opportunity to reach one's full potential. These are important needs and should be met as an obligation of management. A manager should also realize that people vary in the importance they place on various benefits, monetary and nonmonetary. Nevertheless, my experience has indicated that the most appreciated management action is a raise in pay.

OTHER COMPENSATION

What other compensation with a monetary value do you want to offer your employees? An examination of Exhibit 7-4 reveals that there are many possibilities. Determine what the competition is doing and then decide what is best for your firm based on available funds.

Space has been provided in Exhibit 7-4 to list the dollar cost of each potential benefit over a three-year period. You may want to provide additional inducement in the second and third years. After you have determined the total cost of salary and other benefits, compute it as a percentage of your

Exhibit 7-4   Benefit cost worksheet

Dollar Value of Benefits Offered by _____
as of _____, 19_____

	19_____	19_____	19_____
Bonus (cash and/or stock)			
Car			
Club membership			
Cost-of-living increases			
Credit union			
Loans from company			
Maternity leave			
Military leave			
Moving expenses			
Overtime pay			
Pension			
Personal financial and estate counseling			
Profit sharing			
Savings program — employer contributions			
Sick leave			
Social Security			
Stock purchase			
Travel allowance			
Union coverage			
Vacations, paid			
Other[a]			

Total salary and wages _____ _____ _____

Total other benefits _____ _____ _____

Total compensation _____ _____ _____

[a] Space is provided here for other benefits. You are only limited by your imagination as to what financial rewards you might provide that would help you attract and keep good employees. This worksheet permits you to analyze each of the incentives and determine its cost to your firm. Decide what is best with the funds you have available for this purpose.

total costs. This complete package gives you a sound basis for informing employees of the total dollar value of their compensation.[1]

TRAINING

Every small business should provide on-the-job training to improve the skills of its employees. Begin such a program as soon as the new employee reports to work — it is important to get people off to a good start. Emphasize basics, including appearance, safety, courtesy, punctuality, and job skills. In the smallest firms the owner or manager would normally give this instruction. Devote time to part-time help as well as to the regulars. A rude salesperson, temporary or full-time, can lose customers in a hurry, and sloppy janitorial work can cause accidents that may result in costly lawsuits.

In larger small businesses, each activity or department should have considerable latitude in on-the-job training of its personnel. Encourage managers to foster this opportunity for their people. Such a program should stimulate the development of personnel by recognizing the following points:

○ Training is an inherent part of work.
○ Training is an owner's and manager's responsibility.
○ Training must be geared to meet the needs of the business.
○ The best and least costly training is done on the job.
○ Employees have an obligation to exercise initiative in their own development. This includes taking advantage of training opportunities and applying the skills they acquire to their work.
○ Every firm should take advantage of the free training offered by companies who sell and install equipment.

Whenever possible, effective on-the-job training should include giving employees opportunities to assume more important duties. During the temporary absences of supervisors, employees can be appointed to take over the higher positions. This responsibility can be rotated among eligible members of a group to enable management to compare their capabilities. A training program should operate on the premise that, where size permits, each area or function should be at least two-deep in people who are familiar with every supervisory position, so key losses have little adverse effect. Experience has shown the virtue of operating a completely open organization, without any secret operators who will not reveal their duties to others. I recall so well an experience I had shortly after taking over management of a hotel. The front-desk supervisor went on vacation. Soon after his departure, we needed information from him on a legal matter. His assistant said: "Oh, he always locks his desk when he goes, and leaves no address to contact him. He has never told me about his job."

PROMOTION

A good training program simplifies promotion. It permits management to observe staff people in more responsible positions. When vacancies do occur, the department supervisor or owner should be objective and select the best qualified candidate, inside or outside; nevertheless, all other things being equal, it is human nature to select from within the organization. This rule can be highly beneficial if there are competent people available, but to apply it without regard to ability can cause an organization to stagnate. Furthermore, inbreeding can be overdone — a fresh vantage point may be desirable.

In many small businesses, there should be a career promotion pattern. Employees should be told how they can move ahead in the company. Everyone should be notified, for example, of openings that are advertised by the firm. For an employee in a mom-and-pop business, however, chances for advancement from within are often almost nil. Any rewards, assuming no change in duties, must come in the form of pay raises to keep up with the cost of living and merit increases. Make every effort to provide some inducement to retain able people.

If size permits, establish a special management program. This could enable selected young employees to receive limited course instruction and on-the-job training in a variety of tasks in all areas of the business. They would not be assured of new positions after completion of this program, but it would give them added status in applying for managerial openings that do occur. Or your firm may want to pay for an employee's schooling in a local university. Courses would have to increase the employee's value to the company. Small businesses do not sponsor enough of this type of education. Coupled with lack of a definite career promotion pattern, this makes it difficult to keep high-caliber people for the long haul.

TRANSFER, DEMOTION, AND SEPARATION

The removal of unsatisfactory employees from a business is becoming more and more difficult because of government rules. It is true that the individual should be protected from the arbitrary whims of management, but this does not mean that the incompetent should be retained. If a firm has acquired enough evidence, it can normally require an employee to meet established standards or leave. But what often happens? If the firm is large enough, the employee is transferred to another activity. This may continue until the acceptable standard of a particular unit is met. Obviously, an employee may perform better in one work environment than in another, and everyone is entitled to a fair chance. But there is a point of no return. Unfortunately, government review agencies are inclined to accept lack of competence as part of the system. It then becomes a question of whether the government truly desires businesses to be reasonably economical, effective, and efficient. Perhaps the greater obligation is to maintain employment at a high level. If managers of business enterprises are expected to perform efficiently, however, they should be able to remove personnel for failure to meet standards without encountering bureaucratic interference. In order to have a transfer, demotion, and separation system, it is important for the personnel manager to devise necessary written instructions and inform all concerned.

A word of caution: firing can be expensive. Get written resignations whenever possible. Department managers should not be able to fire people without permission of the owner or the personnel manager. In turn, department managers must work in close coordination with the personnel manager to be sure the policies are consistent with regard to transfer, demotion, and separation.

MORALE

Morale may be defined as an individual's enthusiasm, loyalty, and support for a business and its mission. It is that willingness to go the extra mile to get the job done as well as it can be done. One morale-builder is appropriate recognition. There is ample opportunity for managers to recognize people for their contributions to the organization. If you give this recognition fairly, it can be very beneficial. Consider some techniques that have been effective.

An owner of one company remembered the birthday of every member of her firm. She would put a birthday card at the person's place of work before the person arrived on that day. This had a salutary effect; everyone looked forward to receiving this small token. (The thought expressed by the owner illustrated her nature and her way of life. It might be ineffective coming from a supervisor who lacked the warm personality to go with the thoughtful gesture.) On the birthday of each supervisor, the owner also wrote a congratulatory letter. This created an opportunity to say thank you for a job well done and to let supervisors know that their contributions were appreciated. A letter to one supervisor read as follows:

> Many happy returns of the day. It has been my pleasure to work with you during the past ten years, and to note that all of your efforts have been of a high order. I particularly appreciate your interest and efforts that go beyond the normal requirements in helping your employees.
>
> On behalf of your many friends, please accept my sincere good wishes for a
>
> HAPPY BIRTHDAY

In another successful company, the owner personally contacted all employees on their birthdays. Whenever possible, he told them that he appreciated their efforts. This friendly recognition permeated the company, and the firm played a "Happy Birthday" record for the employee.[2] One supervisor provided birthday cards signed by all the co-workers, and certain people brought in boxes of candy or birthday cake to be enjoyed during the coffee break.

Parties on appropriate occasions can keep morale high. Consider Christmas parties, summer picnics, and banquets or festivities in recognition of long and faithful service. The motivation should come from within the firm, and as many people as possible should participate in making it a success.

The natural cheer at Christmas can be fostered not only by a party but by friendly competition in decorating each area of the building. You might also want to send a friendly greeting card to each employee's home. The message might be something like the one below:

> Cordial greetings and best wishes for a Merry Christmas and a Happy New Year. Your friendly spirit of cooperation, loyalty, and achievement during the past year are recognized and deeply appreciated.

A complimentary letter is an excellent method of giving due regard to special accomplishments. A message of appreciation might say something like the following:

> For the past two years you have given a number of orientations to new employees. Your subject area was the history of our uniforms. These presentations required approximately thirty minutes and were well received by all concerned.
>
> These briefings required considerable preparation and were beyond your normal work requirements. You spent many hours of overtime at no expense to the company. I had the pleasure of giving part of the orientation with you, and it was apparent that your entire contribution was outstanding. I wish to take this opportunity to thank you and make this superior performance a matter of record.
>
> A copy of this letter will be sent to our personnel department to be included in your file.

Management may wish to initiate superior accomplishment awards for truly outstanding achievements. Make cash payments to the recipients. The amount should depend on the nature of the contribution and the savings to the firm. Such an award has proved to be a highly coveted honor, prized more than other forms of recognition for exemplary performance because it has dollars-and-cents value.

One very important morale-builder is the effective leadership that produces a successful business. People like to be part of a winning team — nothing succeeds like success. See chapter 9 for a discussion of leadership traits.

DEPARTURE AND RETIREMENT

People who have served their firm well should be honored on leaving the organization. The degree of recognition should be dependent on the length of service and the extent of the person's contribution. The objective is to have people leave the firm with pleasant memories.

People who leave an enterprise after only a few years might be given a letter of appreciation. A farewell ceremony might also be held on company premises, with fellow workers in attendance. The immediate supervisor or owner might present a small gift at this time and make a few appropriate remarks.

Retirement after long and faithful service is worthy of special recognition. On such an occasion, the immediate family might be invited to a dinner party honoring the retiree. Presents could include such items as a cash bonus and watch, appropriately engraved. Plaques have also been well received. They should include the name of the retiree, years of service, and firm insignia. If possible, find out what gift the person would most appreciate — if it is within the means of the company. The owner of one firm found that the following letter, modified to reflect the person's contributions, was greatly appreciated.

> On the occasion of your retirement, I want to express my appreciation for the loyal and efficient service you have rendered to our company for the past twenty-five years.
>
> During this entire period, your skill as a tailor was reflected in the high quality of our uniforms. You must leave with personal satisfaction and pride in the knowledge that you have made an important contribution to the success of our company.
>
> I thank you personally, and on behalf of your friends I extend best wishes for good health and happiness in your retirement years.

At retirement ceremonies it is good to have a photographer present and a story available for release to the press. It is not surprising to hear the importance many people place on having a story and a picture in the hometown paper. Benefits also accrue to the company in the form of excellent free publicity and high morale among other employees who look forward to their day in the sun.

Other forms of recognition that may be given on completion of exemplary service include a festive party. A supervisor at one plant was honored by all 230 employees in a unique surprise ceremony. The program was developed by the plant engineer and patterned after the old television show, *This Is Your Life*. It covered significant phases of the supervisor's life, with emphasis on his forty-five years of company service. The entire sequence was tape-recorded, with friends narrating important events. Such expressions of esteem and interest in people have proved their worth over the years.

SUGGESTION PROGRAM

An employee suggestion program offers a splendid opportunity for members to make contributions to improve the business. Adequate information on the subject should be disseminated to all personnel. Suggestion boxes can be conveniently placed throughout your building. Periodically review the suggestions submitted. Make cash awards promptly and base them on estimated benefits to the company. The stimulus for advancing the program must come from the owner or manager. An excellent opportunity to encourage suggestions is provided at employee meetings. You can place constant emphasis on the program, with gratifying results. At one meeting I attended, an owner remarked: "Maybe you can't build a better mousetrap, but you can improve on a current procedure or eliminate a needless function. Turn your ideas into dollars. Use your suggestion box. It can mean extra money for you in this inflationary era and help assure our firm's survival." The company also invited suggestions from its customers and found many of them helpful.

LABOR RELATIONS

In a very small business with no union, it is relatively easy to maintain good relations with employees. Material presented in this chapter can help you provide a rewarding work environment. Fair pay, appropriate incentives, safety measures, suggestion program, on-the-job training, proper staffing, opportunity for advancement, and clear understanding of responsibilities are all criteria any manager can apply. You must also set the example and motivate your workers to achieve their full potential.

The larger small business may require a separate personnel department to set policies in labor matters. A legal advisor may be necessary in union negotiations and resolving disputes. Nevertheless, the steps listed in the previous paragraph can be helpful in any business.

PERFORMANCE APPRAISAL

What is performance appraisal? It is a measure of the quality of a person's work in comparison with an established standard. In a very small business the owner can observe all the employees daily and inform them how they are doing. As your tiny firm expands, however, you should develop a form to be used for evaluation. The one shown in Exhibit 7-5 is used by a clothing store. You should develop a format to meet your particular needs. Such a formal appraisal should be made every six months to a year. Set aside appropriate time to go over the evaluation in detail with each employee. The purpose of performance appraisal is to:

o Inform employees how they are doing and what actions can be taken to improve.
o Provide a basis for raises and promotions.
o Indicate weaknesses where additional training may be desirable.
o Obtain feedback on the positive and negative aspects of management.

Exhibit 7-5   Performance evaluation form

Date _____

Name _____
            Last   First   Middle

Position _____

Period of evaluation _____

	Outstanding	Good	Fair	Poor
1. Performance of duties				
2. Appearance				
3. Courtesy				
4. Interest in learning				
5. Cooperation				
6. Punctuality				
7. Acceptance of additional responsibility				

Suggestions for improvement

Employee's views   _____

_____

Owner's comments   _____

_____

POSITION CHART AND JOB DESCRIPTIONS

Spell out in writing the duties that are expected of each employee. This can be accomplished by preparing job descriptions. As the term implies, these list in detail what each job is all about. Thus there will be fewer problems if questions arise. New employees should be given written job descriptions promptly along with a spoken explanation.

As your small business expands, you may want to portray the jobs in your organization by using a position chart (Exhibit 7-6). Other organizational charts are also a responsibility of the personnel department. See chapter 2 for a further discussion of charts. The position chart establishes the number of people required to operate a business. It is essential to keep current records on what you have authorized and the actual count. The actual number working at any one time is normally below the authorized figure because of such factors as inability to secure the desired skill in the labor market or budgetary limitations. In any business, it is also important to have a good mix in age, sex, and experience. One approach is to keep information in tabular form (Exhibits 7-7 and 7-8). Exhibit 7-7 shows age spread, which can be important to management. If too many are bunched together at one end of the spectrum, the firm may be losing too many. personnel at one time. It is good to have a broad distribution. A length-of-service chart (Exhibit 7-8) permits a determination of the rate of turnover. This one also allows you to determine if minorities are properly represented.

HEALTH PROGRAM

A good health program can be a rewarding investment. It can reduce sick leave, build morale, and help you retain quality personnel. You may want to provide such health inducements as an annual physical examination, periodic dental checkups, and membership in a physical fitness program. The availability of funds for this purpose must be the major factor in deciding what kind of health program you adopt. Some firms provide a portion of the membership fee in a local health club like the YMCA.

SAFETY

As an owner of a business, you must take appropriate safety measures. These should include purchasing necessary equipment to protect your employees and having safety experts make inspections.

Fire losses, for example, are on the increase throughout the nation. This has resulted in considerable loss of life and property, but there are precautions that can be taken. Of prime importance is a plan of escape for all

Exhibit 7-6   Position chart of XYZ Corporation

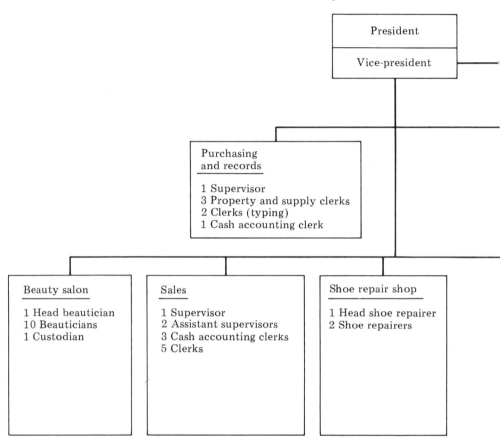

people on the premises. Exhibit 7-9 is a checklist to reduce the risk of fire and, if one should occur, to help people get out in time.

Commercial fires can be costly. In addition to possible business losses, irreplaceable valuables can be destroyed. Insurance may not cover replacement costs, and temporary moving to another place can be expensive and cause the firm to lose income. One fire chief put it well:

Many commercial fires could be prevented with appropriate fire prevention measures. I am really concerned today about some businesses not making periodic inspections. Taking all precautions possible ahead of time can prevent tragedies. The old adage, "an ounce of prevention is worth a pound of cure" is so true.

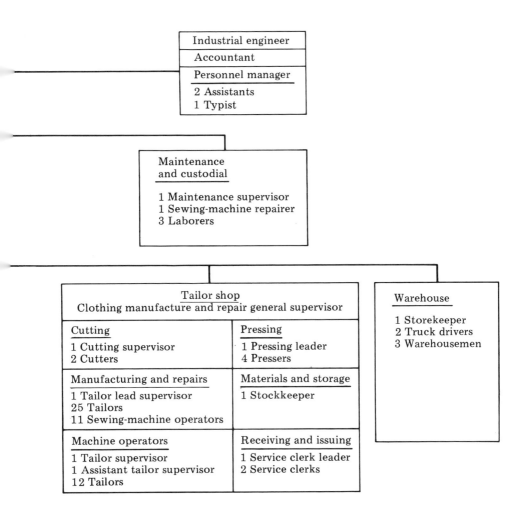

| Industrial engineer |
| Accountant |
| <u>Personnel manager</u> |
| 2 Assistants
1 Typist |

| Maintenance
<u>and custodial</u> |
| 1 Maintenance supervisor
1 Sewing-machine repairer
3 Laborers |

Tailor shop
Clothing manufacture and repair general supervisor

Cutting	Pressing
1 Cutting supervisor 2 Cutters	1 Pressing leader 4 Pressers
Manufacturing and repairs	Materials and storage
1 Tailor lead supervisor 25 Tailors 11 Sewing-machine operators	1 Stockkeeper
Machine operators	Receiving and issuing
1 Tailor supervisor 1 Assistant tailor supervisor 12 Tailors	1 Service clerk leader 2 Service clerks

| Warehouse |
| 1 Storekeeper
2 Truck drivers
3 Warehousemen |

Approved: Narco Namllits, President
6/17/83

A variety of measures can be taken to protect your business from crime. Some, like alarm systems and iron doors, are expensive. Other actions can be taken for little or no cost. These include working with the police, marking valuable items, and installing locks yourself.

The best time to determine your security requirements is during the

Exhibit 7-7 Age and sex comparison, Company A, January 1, 1983

Ages	Male	Female	Total
18 – 21		3	3
22 – 25	2	2	4
26 – 29	2	2	4
30 – 33	8	3	11
34 – 37	5	4	9
38 – 41	7	3	10
42 – 45	6	6	12
46 – 49	16	6	22
50 – 53	6	8	14
54 – 57	10	5	15
58 – 61	11	1	12
62 – 65	6		6
66 – 69	6		6
Totals	85	43	128

planning phase of starting your business. You can then allocate a specified amount of money within your total budget for protective devices. If you wait, installation costs will be higher, interest charges will be greater, and you will not have the desired protection from the moment you open your business.

You should have adequate protection to give you a sense of security and

Exhibit 7-8 Length of service comparison, Company A, January 1, 1983

Years	Male	Female	Total
0 – 6	36 (6)[a]	29 (3)	65 (9)
7 – 13	18 (3)	12 (4)	30 (7)
14 – 20	14 (2)	0	14 (2)
21 – 27	8 (5)	0	8 (5)
28 – 34	5 (1)	1	6 (1)
35 – 41	4 (2)	1 (1)	5 (3)
Totals	85	43	128 (27)

[a] Figures in parentheses represent minorities. Such records are essential and permit a rapid determination of problems you might have in complying with federal regulations.

Exhibit 7-9   Fire prevention checklist

		Yes	No
Date last checked _____			
1. Smoke and fire detectors are installed. These should be checked periodically for proper operation. This check should include an examination of the batteries.		____	____
2. Electric wiring is appropriate for business needs.		____	____
3. Trash is kept in a safe place.		____	____
4. Flammables, such as gasoline, turpentine, and mineral spirits, are stored away from water heaters, clothes dryers, or any other source of high heat or open flames. Such flammables should be kept in metal containers with appropriate expansion vents.		____	____
5. Ashtrays are checked when visitors leave.		____	____
6. There are fire extinguishers that meet your needs.		____	____
7. The fire department has made a free inspection of your business.		____	____
8. Regular monthly fire drills conducted to include explanation of all fire escape routes.		____	____
9. Other. (Itemize.)		____	____

peace of mind. This may require enough equipment to discourage an intruder and make him decide it would be easier to go elsewhere. You can help an intruder make this decision by using whatever devices are at your disposal. Remember that security is only as good as you make it. If you fail to lock your doors or turn on your alarm system, these measures are a wasted expense.

SUMMARY

Every business, regardless of size, must make effective use of available human resources. Personnel responsibilities may include staffing; determining salaries, wages, and other compensation; training; keeping morale high; running a suggestion program; labor relations; preparing job descriptions and conducting performance appraisals; and maintaining safety and health programs. Larger small businesses may require a separate personnel department to accomplish these duties. Even the smallest business owner or manager, however, must give appropriate attention to these matters to obtain best results. The challenge in the United States is to take a heterogeneous group of people and bring out the best qualities of each in order to create "a true whole that is larger than the sum of its parts, a productive entity that turns out more than the sum of the resources put into it."[3] If done effectively, this can produce remarkable results; but with poor personnel management it can result in dismal failure.

NOTES

1. You may want to use Exhibit 7-4 for another purpose. Competition is always keen for able people. Look at your firm and rate the benefits you offer your employees against comparable businesses in the area, replacing the year column headings with the names of the other companies.

2. The company has a record player that is used for several hours a day. On occasion there has been controversy over certain selections and the length of time music is to be played. To eliminate this problem, a committee of workers has been established. They select the records to be purchased and played. This committee approach has been successful to date.

3. Drucker, Peter, *An Introductory View of Management*, New York: Harper's College Press, 1977, p. 214.

Chapter 8
Insurance

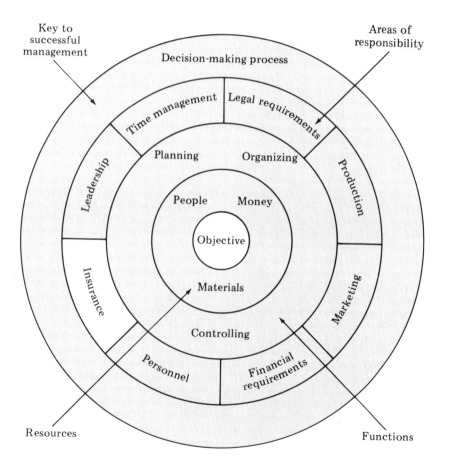

Key to
successful
management

Areas of
responsibility

Decision-making process

Time management · Legal requirements

Planning · Organizing

People · Money

Objective

Leadership

Production

Insurance

Materials

Controlling

Marketing

Personnel · Financial requirements

Resources

Functions

Exhibit 8-1 Stillman's Small Business Management Model: An overview of the five major components of management with emphasis on insurance

> I sleep better with my insurance premiums paid.
> My only regret — I can't eliminate the ultimate
> risk.
>
> — Philip Joseph

This chapter will discuss the insurance needs of the small business owner. As owner, or manager, you are responsible for seeing that your firm has the necessary protection. The amount and kind will vary based on such factors as size, type of ownership (proprietorship, partnership, or corporation), nature of business, and location.

How does insurance fit into the total approach emphasized throughout this text? Exhibit 8-1 highlights the area of insurance responsibility. The objective also is emphasized to indicate that it must be considered in arriving at all insurance decisions. Here, as before, every other topic in this book is interrelated to the topic of this chapter. Resources (people, money, materials), for example, must be adequately protected against potential losses. This requires planning to develop an appropriate insurance program in accordance with your company's objectives. The plan, in turn, must be implemented. You will also need to make frequent checks to determine if the plan is being implemented properly. If it is not, make the appropriate modifications. An owner can make sound decisions about insurance by understanding all aspects of management. This requires taking into consideration the objective, resources, functions, and responsibilities of the firm. Let us look at the purpose of insurance and the various policies available to businesses.

PURPOSE

Insurance has been defined as "coverage by contract whereby one party undertakes to indemnify or guarantee another against loss by a specified contingency or peril."[1]

Insurance provides protection against loss. Without this protection a business may have to assume the cost of extraordinary losses. For example, if $2,700 in equipment is stolen from your store, you may need to come up with another $2,700 to replace it unless you are able to shift the burden of loss elsewhere. If the thief is found, you may recover the merchandise, or the courts may require him to pay the damages — if he has the money to do so.

If you assume the risk (burden of loss) yourself, you may set aside so much of the firm's budget each year for such losses. This can become a prohibitive risk, however, in the event of loss of your building or severe personal injury for which you are liable. Thus, as the definition of insurance indicates, the burden of loss can be shifted by one party to another. Coverage by contract for a specified loss appears in each insurance policy.

KEY TERMS

Before buying insurance, you should be familiar with four important terms.

Contract

The definition referred to a contractual agreement. Insurance agreements are spelled out in written documents called contracts. Each contract specifies the set of conditions under which the insured person or firm will be paid, including the dollar amount. The written provisions of contracts are normally long and complicated. The language is often difficult to understand. The terms of the contract include policy limitations, special assessments, and exclusions.

It is essential to read and understand the exclusions and limitations before buying a policy. Even after thorough reading, you may find the policy couched in language that requires you to ask advice from your firm's lawyer.

Insurer

The firm that accepts the risk and responsibility, and administers the insurance policy, is the *insurer.* Insurers may be organized as associations, corporations, partnerships, or groups of underwriters formed into syndicates. The insurer depends on having enough clients to spread the risk adequately. The insurer is also careful who gets insurance. Too many bad risks can bankrupt a firm.

Underwriter

An individual who determines the eligibility of the insured and the premium the insured should pay for a policy is an *underwriter.* [2] Fairness in establishing rates is one of the most difficult problems of underwriters. Get to know your underwriter as well as you know your banker. If possible, have the underwriter visit your firm to see that you deserve a lower-than-average rate.

Actuary

The person who determines insurance premiums, dividends, and reserves is an *actuary*. Some actuarial work may be done by underwriters but actuarial work is a highly skilled profession, and there is a limited number of certified actuaries throughout the country. They have strong backgrounds in mathematics, and in their work for life insurance companies they develop options for settlements and prepare complex formulas to determine costs of a variety of policies. Accurate actuarial information is essential to the success of every insurance company.

INSURANCE COMPANY RATINGS

In arriving at a sound insurance program for your firm, you should read and understand the policies you are considering, and examine appropriate statistical data before selecting a company. A fine source for background information is the Alfred M. Best Company of Old Wick, New Jersey, which publishes two books each year — one on life and health insurance companies and the other on property and casualty firms.

In its publications, *Best's* places companies it rates into one of the five categories shown in Exhibit 8-2.[3]

Best's bases its ratings on five factors — competent underwriting, cost control and efficient management, adequate reserves for undischarged liabilities of all types, net resources to absorb unusual shock, and soundness of investment.

In addition to rating insurance companies, *Best's* provides a financial size category rating, as shown in Exhibit 8-3. "This size category," they state, "is determined by the surplus to policyholders, conditional or technical reserves, plus equities in unearned premiums and loss reserves, or less indicated shortages in reserves, if any."[4]

Exhibit 8-2 Ratings given insurance companies in *Best's Insurance Reports*

Classification	Rating
A+ and A	Excellent
B+	Very good
B	Good
C+	Fairly good
C	Fair

Exhibit 8-3 Financial size categories of
insurance companies rated in *Best's
Insurance Reports*

Class	Financial size (in dollars)[a]	
I	250,000	or less
II	250,000 to	500,000
III	500,000 to	750,000
IV	750,000 to	1,000,000
V	1,000,000 to	1,500,000
VI	1,500,000 to	2,500,000
VII	2,500,000 to	3,750,000
VIII	3,750,000 to	5,000,000
IX	5,000,000 to	7,500,000
X	7,500,000 to	12,500,000
XI	12,500,000 to	25,000,000
XII	25,000,000 to	50,000,000
XIII	50,000,000 to	75,000,000
XIV	75,000,000 to	100,000,000
XV	100,000,000	or more

[a] Financial size is determined by the surplus to
policyholders and conditional or technical reserves,
plus equities in unearned premiums and loss reserves, or minus any indicated shortage of reserves.

THE INSURANCE POLICY

Once you find a first-rate insurance company, decide on a policy that
meets the particular needs of your firm. The agreement between the insured and the insurer should spell out all of your requirements. An insurance
policy is normally divided into two sections. The first section lists the
specified coverage agreed to by the policyholder and the insurer. The second section covers general provisions.

POLICIES AVAILABLE

Many different types of insurance policies are available to a small business. They may be classified as follows.

Life Insurance

Business life insurance[5] can be written for numerous specific purposes.
Chief among these are:

○ A sole proprietorship insurance plan. To provide for maintenance of a business upon the death of the sole proprietor.

○ A partnership insurance plan. To retire a partner's interest at death.

○ A corporate insurance plan. To retire a shareholder's interest at death.

○ Key-person protection. To reimburse for loss and to provide funds for securing a replacement in the event of a key employee's death. Such insurance helps to prevent a setback that might develop when you lose a vital employee.

○ Group plan for employees. A group annuity or pension plan may be desirable if you have enough employees. Where only a few are involved, some form of individual retirement policy could be used, with the cost shared by employer and employee in any proportion you choose.

○ Reserve for emergencies. Most business life insurance plans use cash value life insurance. This cash value, growing over the years, provides the firm with an important reserve for emergencies in the event of any sharp dislocation in business conditions. When necessary, the cash value of the policy can be used to secure loans.[6]

○ Where an estate consists entirely of an interest in a business, life insurance payable to the beneficiary on the insured's death provides ready cash and aids in liquidating the insured person's interest in the business.

Business life insurance should cover every aspect of your business. You can accomplish this by checking with people who know about life insurance and about your business. Among those who can help are your lawyer, your accountant, your banker, and your life insurance agent or broker. An agent or broker can provide technical advice about the selection of policies available.[7] The others will provide essential information on which you can base a sound insurance program. They can also help you see that you are meeting legal requirements. Expert assistance should include advice on the impact of taxes on insurance and vice versa. In view of frequent changes in the tax laws, however, it is important that you keep your program current.

Fire Insurance

You should carry enough fire insurance to cover the kind of losses a fire can inflict.[8] You can obtain coverage for such other perils as windstorm, hail, smoke, explosion, vandalism, and malicious mischief at relatively little extra cost. If you need comprehensive coverage, your best buy may be an all-risk contract, which offers the broadest protection available for the money.

The insurance company may compensate your firm for losses in one of several ways:

○ It may pay actual cash value of the property at the time of the loss.

○ It may repair or replace the property with material of like kind and quality.

○ It may take all the property at the agreed or appraised value and reimburse you for your loss.
○ If you sell your business or property, you cannot assign the insurance
policy along with the property unless you receive permission from the
insurance company.

Even if your firm has several policies on its property, it can still collect
only the amount of the actual cash loss. All the insurers share the payment
proportionately. Suppose, for example, that you carried two policies — one
for $20,000 and one for $30,000 — on a $40,000 building, and fire causes
damage to the building amounting to $12,000. The $20,000 policy will pay
$4,800; that is,

$$\frac{20,000}{50,000} \times \$12,000 = \$4,800$$

The $30,000 policy will pay $7,200; that is,

$$\frac{30,000}{50,000} \times \$12,000 = \$7,200$$

Liability Insurance

Most liability policies may now be extended to cover personal injuries
(libel, slander, and the like) in addition to bodily injuries. Insurance companies normally require a firm to notify them immediately after any incident
on the property that might cause a future claim. This holds true no matter
how unimportant the incident may seem at the time it happens. Under
certain conditions, a business may be subject to damage claims even from
trespassers, and it may be legally liable for damages even in cases where
reasonable care is used.

Liability lawsuits against businesses are on the rise, so adequate protection is essential. Legal liability limits of $1 million to $2 million are no longer
considered high or unreasonable even for a small business.

Automobile Insurance

There are six major categories of automobile insurance coverage —
bodily injury liability, property damage liability, medical payments, comprehensive excluding collision, collision, and uninsured motorists. Look at
each kind of coverage, remembering that company terms vary; it is important to read the fine print with care before buying a policy.

Bodily injury liability insurance pays for injury to others, or sickness or
disease of others — including death resulting therefrom — for which the

insured may be legally liable. This includes damages for medical care and loss of services that may result from an accident involving the firm's automobile. This policy also protects your business from claims or suits that may arise as a result of an accident.

Property damage liability coverage protects the insured from financial loss brought about by injury to, or destruction of, the property of others. This protection includes damage to other cars, homes, and buildings. It does not provide protection for destruction of the covered car — only the property of others.

Medical coverage pays all reasonable expenses incurred within one year of the date of an accident for necessary medical, surgical, X-ray, and dental services.

Comprehensive coverage protects the insured against loss caused by an event other than a collision. This coverage includes breakage of glass and loss caused by missiles, falling objects, fire, theft, windstorm, hail, water, flood, and larceny.

Collision insurance pays for loss to the insured automobile or an uninsured vehicle and does not include other cars involved in an accident. This is the most expensive type of policy if you want complete coverage, but the majority of contracts are written with a deductible clause. This means that the insurance company agrees to pay only for the amount of each loss in excess of the established deduction. Most deductible clauses provide that the insurer pay the actual cash value less $50, $100, $150, or other round number up to $500.

Uninsured motorist coverage provides protection for accidents caused by an uninsured motorist or a hit-and-run driver. It covers expenses resulting from bodily injury or death of the driver of your vehicle or other person or persons occupying the policyholder's vehicle. Subject to the limits for uninsured motorist coverage stipulated in the policy, the insurer will pay the amount that would normally be paid by the legally responsible party if insured.

Other special types of coverage may also be available, such as emergency road service.

As your firm expands, ask about reduced rates. Five or more automobiles or motorcycles under one ownership and operated as a fleet for business purposes can generally be insured against both material damage to the vehicle and liability to others for property damage or personal injury under a low-cost fleet policy. Shop around to obtain the best rates. Use Exhibit 8-4 to help make comparisons.

Personal property stored in an automobile and not attached to it (for example, merchandise being delivered) is not covered under an automobile policy.

Exhibit 8-4   Automobile insurance rate comparison worksheet

Coverage	Annual premium		
	Company A	Company B	Company C
Bodily injury liability			
Property damage liability			
Medical payments			
Comprehensive (excluding collision and personal effects)			
Collision			
Uninsured motorists			
Other			
Total annual premium			
Less estimated annual dividend			
Net annual premium			

Workers' Compensation

Federal and common law require that an employer (1) provide employees a safe place to work, (2) hire competent fellow employees, (3) provide safe tools, and (4) warn employees of an existing danger. An employer who fails to make these provisions is liable for damages in suits brought by employees, and for possible fines or prosecution. It is essential to have appropriate Workers' Compensation coverage. In nearly all states, a firm is legally required to have such coverage.

Rates for Workers' Compensation insurance vary from 0.1 percent of the payroll for "safe" occupations to 25 percent or more of the payroll for very hazardous occupations. Make every effort to keep accidents below the norm for the industry; this can result in lower Workers' Compensation premium costs.

Business Interruption Insurance

Insurance is available to cover fixed expenses that continue if a fire or other catastrophe shuts down the business. This coverage includes expenses such as salaries to key employees, taxes, interest, depreciation, and utilities — as well as lost profits.

Crime Insurance

Burglary insurance excludes such property as records and accounts, fur articles in a showcase window, and manuscripts. The insurance can, however, be written to cover inventoried merchandise and damage incurred in the course of a burglary, in addition to money in a safe.

A comprehensive crime policy written just for small business owners is available. In addition to burglary and robbery, it covers other types of loss by theft, destruction, and disappearance of money and securities. It also covers thefts by employees.

If your business is located in a high-risk area and you cannot get crime insurance through normal channels except at excessive rates, you may be able to get help through the federal crime insurance plan. An insurance agent or state insurance commissioner can tell you where to get information about this plan.

Glass Insurance

A special glass insurance policy can be purchased to cover all risks to plate glass windows, glass signs, motion picture screens, glass bricks, glass doors, showcases, countertops, and insulated glass panels. The glass insurance policy can cover not only the glass itself but also its lettering and ornamentation, if these are specifically insured, and the cost of temporary plates or boarding up, if necessary.

Rent Insurance

You can get rent insurance that will pay your rent if the leased property becomes unusable because of fire or other insured perils and the lease calls for continued payments. Also, if you own property and lease it to others, you can insure against loss if the lease is cancelled because of fire or other peril and it is necessary to rent the property again at a reduced rate.

Employee Benefit Coverage

Insurance coverage that can be used to provide employee benefits includes group life insurance, group health insurance, disability insurance, and retirement income. Key-person insurance protects your company against financial loss caused by the death of a valuable employee or partner.

Keep a list of your insurance policies, using a format similar to Exhibit 8-5. Conduct periodic reviews to determine if you should modify your program.

GUIDELINES FOR BUYING INSURANCE

You may want to consider the following guidelines in arriving at insurance decisions.

- Deal only with reputable firms that have been in business a long time.
- Shop around to secure the best price from among reputable firms. Make

Exhibit 8-5 Insurance policy review worksheet

Reviewed as of _____

Type of insurance	Annual premium	Dollar amount of protection	Planned increase or decrease in coverage	Name of company	Agent's phone number	Policy number
Life						
Fire						
Liability						
Automobile						
Bodily injury liability						
Property damage liability						
Medical payments						
Comprehensive (excluding collision and personal effects)						
Collision						
Uninsured motorists						
Other						

Workers' compensation

Business interruption

Crime

Glass

Rent

Employee benefits
  Group life
  Group health[a]
  Disability
  Retirement
  Key-person

---

[a] Consider an alternative to a conventional health insurance plan. Over 10 million Americans are members of health maintenance organizations (HMOs). The typical HMO provides unlimited doctor visits, diagnostic tests, and hospitalization. An HMO gives your employees greater protection at lower cost. The main drawback is that members cannot select their own doctor, or have limited choice. Furthermore, an HMO may not be available in your community, or may be too far away to be useful to all your employees.

your selection from among at least three bids that offer comparable protection.

○ Buy insurance for protection *only* and buy only the amount your business *needs*.

○ Review your insurance needs annually and make appropriate changes. This review should include rereading your policy agreements. Also, modify your program each time changing circumstances require it.

○ Do not be insurance-poor. Get adequate coverage, but don't tie up your funds in excessive coverage and neglect other needs.

○ Read and understand your policy before accepting it.

○ Read the appropriate *Best's Insurance Reports* before buying insurance, to obtain statistical information on companies. Check each new edition of *Best's* to see if there have been any significant changes regarding the insurance companies with which your firm has policies.

○ If possible, let all your policies have the same anniversary month.

○ Examine savings at various levels of coverage and deductibility. There may, for example, be little difference between the cost of $2 million of liability coverage and the cost of $1 million.

○ In deciding how much insurance to buy, keep in mind rising replacement costs and ever-increasing damage judgments.

SUMMARY

It is important to understand what insurance is all about before spending money on it. Read this chapter carefully, for it provides background information on the principles of insurance. An understanding of this material will help you decide on your firm's needs for property, casualty, health, and life insurance.

One dictionary defines insurance as "coverage by contract whereby one party undertakes to indemnify or guarantee another against loss by a specified contingency or peril." By purchasing an insurance policy, your business transfers risk from itself to the insurance company. Your company receives protection against loss in the dollar amount of its coverage. You may want to assume certain risks or losses, but this can be prohibitive in such areas as personal injury liability.

Before buying protection against various risks you should be familiar with the principles of insurance. By understanding basic concepts and using a wise managerial approach, you should be able to establish an insurance program to meet the needs of your company. Insurance is only one part of a balanced managerial program. It is important, therefore, that you spend as little as you reasonably can for needed protection against financial loss.

Management steps that you should take to get the desired program are as follows:

○ *Determine your objectives.* What are your firm's insurance needs? This requires checking to find out what life, property, casualty, and health insurance is appropriate. A review of your company's debts and obligations is essential in determining life insurance requirements.

○ Spend time in *planning* a sound insurance program. This includes selecting the right companies and determining costs. Study costs carefully to see, for example, if you are spending too much of your budget for insurance.

○ Once you determine your course of action, take steps to *implement* your plan.

○ Then institute appropriate *controls*, including reviews of your plans to see that policies are modified as changes occur.

NOTES

1. *Webster's New Collegiate Dictionary*, Springfield, Mass.: G. & C. Merriam Company, 1981.

2. An underwriter may also be defined as one who underwrites or guarantees a policy. By this definition, the underwriter would normally be the insurer discussed in the previous paragraph.

3. If an insurance company does not provide appropriate information, it is not rated.

4. *Best's Insurance Reports: Property-Casualty*, Old Wick, N.J.: Alfred M. Best Company, Inc., 1981, p. 12.

5. The material on life insurance is based on the SBA Management Aids for Small Manufacturers pamphlet no. 222, *Business Life Insurance*, by the Institute of Life Insurance, Washington, D.C.: U.S. Government Printing Office, 1979.

6. Some small business owners believe whole life insurance is a bad investment. They recommend term insurance, in the view that the cost savings can be invested at a higher rate of return than is provided by insurance companies.

7. Don't forget that the more your insurance agent sells you, the more your insurance agent earns. Many insurance agents will try to work out the best possible deal for you, so it is important to get competitive bids every year.

8. The material on fire and other insurance is based on the SBA pamphlet *Insurance Checklist for Small Businesses*, by Mark R. Greene, Washington, D.C.: U.S. Government Printing Office, 1980.

Part III
The Personal Factor — You

Do you have the qualities needed to become a successful small business owner? Can you acquire the skills demanded of a leader? This final section examines the personal factor. Chapter 9 points out the responsibilities of a leader and concludes that many people can develop the traits that are essential if they are to succeed in business. Chapter 10 presents information on how you can manage your time wisely. It also provides forms that permit you, as a business owner or manager, to see how you are now spending your hours at work and to determine where improvements can be made. The important thing is not how hard you work but how productively.

Chapter 9
Leadership

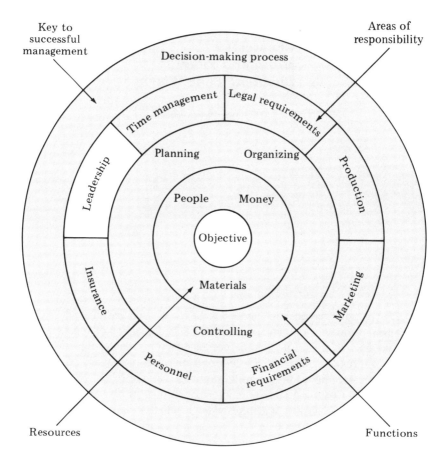

Key to successful management

Areas of responsibility

Decision-making process

Time management

Legal requirements

Planning

Organizing

Leadership

Production

People

Money

Objective

Materials

Insurance

Marketing

Controlling

Personnel

Financial requirements

Resources

Functions

Exhibit 9-1 Stillman's Small Business Management Model: An overview of the five major components of management with emphasis on leadership

> The final test of a leader is that he leaves behind
> him in other men the conviction and the will to
> carry on.
>
> — Walter Lippmann

What are the leadership responsibilities that a small business manager must perform successfully? This chapter will explain these responsibilities and allow you to look at your qualifications as a manager. Other topics covered here include the traits of a leader; effective communication, both oral and written; and the importance of providing leadership opportunities in your organization. Let us first see how the element of leadership fits into the total approach emphasized throughout this text. The white area in Exhibit 9-1 represents leadership. The objective is also white, to emphasize that you must consider it in arriving at all managerial decisions. Take time to study Exhibit 9-1. The leader (boss, manager, owner) is the person who makes it all happen, whose job it is to see that the goals are achieved. This requires the effective use of resources (people, money, materials) and careful attention to the functions of planning, organizing, and controlling. It also requires the coordination of all aspects of the business — legal, financial, marketing, and all the rest. An understanding of these responsibilities enables the leader to make wise decisions.

QUALIFICATIONS

Are you qualified to be a small business owner? The job requires effective leadership skills. You should make a self-evaluation before starting your own business, or when you feel you need to upgrade the leadership you are currently providing your firm. Exhibit 9-2 permits you to make such an examination. Once you have filled out the form, analyze it; if there are major weaknesses, decide how to make improvements. You can often do this by attending evening classes offered at many colleges and universities. A successful real-estate developer and former member of my management class commented on the value of going back to school.

I wanted very much to have my own business. This became an obsession with me after ten years of working for other people. However, I had no knowledge of the leadership problems facing a small business owner. More

155

important, I was afraid to speak before a group and had no writing experience. This situation was corrected as a result of my taking evening courses in such areas as management, accounting, marketing, computers, production, finance, public speaking, and English. My only regret — I did not return to school earlier. It gave me the confidence and the skills to be successful.

LEADERSHIP RESPONSIBILITIES AND QUALIFICATIONS

What are the obligations of a leader? As Exhibit 9-3 indicates, the duties are fivefold. They include: providing guidance to achieve the *objectives* of the firm; performing the *functions* of planning, organizing, and controlling; using *resources* wisely; and making sound *decisions*. In addition, a leader must possess certain *traits* in order to do his job well. Let us discuss each one as it appears in the fourth circle of Exhibit 9-3. I begin with charisma because it is so important and so debatable.

Charisma

Charisma may be defined as a personal quality of a leader that arouses in others great loyalty or support. Such loyalty can be an important factor in achieving company goals. Subordinates, for example, will go the extra mile if they admire and respect their boss. Some say that charismatic leaders are born with this quality. Others believe that people acquire charisma over a period of time. An examination of people with this quality reveals that they have been given ample opportunity to sharpen their leadership skills. John F. Kennedy and Winston Churchill, for instance, received first-rate educations and strong family support. Their charisma evolved as they assumed ever-increasing responsibilities. John Kennedy was a rather shy person at Harvard. The Kennedy family's hope for the presidency rested in the eldest son, Joseph, Jr. John became the heir apparent when his brother was killed in World War II. After John returned home from combat duty in the Pacific, he was guided by a wise old politician who knew the Boston area well. This assistance was an important factor in his being elected to the House of Representatives. He grew in the job, and with strong family backing later became a United States senator and finally president of the United States. John F. Kennedy, it would appear, acquired this charismatic quality.

It must also be recognized that some people automatically gain respect by the nature of their positions. The president of a corporation, for example, has access to the symbols of power. There is an aura around such a person by virtue of holding the office. Think about it! If you are being introduced to someone and you hear the statement, "This is Joan Smith, president of the XYZ Corporation," doesn't it have a different impact upon you than if the

Exhibit 9-2   Self-evaluation worksheet

	Outstanding	Good	Fair	Weak
1. Desire to have your own business.				
2. Understanding of ownership responsibilities.				
3. Willingness to take risks.				
4. Ability to have other people carry out your instructions.				
5. Speaking ability.				
6. Writing ability.				
7. Relationships with other people.				
8. Creativity.				
9. Organizational talents.				
10. Response to stress.				
11. Health.				
12. Impartiality.				
13. Integrity.				
14. Capability of making unpleasant decisions.				
15. Acceptance of community and business club positions.				
16. Flexibility.				
17. Capacity for leadership.				
18. Financial skills.				

Ratings
1 Outstanding
2 Good
3 Fair
4 Weak

introduction had been, "This is Joe Jones, a sales representative for the XYZ Corporation"? Other titles — like Dr. James instead of Mr. James — can also lend a person this status.

Charisma, to a degree, is conferred upon people who hold key positions in organizations. People also need to be given the opportunity to grow into these positions. During World War II, it was my good fortune to serve with General George S. Patton. I was a briefing officer, liaison between Patton's headquarters and General Omar N. Bradley's headquarters, and finally secretary of the general staff with an office next door to Patton. The charisma of General Patton, in my view, was partly his own creation. He was mindful of

Exhibit 9-3   Stillman's Leadership Model: An overview of the five major components of leadership

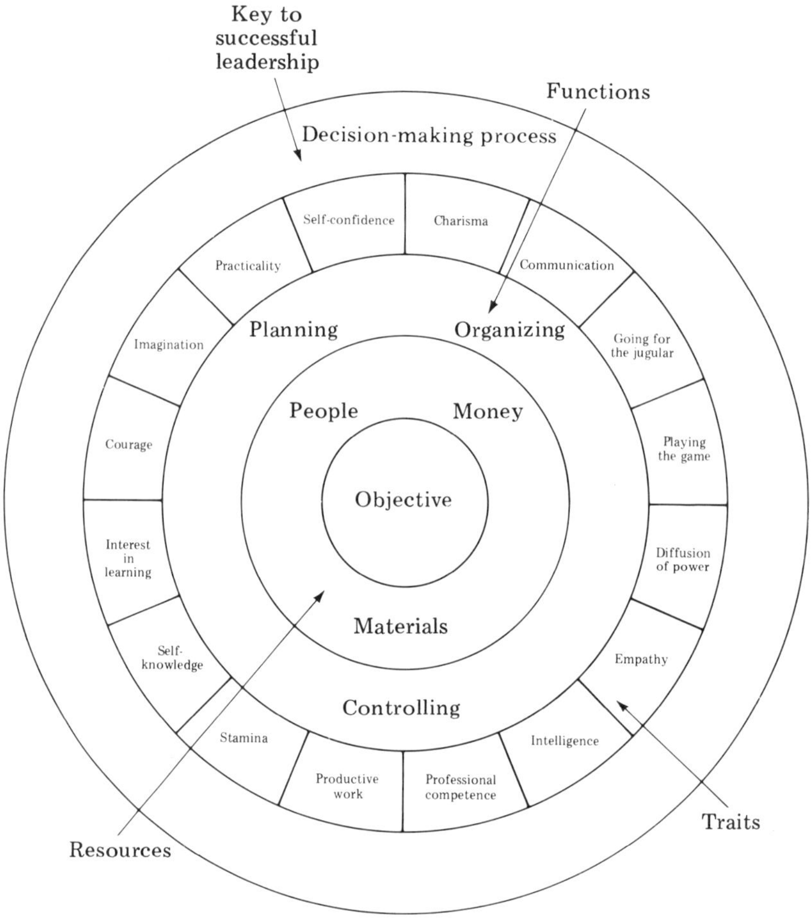

public relations and took full advantage of his opportunities. He covered his high squeaky voice and his shyness with profanity and glamorous uniforms. He conducted his affairs so as to place himself in the limelight. The loyalty of his staff was remarkable. I also had an opportunity to observe General Bradley. He, too, had charisma, although his approach to leadership was entirely different. The loyalty of Bradley's staff was also total. My observation of political, military, and business leaders indicates that all have some degree of charisma by virtue of their status. Small business owners should capitalize on their positions and take every opportunity to grow on the job.

Communication

A leader must be able to communicate well, both orally and in writing. The more opportunities you take to speak and write, the better you become.

Later in the chapter (pp. 164 – 166), there is information on how to improve speaking skills in a business organization.

Going for the Jugular

A leader must go for the jugular. This can be restated as, be tough-minded. Malcolm P. McNair, a distinguished professor at the Harvard Business School, commented as follows:

> William James, a great teacher of philosophy at Harvard during the early years of this century, made the useful distinction between people who are "tough-minded" and the people who are "tender-minded." These terms have nothing to do with levels of ethical conduct; the "toughness" referred to is "toughness" of the intellectual apparatus, hardihood of the spirit, not "toughness" of the heart. The tough-minded have a zest for tackling hard problems; they dare to grapple with the unfamiliar and wrest useful truth from stubborn new facts; they do not wall themselves in with comfortable illusions. [1]

Leo Durocher used to say, "Nice guys finish last." Business leaders must be strong in their convictions. The successful owner of a real-estate agency told me: "I own properties and collect rents for various other property-owners. My instructions to my assistant made it clear that payments were to be made by the tenth of the month with no exceptions. The second time he failed to follow my instructions, I fired him. Word gets around quickly in an organization. If you don't enforce the rules, how can you expect your employees to follow them? My policy is if an error is made, I warn them the first time and replace them the next time. This may seem drastic, but if I can't pay my bills because I don't have enough cash, my company will fail and no one will have a job."

Playing the Game

"Playing the game" means getting along with people in your organization as well as bankers, suppliers, competitors, and government officials. Know the power structure in any group and use it to your advantage. This does not mean lowering your standards or compromising your integrity.

Diffusion of Power

As a manager, you should distribute responsibilities equitably among subordinates. If you appoint an heir apparent to succeed you in business, you leave little incentive for others who want to advance to the top rung in the organization. Result: capable people leave. Such problems occur frequently in very small businesses where relatives are often heirs apparent. Select the best-qualified people for the key jobs and keep them guessing who will receive the ultimate prize.

Empathy

Empathy is participation in the thoughts and feelings of another person. If you understand the interests and goals of the people in your organization, you are better able to motivate them. How often have you heard an owner make this complaint? "I am working twelve to fourteen hours a day to get my job done, but I can't get my employees to work hard. I'm lucky if they put in a day's work for a day's pay." Think about this remark — doesn't the boss have greater motivation to be productive? After all, the profits go to him. If the employees are on salary or an hourly wage, what is their incentive to succeed? One successful owner talked with his employees and found out they could be similarly motivated to put in the extra hours if a profit-sharing plan were instituted. One was adopted promptly, and it paid off. There may be other incentives that would motivate people, besides money. It is up to the leader to look at the problems from the subordinate's point of view.

Intelligence

Before starting a business, ask yourself: "Do I have the basic intelligence to be a successful boss?" God has given people different levels of intelligence; we were not all born equal in intellectual ability. Without a sharp mind, it is impossible to succeed in business. Many people have the necessary IQ and can build upon this foundation with appropriate education and on-the-job experience. Take full advantage of all your opportunities.

Professional Competence

Know your job well. This requires learning as much as possible about your work before opening your business. You can gain professional competence by reading available literature on the subject, and you can learn by working for others — at the other person's expense.

Productive Work

You can be a hard worker and still not be a productive worker. Most successful business leaders, however, put in long *and* productive hours. If you want to go into business, especially a proprietorship, expect to be busy seven days a week. This will be especially true if you open a restaurant, bar, hotel, or other business that caters to the public around the clock. After all, as proprietor you have sole responsibility for the success or failure of your business. The presence of the boss is an important factor in getting things done properly. Wise management of your time (chapter 10) can, however, reduce your work load and increase productivity.

Stamina

Having stamina doesn't mean you have to be a super athlete. Franklin D. Roosevelt is a fine example: a man in a wheelchair who was a most effective leader at a most difficult time. FDR did, however, take a daily swim and do other exercises that were within his capabilities. He took periodic vacations to his mother's home in New York as well as Warm Springs, Georgia. The president was also emotionally strong, and this somewhat compensated for his physical handicap. Today most business leaders must cope with considerable stress. It helps to take time each day for some form of physical exercise. This may include visits to physical fitness centers like the YMCA to participate in a sport like handball, running, or tennis. One construction company owner finds relief from mental pressures by going away for a long fishing weekend with friends every month. You must decide what type of recreation can enable you to meet the stress of your managerial responsibilities.

Self-Knowledge

Look at yourself objectively and determine your strengths and weaknesses. This candid self-evaluation can help you determine if you are really capable of starting and staying in business. Such an evaluation may also enable you to take corrective measures when your business is in trouble. (See Exhibit 9-2 for a list of the qualities required of a small business owner.

Interest in Learning

Our rapidly changing society requires that we keep abreast of events and their impact on our own businesses. To do this, become a member of business associations, read pertinent literature, and go back to school. You can take courses at a local university after work. Leading schools such as Harvard, Stanford, and Wharton provide special programs that last from one to six months. Small business management courses are also put on in various communities throughout the United States by management experts.

Courage

Hemingway spoke of courage as "grace under pressure." Time and again you as a business leader will be challenged, and it will be necessary for you to take courageous action if you are to survive.

One small manufacturer of automobile batteries was hurt badly by the recession of 1981 – 82. He talked with the local union leader about the possibility of his employees' accepting a reduction in wages and some benefits in order to keep the business operating. Initially, the union boss threatened the owner. He didn't want to lose the hard-earned concessions of past bargaining negotiations, and said he preferred the company to go under. In spite of threats to himself and his family, the owner appealed personally to the workers and made his financial records available to a committee of the employees. After a series of meetings, that included representation from the union's national headquarters, the workers voted almost unanimously to accept management's conditions until business improved.

Imagination

A business has to come up with fresh ideas in order to keep pace with its competitors. You are only limited by your own imagination. You must also provide a climate where other people in your organization can be encouraged to present their visionary thoughts. To be effective, however, the creative suggestions must be realistic — you've got to be able to implement them.

Practicality

The brightest ideas are valueless if they aren't practical. Every business has limited resources — people, money, materials, and equipment. A leader must therefore make decisions that can be put into effect.

Self-Confidence

You have to believe in yourself. There is no substitute for the knowledge that you can do the job. Without this self-confidence it is impossible to succeed in business.

QUANTIFYING THE LEADERSHIP MODEL

You can make further use of the leadership model portrayed in Exhibit 9-3 by quantifying the data, placing weights and values on the traits, functions, resources, and decision-making process. Exhibit 9-4 presents a mathematical formula applied to sales personnel. This equation can be used to assist in the selection of the most effective leader within the sales staff as its manager. A similar approach could be used in choosing managers from within each of the other areas of a small business, such as finance and

Exhibit 9-4 Stillman's Quantitative Leadership Model with focus on the sales manager

Leadership
Effectiveness $= 1/15 \; T \sum\limits_{i=1}^{15}(X_iV_i) + 1/3 \; F \sum\limits_{i=1}^{3}(Y_iU_i) + 1/3 \; R \sum\limits_{i=1}^{3}(Z_iW_i) + K(DP)$
i = 1 to N

$(200) \cdot (.38) + (100) \cdot (.28) + (50) \cdot (.18) + (200) \cdot (.1) = 133$ Maximum = 464

X = Weights for traits	Z = Weights for resources
V = Values for traits	W = Values for resources
Y = Weights for functions	D = Weights for key
U = Values for functions	P = Values for key

Traits "T" = 200

	Weights	Values	
Charisma	X2 = .7	V2 = .1	.07
Communication	X3 = 1.0	V3 = .3	.30
Going for the jugular	X4 = .2	V4 = 1.0	.20
Playing the game	X5 = .7	V5 = .9	.63
Diffusion of power	X6 = .5	V6 = 1.0	.50
Intelligence	X7 = .6	V7 = 1.0	.60
Professional competence	X8 = 1.0	V8 = .2	.20
Productive work	X9 = .6	V9 = 1.0	.60
Stamina	X10 = .4	V10 = 1.0	.40
Self-knowledge	X11 = .5	V11 = .2	.10
Interest in learning	X12 = .8	V12 = 1.0	.80
Courage	X13 = .7	V13 = 1.0	.70
Imagination	X14 = 1.0	V14 = .3	.30
Practicality	X15 = .6	V15 = .1	.06
Self-confidence	X1 = 1.0	V1 = .2	.20

Total = 10.3   Superior = .5 to .69   Total = 5.66
÷ 15 = .69   Average = .31 to .49   ÷ 15 = .38
                    Low = 0 to .30

Functions "F" = 100

Planning	Y1 = 1.0	U1 = .3	.30
Organizing	Y2 = .6	U2 = .4	.24
Controlling	Y3 = 1.0	U3 = .3	.30

Total = 2.6   Total = .84
÷ 3 = .86   ÷ 3 = .28

Resources "R" = 50

People	Z1 = 1.0	W1 = .2	.20
Money	Z2 = .7	W2 = .3	.21
Materials	Z3 = .7	W3 = .2	.14

Total = 2.4   Total = .55
÷ 3 = .8   ÷ 3 = .18

Key "K" = 200

Decision-making process	D = 1.0	P = .10	.10

Maximum = 1.0   Total = 1.0

production. Vary the weights and values for each area using the following formula:

Leadership effectiveness

$$= 1/15T \sum_{i=1}^{15} (X_iV_i) + 1/3F \sum_{i=1}^{3} (Y_iU_i) + 1/3R \sum_{i=1}^{3} (Z_iW_i) + K(DP)$$

$$X = \text{weights for traits}$$
$$V = \text{values for traits}$$
$$Y = \text{weights for functions}$$
$$U = \text{values for functions}$$
$$Z = \text{weights for resources}$$
$$W = \text{values for resources}$$
$$D = \text{weights for key}$$
$$P = \text{value for key}$$

This approach may have exciting possibilities with the increased availability of computers for use by small firms.

LEADERSHIP OPPORTUNITIES

Provide leadership opportunities for staff members in your business. All employees should become familiar with duties of their superiors.

Ways for people to grow include the experience of speaking formally at group meetings. They can research and present reports of interest to the business. One successful company has a rotation system in which every supervisor in the firm speaks on a topic pertaining to his area of responsibility. After every talk, the other members offer constructive comments — good points and areas where improvements can be made. These comments pertain not only to the talk but to the speaker as well (self-improvement suggestions). A copy of the critique format appears in Exhibit 9-5. The result of this program is apparent in the comments of the vice-president for sales:

> Everyone in the company acquired more self-confidence. After twelve months we could see this self-assurance in dollar terms. Our sales representatives all showed increases and gave credit to the program for their ability to get their message across to potential buyers. In addition, they joined local business clubs and received recognition for their speaking

Exhibit 9-5 Form for critique of oral presentations

Critique of _____

Factors	Maximum score	Individual's score
1. Knowledge of the subject	30	
2. Format (logical flow of ideas; within the prescribed time)	20	
3. Creativity (innovative ideas that are also practical)	20	
4. Delivery (gestures, voice, eye contact)	10	
5. Appearance	10	
6. Visual aids	10	
Total	100	_____

Remarks: Itemize good points and specific suggestions for improvement.

ability. I had taken both sixty-hour EST training and the Dale Carnegie course, but I thought our in-house program more effective. We provided the type of training best suited for us at negligible cost.

Another speaking program that proved effective for a small firm was one that required supervisors to report orally as a group on a project that had impact on the entire business. The topics that came up for discussion included: buying a computer; expanding the plant; modernizing equipment; hiring summer help. The fact that people had to work as a team to complete the presentation produced camaraderie and respect for the other person's requirements. The semiannual talks were held at a leading restaurant in the community. The rules were as follows:

○ Each manager will be given approximately the same amount of speaking time within the forty-five minutes provided for making the oral presentation.
○ Before the presentation, the president will be given a list of the speakers, with the times allotted for each person and the topics to be covered. In fairness to all speakers, it is essential to stay within the time provided.
○ There should be an introduction indicating the subject to be presented and the interrelatedness of the various topics. Team captains should give a summary pointing out the conclusions and recommendations.

o This should be a formal presentation. Use of blackboards, charts, drawings, and handouts is encouraged.
o Each speaker should highlight primary research that he or she has accomplished. Be specific and emphasize managerial aspects, including those based on your own observations.

SUMMARY

Effective leadership is essential to the success of a business. Look at your own qualifications to determine whether you are capable of heading a company. If not, perhaps you can acquire traits of leadership. You can work on such areas as charisma, communication, toughness, getting along with others, spreading power around, empathy, knowledge, specialized skills, work productivity, physical fitness, self-understanding, interest in learning, courage, creativity, practicality, and self-confidence.

A leader should provide opportunities for people in the organization to develop their leadership skills. You can do a lot to enable them to communicate better — orally and in writing. The results are twofold — employees can more readily move into positions of greater responsibility, and the business can become more successful.

NOTES

1. McNair, Malcolm P., "On the Importance of Being Tough-Minded," *Harvard Business School Bulletin*, May–June 1969, p. 2.

Chapter 10
Managing Your Business Time Wisely

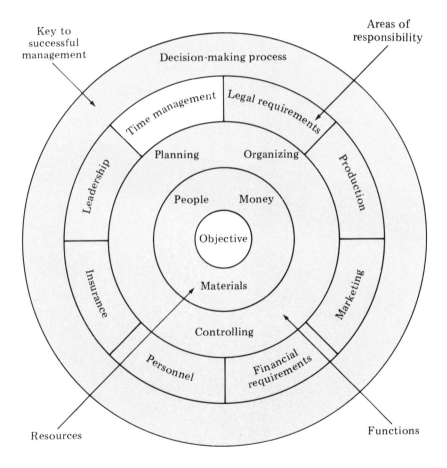

Key to successful management

Areas of responsibility

Decision-making process

Time management

Legal requirements

Planning

Organizing

Leadership

People

Money

Production

Objective

Insurance

Materials

Marketing

Controlling

Personnel

Financial requirements

Resources

Functions

Exhibit 10-1 Stillman's Small Business Management Model: An overview of the five major components of management with emphasis on time management

> Dost thou love life? Then do not squander time,
> for that's the stuff life is made of.
>
> — Benjamin Franklin

What duties must a small business manager perform to be successful? Exhibit 10-1 highlights the topic of time management. The objective also is highlighted to point up that it must be considered in arriving at all managerial decisions.

BUDGETING YOUR TIME

As a business owner or manager you have a multitude of responsibilities. This is readily apparent from a review of the previous nine chapters and an examination of Exhibit 10-1. The boss must give attention to marketing, production of goods or services, finance, legal requirements, personnel, insurance, leading, planning, organizing, controlling, use of resources (people, money, materials) and decision-making. To cope with these duties, you must use your time wisely. Remember: time is an irreplaceable asset. Money lost can be replaced, but not time.

PREPARATION OF A TIMETABLE

How are you using your time in running your business? Exhibit 10-2 provides a way to indicate what you do in a day. Keep such a schedule for one week of normal business activities. In addition, keep a record of what you do for the remainder of the twenty-four-hour day. You may be surprised to see how much time you spend on trivial matters.

The categories listed in Exhibit 10-3 may be helpful in posting your daily activities to a chart like the one shown in Exhibit 10-2. Be specific and state precisely what you do within these broad categories. For example, in regard to a financial matter you might list an hour spent at a bank meeting with the loan officer as follows:

Fin.: Bank meeting with RJS.

Exhibit 10-2   Personal timetable worksheet

My 24-hour day
(Business and nonbusiness activities)
_____ _____, 19_____

	A.M.	P.M.
12:00-12:30		
12:30-1:00		
1:00-1:30		
1:30-2:00		
2:00-2:30		
2:30-3:00		
3:00-3:30		
3:30-4:00		
4:00-4:30		
4:30-5:00		
5:00-5:30		
5:30-6:00		
6:00-6:30		
6:30-7:00		
7:00-7:30		
7:30-8:00		
8:00-8:30		
8:30-9:00		
9:00-9:30		
9:30-10:00		
10:00-10:30		
10:30-11:00		
11:00-11:30		
11:30-12:00		

A twenty-minute conversation on a charity drive you have been asked to lead could be summarized in this manner:

Phone: TSS re: Red Cross.

The times in Exhibit 10-2 have been divided into half-hour increments. Your day will not fit precisely into these groupings, so you should modify the figures to meet your requirements. And don't count time twice. If you eat and hold a meeting at the same time, credit only one category.

Once you have listed the time spent on your business and nonbusiness activities (Exhibit 10-2) you should post it to a weekly summary sheet (Exhibit 10-4).

Exhibit 10-3   Broad categories for use in preparing a timetable

Business	Nonbusiness
Travel from home	Sleep
Travel to home	Family activities
Other travel	Study
Telephone	Entertainment
Meetings	Exercise
Marketing	Recreation and hobbies (other than TV)
Legal	Watching TV
Personnel	Eating
Insurance	Travel (other than work)
Finance	Bathing
Production (goods or services)	Wash
Planning	Shave
Organizing (includes running the business)	Shower
Controlling	Shopping
Decision-making	Food
Leading	Clothing
Other	Church
	Medical and dental care
	Money matters (banking, loans, insurance, preparing tax statements)
	Work (around the house, do-it-yourself, etc.)
	Other

ANALYSIS OF TIME USE

On completion of the summary, analyze it with care. Is this the way you want to spend your time? You may want to review your goals in life and ask: Is this work and nonwork program what I want out of life? Your analysis should consider such points as: Am I devoting too much time to my business? Can I be more efficient and have more time to enjoy my family? Am I allocating enough time to recreation, health, and physical fitness? Is the boob tube consuming more of my time than I had realized? Should I live closer to work? Travel in a car pool? Do I allow enough time for proper eating habits?

If you find that changes are desirable, make up a new schedule indicating how you will spend your time in the future. This can be accomplished by setting up your proposed timetable using the format of Exhibit 10-4. Be precise, itemizing exactly what categories you will increase and where you will make the deductions. Say one important change is in recreation. You make the decision to reduce your TV viewing by ten hours a week. The time

Exhibit 10-4   Weekly summary worksheet
Business and Nonbusiness Activities

	Mon	Tue	Wed	Thu	Fri	Sat	Sun	Total
Business								
Travel from home								
Travel to home								
Other travel								
Telephone								
Meetings								
Marketing								
Legal								
Personnel								
Insurance								
Finance								
Production (goods or services)								
Planning								
Organizing (includes running the business)								
Controlling								
Decision-making								
Leading								
Other								
Nonbusiness								
Sleep								
Family activities								
Study								
Entertainment								
Exercise								
Recreation and hobbies (other than TV)								
Watching TV								
Eating								
Travel (other than work)								

Exhibit 10-4 Continued

	Mon	Tue	Wed	Thu	Fri	Sat	Sun	Total
Bathing								
Wash								
Shave								
Shower								
Shopping								
Food								
Clothing								
Church								
Medical and dental care								
Money matters (banking, loans, insurance, preparing tax statements)								
Work (around the house, do-it-yourself, etc.)								
Other								

saved will be spent exercising each afternoon for two hours, five times a week, at the YMCA. The two hours include travel to and from work. Most important, check to see that you follow your new program by using the format of Exhibits 10-2 and 10-4.

ESTABLISHING PRIORITIES

Assume you have analyzed Exhibit 10-4 and find you are spending fifty hours a week at work. Can you improve your efficiency by doing your most important tasks first? I think so. List your daily goals in order of importance. This forces you to determine which have priority. Debbie S., for example, is a successful owner of a small hotel. On April 15, she listed her goals as:

○ Get gas for the company car (tank nearly empty).
○ Take bookkeeper to work and return him home (bus drivers on strike).
○ Meet with Mr. Thomas re: convention in hotel.
○ Renew driver's license (expires today).
○ Mail federal income tax to IRS.

○ Stop by bank and deposit funds in interest-bearing checking account (current balance below minimum for no charge).
○ Attend evening hotel management class.
○ Interview custodian for possible job.
○ Inspect all units for cleanliness (respond to a letter complaint from BBB).
○ Call architect to prepare plans for eighteen additional rooms.
○ Meet with attorney to discuss incorporating.
○ Call fire chief to have site inspected for possible fire hazards (major fire occurred in a neighboring hotel).

In addition to listing your daily goals, determine which ones you have actually completed. Remember the management functions of *planning, doing,* and *checking.* First, using the format shown in Exhibit 10-5, decide which goals you want to achieve on a particular day (*planning*). Next,

Exhibit 10-5   Daily goals worksheet

Daily goals as of _____
                              (date)

Goal[a]	Planned	Completed
1.		
2.		
3.		
4.		
5.		
6.		
7.		
8.		
9.		
10.		
11.		
12.		

[a] Remember to list goals in order of importance from first to last and accomplish highest-priority goals first.

implement your plan (*doing*), and finally, review it the following day to see if you completed your goals, in order of priority (*checking*). In Debbie's case, she decided that the first nine goals were really important. Her review the next day indicated she hadn't had the time to achieve the other goals. She recognized, however, that the remaining three should be done soon, and arranged to attend to them the next day.

TIME-SAVERS

In listing and performing your daily goals, keep the following points in mind. They can be real time-savers.

- Remember that time is money. There is only so much available, and using it wisely can enable you to achieve important daily goals.
- Do one thing at a time. In most cases it is best to complete one project, or a specific portion of a project, before taking on another task.
- Do the most difficult assignment while you are at the peak of your efficiency.
- Minimize the time spent on insignificant matters.
- Have a time established to write down your daily goals.
- List your daily goals in order of importance. Attend to them in that order.
- List only those goals that you can realistically reach.
- Each day, set aside at least one or two hours of quiet time for yourself — either before or after business hours. Allow no interruptions. One successful entrepreneur found that she could do her most productive and creative work by arriving at the office by 6:00 A.M. She also avoided the traffic and the aggravation of waiting in line.
- Be flexible. You should, for example, be able to adjust your priorities as required.
- Learn to say no.
- Delegate responsibilities to other members of the business.
- Consider how much time you are spending on the telephone each day. Are all outgoing calls necessary? When the telephone rings, answer it promptly and courteously.
- Make a decision on each piece of your mail after opening it — discard, hold, or respond. If possible, open and sort all incoming mail. It can be a valuable source of information.
- Join only those organizations that you really enjoy and that are beneficial to your business.
- Take time to smell the roses.

SUMMARY

There is only so much time available to the small business owner. Wise use of this time can help you achieve your goals. One approach is to find out how you are currently using your week. Analyze the data; you may find that you can be far more productive and get more work done in less time. Another approach is to set priorities each day and accomplish the most important tasks first.

In summary and in conclusion, I would like to wish you every success in your small business. Here is a timely thought you might enjoy:

> Time is . . .
>   Too slow for
>   those who wait.
>   Too swift for
>   those who fear.
>   Too long for
>   those who grieve.
>   Too short for
>   those who rejoice.
>   But for those
>   who love . . .
>   Time
>   is Eternity.
>
> — *Anonymous*

Appendix A
Publications Available from the Small Business Administration

The following literature is available from the Small Business Administration. Many publications can be obtained free and the others at modest cost. Visit an SBA office if one is convenient. It can provide helpful advice and should have some of this material on hand.

MAs (MANAGEMENT AIDS)

170. *The ABC's of Borrowing*
171. *How to Write a Job Description*
178. *Effective Industrial Advertising for Small Plants*
186. *Checklist for Developing a Training Program*
187. *Using Census Data in Small Plant Marketing*
189. *Should You Make or Buy Components?*
190. *Measuring Sales Force Performance*
191. *Delegating Work and Responsibility*
192. *Profile Your Customers to Expand Industrial Sales*
193. *What Is the Best Selling Price?*
194. *Marketing Planning Guidelines*
195. *Setting Pay for Your Management Jobs*
197. *Pointers on Preparing an Employee Handbook*
200. *Is the Independent Sales Agent for You?*
201. *Locating or Relocating Your Business*
203. *Are Your Products and Channels Producing Sales?*
204. *Pointers on Negotiating DOD Contracts*
205. *Pointers on Using Temporary-Help Services*
206. *Keep Pointed Toward Profit*
207. *Pointers on Scheduling Production*
208. *Problems in Managing a Family-Owned Business*
209. *Preventing Employee Pilferage*
211. *Termination of DOD Contracts for the Government's Convenience*
212. *The Equipment Replacement Decision*

SMALL BUSINESS MANAGEMENT SERIES

The booklets in this series provide discussions of special management problems in small companies.

1. *An Employee Suggestion System for Small Companies.* Explains the basic principles for starting and operating a suggestion system. It also warns of various pitfalls and gives examples of suggestions submitted by employees.

9. *Cost Accounting for Small Manufacturers.* Assists managers of small manufacturing firms, producing a broad range of products, establish accounting procedures that will help to document and to control production and business costs.

15. *Handbook of Small Business Finance.* Written for the small business owner who wants to improve financial management skills. Indicates the major areas of financial management and describes a few of the many techniques that can help the small business owner.

20. *Ratio Analysis for Small Business.* Ratio analysis is the process of determining the relationships between certain financial or operating data of a business to provide a basis for managerial control. The purpose of the booklet is to help the owner/manager in detecting favorable or unfavorable trends in the business.

22. *Practical Business Use of Government Statistics.* Illustrates some practical uses of Federal Government statistics, discusses what can be done with them, and describes major reference sources.

25. *Guides for Profit Planning.* Guides for computing and using the break-even point, the level of gross profit, and the rate of return on investment. Designed for readers who have no specialized training in accounting and economics.

Appendix B
Business Definitions

The following definitions may be helpful to small business managers. They include management and finance, insurance, and housing terms.

MANAGEMENT AND FINANCE

Accrued interest The interest that has accumulated on a bond between its issuance and a sale. Describes the way bonds are priced. When a bond is purchased, the buyer pays the agreed price plus accrued interest.

Affirmative action Action by the federal government that requires companies (fifty or more workers) receiving federal contracts (more than $50,000) to establish goals for hiring and using minorities and women and to have specific programs to achieve these goals.

Age Discrimination in Employment Act of 1967 An action by the federal government to protect older people (between the ages of forty and seventy) from being discriminated against at work.

Assets What an organization owns plus what is owed to it. Assets may be tangible, like a house, or intangible, like good will.

Balance sheet A financial report of an organization, listing its assets, liabilities, and net worth for one particular period of time.

Bond A formal evidence of a debt, in which the borrower agrees to pay the lender a specified amount, with interest at a fixed rate payable on specified dates.

Book value A computation arrived at by taking the assets of an organization at the balance-sheet values and subtracting all liabilities and the liquidation price of preferred stock, if any.

Budget A schedule for estimating income and expenses for a given period. It can be used by management as both a planning and a control document.

Callable bonds Bonds that may be redeemed by the issuing corporation before the maturity date. Usually the company is required to pay a premium over their face value when they are called before maturity.

Capital structure or capitalization The amount and type of securities authorized and issued by an organization.

Cash flow   The complete series of new proceeds and new outlays of cash related to a business activity.

Cash items   Cash, bank deposits, U. S. government issues, and other securities that are considered the same as cash.

Caveat emptor   "Let the buyer beware."

Civil Rights Act of 1964   An action by the Federal Government to protect individuals from job discrimination based on race, religion, sex, or national origin. This congressional act pertains to all firms having fifteen or more workers and covers such areas as hiring, promotion, salaries, and assignments.

Collateral   An obligation or security attached to another to secure its performance.

Common stock   Securities that have a right to dividends subordinate to all other stock of the organization.

Communication   The giving and receiving of information.

Consolidated financial statement   An accounting report that gives an insight into the overall picture only. The parent company and its subsidiaries are treated as one organization.

Convertible bonds   Bonds that may, at the option of the holder, be exchanged for a specified amount of other securities of the issuing firm.

Convertible preferred stock   Preferred stock that may be converted, at the option of the holder, into common stock, on stated terms, within a specified period of time.

Conveyance   An instrument by which the title to property is conveyed.

Coordination   Effective communication among members of an organization to permit them to function in harmony.

Cumulative preferred stock   Preferred stock on which the dividends, if not paid in full, accumulate. The accumulations must be paid before any dividends can be paid on the corporation's common stock.

Current assets   Cash, cash items, inventories, and notes and accounts receivable due within one year.

Current liabilities   Accounts and notes payable, accrued taxes, interest, declared dividends, and other claims that are payable within one year.

Debenture   A long-term debt supported by the general credit of the issuing corporation.

Decision-making process   The decision-making process draws upon the following management components to arrive at a sound solution: objective, resources, areas of responsibility, and functions. In arriving at management decisions, these questions should be kept in mind: (1) What is your objective? (2) Do you have the necessary facts to make a sound decision? (3) What are your alternatives? (4) Have you chosen the most profitable alternative?

Depreciation   A periodic charge against income to spread the cost of such items as building and equipment over their estimated useful life.

Dividend   The payment made by a corporation to its stockholders as a return on their investment.

Equal Employment Opportunity Commission (EEOC)   The enforcement arm of Civil Rights Act of 1964. This commission has the authority to see that firms comply with the requirements of the 1964 Act.

Equity   The net worth of an organization; the money value owned by the stockholders.

Ex dividend   Of a stock, without the dividend. The purchaser of the stock on or after the ex dividend date will not receive payment of the dividend even though it is made at a later date.

Feedback   The receipt of information by management from both within and outside an organization. A primary means of effective feedback is conversation with employees.

First mortgage   A mortgage having precedence over all others.

First mortgage bond   A bond secured by a first mortgage on property of the issuing corporation.

Fixed charges   Relatively constant expenses such as property rental and the interest on notes.

Funded debt   Long-term debt normally maturing more than one year from date of issue.

Funds flow   The complete series of proceeds and outlays of funds related to a business activity.

Gresham's law   Bad money tends to drive good money out of circulation. Sir Thomas Gresham pointed out an economic fact of life that when two coins of equal value can be used in trade the one with the greater intrinsic value will be removed from circulation. Recent examples are the U. S. coins containing silver (dollar, half-dollar, quarter, and dime), which were replaced by cheaper non-silver coins in the 1960s. The silver coins were rapidly hoarded and have disappeared from circulation.

Human understanding   Respect and compassion for people in an organization.

Incentives   Payments or other rewards used to motivate individuals in an organization to achieve specified goals.

Leader   The boss, manager, or head of any organization

Liabilities   What an organization owes.

Line   An organizational structure in which the superior – subordinate relationship is delineated.

Listed securities   Corporation shares that have been approved for listing by a stock exchange.

Maintenance   Work required to keep equipment operating.

Management   The achievement of objectives by effective use of resources (people, money, and materials). It involves performing the functions of planning, organizing, and controlling; working within a framework of line, staff, and service responsibilities to arrive at sound decisions.

Mortgage   A giving of property as security for payment of a debt.

Motivate   Encourage individuals in an organization to improve their productivity.

Net income   The true corporate profit after deducting all expenses, including taxes.

Net working capital   Current assets minus current liabilities.

Net worth   The true financial worth of an organization. It can be determined by subtracting liabilities from assets.

Objectives   Specific goals toward which managerial efforts are concentrated.

On-the-job training (OJT)   A training program in which the new employee receives instructions from the supervisor, at the work site, on the specific duties that must be performed.

Organization chart   A schematic drawing portraying the formal relationships among the various activities of an organization.

Over-the-counter   The market for securities not listed on an exchange.

Par   The dollar value assigned to shares by the corporate charter.

Participating bonds   Bonds that are entitled to a stated rate of interest and may also share in the profits of the issuing corporation.

Participating preferred stock   Stock that has an established rate of dividend and may be entitled to additional dividends.

PERT (Program Evaluation and Review Technique)   Serves as a manager's tool for defining and coordinating what must be done to accomplish the objectives of a project successfully within an established time.

Preferred stock   A category of stock with priority over common stock in the distribution of dividends and assets.

Prior preferred stock   A category of stock with priority in the distribution of dividends and assets over either preferred stock or common stock.

Prospectus   A pamphlet that describes in detail a security offered for sale. It contains information about the corporation's business and its financial condition.

Proxy   A written authority given by a shareholder to another person empowering the latter to vote stock owned by the former.

Refunding   Refinancing a debt before maturity to secure better terms for the debtor.

Right   A privilege granted to stockholders to buy new securities at a price generally below the prevailing market.

SEC   Securities and Exchange Commission.

Second mortgage   An additional mortgage placed on property already encumbered by a first mortgage.

Span of control   The number of people in an organization reporting to a given supervisor.

Statement of income   A financial report of an organization listing its income, expenses, and profit or loss for a given period, normally one year.

Stock   See common stock; convertible preferred stock; cumulative preferred stock; preferred stock; and prior preferred stock.

Stock dividend   Additional shares of stock issued by a corporation to its stockholders.

Stock split   The division of each present share of stock into more shares.

Stop order   An order instructing a broker to buy or sell at the market, if and when the price of the stock reaches a certain figure.

INSURANCE[1]

Actuary   A person professionally trained in the technical aspects of insurance and related fields, particularly in the mathematics of insurance, such as the calculation of premiums, reserves, and other values.

Agent   A sales and service representative of an insurance company. Life insurance agents may also be called underwriters.

Annuitant   The person during whose life an annuity is payable, usually the person to receive the annuity.

Annuity   A contract that provides an income for a specified period of time, such as a number of years or for life.

Annuity certain   A contract that provides an income for a specified number of years, regardless of life or death.

Beneficiary   The person named in the policy to receive the insurance proceeds at the death of the insured.

Business life insurance   Life insurance purchased by a business enterprise on the life of a member of the firm. It is often bought by partnerships to protect the surviving partners against loss caused by the death of a partner, or bought by a corporation to reimburse it for loss caused by the death of a key employee.

Cash-surrender value   The amount available in cash upon voluntary termination of a policy before it becomes payable by death or maturity.

Claim   Notification to an insurance company that payment of an amount is due under terms of a policy.

Convertible term insurance   Term insurance that can be exchanged, at the option of the policyholder and without evidence of insurability, for another plan of insurance.

Deferred group annuity   A type of group annuity providing for the purchase each year of a paid-up deferred annuity for each member of the group, the total amount received by the member at retirement being the sum of these deferred annuities.

[1] Definitions in this section are from *Life Insurance Fact Book*, published in 1981 by the American Council of Life Insurance, 1850 K Street, Washington, D. C. 20006.

Disability benefit   A provision added to a life insurance policy for waiver of premium and sometimes payment of monthly income, if the insured becomes totally and permanently disabled.

Grace period   A period (usually 31 days) following the premium due date, during which an overdue premium may be paid without penalty. The policy remains in force throughout this period.

Group annuity   A pension plan providing annuities at retirement to a group of persons under a single master contract, with the individual members of the group holding certificates stating their coverage. It is usually issued to an employer for the benefit of employees. The two basic types are *deferred* and *deposit administration* group annuities.

Group life insurance   Life insurance issued, usually without medical examination, on a group of persons under a single master policy. It is usually issued to an employer for the benefit of employees.

Individual policy pension trust   A type of pension plan, frequently used for small groups, administered by trustees who are authorized to purchase individual level-premium policies or annuity contracts for each member of the plan. The policies usually provide both life insurance and retirement benefits.

Insurance examiner   The representative of a state insurance department assigned to participate in the official audit and examination of the affairs of an insurance company.

Lapsed policy   A policy terminated for nonpayment of premiums. The term is sometimes limited to a termination occurring before the policy has a cash or other surrender value.

Legal-reserve life insurance company   A life insurance company operating under state insurance laws specifying the minimum basis for the reserves the company must maintain on its policies.

Level-premium insurance   Insurance for which the cost is distributed evenly over the period during which premiums are paid. The premium remains the same from year to year and is more than the actual cost of protection in the earlier years of the policy and less than the actual cost in the later years. The excess paid in the early years builds up the reserve.

Life annuity   A contract that provides an income for life.

Limited-payment life insurance   Whole life insurance on which premiums are payable for a specified number of years or until death if death occurs before the end of the specified period.

Mortality table   A statistical table showing the death rate at each age, usually expressed as so many per thousand.

Mutual life insurance company   A life insurance company without stockholders, whose management is directed by a board elected by the policyholders. Mutual companies, in general, issue participating insurance.

Nonparticipating insurance   Insurance on which the premium is calculated to cover as closely as possible the anticipated cost of the insurance protection and on which no dividends are payable.

Ordinary life insurance   Life insurance usually issued in amounts of $1,000 or more with premiums payable on an annual, semiannual, quarterly, or monthly basis. The term is also used to mean straight life insurance.

Paid-up insurance   Insurance on which all required premiums have been paid. The term is frequently used to mean the reduced paid-up insurance available as a nonforfeiture option.

Participating insurance   Insurance on which the policyholder is entitled to receive policy dividends reflecting the difference between the premium charged and actual experience. The premium is calculated to provide some margin over the anticipated cost of the insurance protection.

Permanent life insurance   A phrase used to cover any form of life insurance except term; generally, insurance that accrues cash value, such as whole life or endowment.

Policy loan   A loan made by an insurance company to a policyholder on the security of the cash value of his policy.

Policy reserves   The amount that an insurance company allocates specifically for the fulfillment of its policy obligations. Reserves are so calculated that, together with future premiums and interest earnings, they will enable the company to pay all future claims.

Premium   The payment, or one of the periodic payments, a policyholder agrees to make for an insurance policy.

Rated policy   An insurance policy issued at a higher-than-standard premium rate to cover the extra risk involved in certain cases where the insured has impaired health or a hazardous occupation.

Renewable term insurance   Term insurance that can be renewed at the end of the term, at the option of the policyholder and without evidence of insurability, for a limited number of successive terms. The rates increase at each renewal as the age of the insured increases.

Revival   The reinstatement of a lapsed policy by the company upon receipt of evidence of insurability and payment of past-due premiums with interest.

Stock life insurance company   A life insurance company owned by stockholders, who elect a board to direct the company's management. Stock companies, in general, issue nonparticipating insurance, but may also issue participating insurance.

Straight life insurance   Whole life insurance on which premiums are payable for life.

Supplementary contract   An agreement between a life insurance company and a policyholder or beneficiary by which the company retains the cash sum payable under an insurance policy and makes payments in accordance with the settlement option chosen.

Underwriting The process by which an insurance company determines whether or not and on what basis it will accept an application for insurance.

Variable annuity An annuity contract in which the amount of each periodic income payment fluctuates. The fluctuation may be related to security-market values, a cost-of-living index, or some other variable factor.

Whole life insurance Insurance payable to a beneficiary at the death of the insured whenever that occurs. Premiums may be payable for a specified number of years (limited-payment life) or for life (straight life).

HOUSING[2]

Abstract (of title) A summary of the public records relating to the *title* to a particular piece of land. An attorney or title insurance company reviews an abstract of title to determine whether there are any title defects which must be cleared before a buyer can purchase clear, marketable, and insurable title. See *title*.

Acceleration clause Condition in a mortgage that may require the balance of the loan to become due immediately, if regular mortgage payments are not made or for breach of other conditions of the mortgage.

Agreement of sale Known by various names, such as *contract of purchase, purchase agreement*, or *sales agreement* according to location or jurisdiction. A contract in which a seller agrees to sell and a buyer agrees to buy, under certain specific terms and conditions spelled out in writing and signed by both parties.

Amortization A payment plan which enables the borrower to reduce his debt gradually through monthly payments of principal.

Appraisal An expert judgment or estimate of the quality or value of real estate as of a given date.

Assumption of mortgage An obligation undertaken by the purchaser of property to be personally liable for payment of an existing *mortgage*. In an assumption the purchaser is substituted for the original mortgagor in the mortgage instrument and the original mortgagor is released from further liability under the mortgage. Since the mortgagor is to be released from further liability in the assumption, the mortgagee's consent is usually required.

The original mortgagor should always obtain a written release from further liability if he desires to be fully released under the assumption. Failure to obtain such a release renders the original mortgagor liable if the person assuming the mortgage fails to make the monthly payments.

An "assumption of mortgage" is often confused with "purchasing subject to a mortgage." When one purchases subject to a mortgage, the purchaser agrees

---

[2] Definitions in this section are adopted from the U. S. Department of Housing and Urban Development booklet *Home Buyer's Vocabulary*. The terms listed do not cover all possible meanings or nuances that a term may acquire in legal use. State laws and custom in use in various states may modify or completely change the meaning of certain terms defined.

to make the monthly mortgage payments on an existing mortgage, but the original mortgagor remains personally liable if the purchaser fails to make the monthly payments. Since the original mortgagor remains liable in the event of default, the mortgagee's consent is not required to a sale subject to a mortgage.

Both "assumption of mortgage" and "purchasing subject to a mortgage" are used to finance the sale of property. They may also be used when a mortgagor is in financial difficulty and desires to sell the property to avoid foreclosure.

Binder or offer to purchase A preliminary agreement, secured by the payment of *earnest money*, between a buyer and seller as an offer to purchase real estate. A binder secures the right to purchase real estate upon agreed terms for a limited period of time. If the buyer changes his mind or is unable to purchase, the earnest money is forfeited unless the binder expressly provides that it is to be refunded.

Broker See *real estate broker.*

Building line or setback Distances from the ends and/or sides of the lot beyond which construction may not extend. The building line may be established by a filed plat of subdivision, by restrictive covenants in deeds and leases, by building codes, or by zoning ordinances.

Certificate of title A certificate issued by a title company or a written opinion rendered by an attorney that the seller has good marketable and insurable *title* to the property which he is offering for sale. A certificate of title offers no protection against any hidden defects in the title which an examination of the records could not reveal. The issuer of a certificate of title is liable only for damages due to negligence. The protection offered a homeowner under a certificate of title is not as great as that offered in a title insurance policy. See *title; title insurance.*

Closing costs The numerous expenses which buyers and sellers normally incur to complete a transaction in the transfer of ownership of real estate. These costs are in addition to price of the property and are paid only once, at the closing day. This is a typical list:

Buyer's expenses and *Seller's expenses*

documentary stamps on notes	cost of abstract
recording deed and mortgage	documentary stamps on deed
escrow fees	real estate commission
attorney's fee	recording mortgage
title insurance	survey charge
appraisal and inspection	escrow fees
survey charge	attorney's fees

The agreement of sale negotiated previously between the buyer and the seller may state in writing who will pay each of the above costs.

Closing day The day on which the formalities of a real estate sale are concluded. The *certificate of title, abstract,* and *deed* pass from the seller to the buyer, the buyer signs the mortgage, and closing costs are paid. The final closing merely confirms the original agreement reached in the agreement of sale.

Cloud (on title) An outstanding claim or encumbrance which adversely affects the marketability of title.

Commission Money paid to a real estate agent or broker by the seller as compensation for finding a buyer and completing the sale. Usually it is a percentage of the sale price — 6 to 7 percent on houses, 10 percent on land.

Condemnation The taking of private property for public use by a government unit against the will of the owner but with payment of just compensation under the government's power of eminent domain. Condemnation may also be a determination by a governmental agency that a particular building is unsafe or unfit for use.

Condominium Individual ownership of a dwelling unit and an individual interest in the common areas and facilities which serve the multiunit project.

Contract of purchase See *agreement of sale.*

Contractor In the construction industry a contractor is one who contracts to erect buildings or portions of them. There are also contractors for each phase of construction: heating, electrical, plumbing, air conditioning, road building, bridge and dam erection, and others.

Conventional mortgage A mortgage loan not insured by HUD or guaranteed by the Veterans' Administration. It is subject to conditions established by the lending institution and state statutes. The mortgage rates may vary with different institutions and between states. (States have various interest limits.)

Cooperative housing An apartment building or a group of dwellings owned by residents (generally a corporation) and operated for their benefit by their elected board of directors. In a cooperative the corporation or association owns title to the real estate. A resident purchases stock in the corporation which entitles him to occupy a unit in the building or property owned by the cooperative. While the resident does not own his unit, he has an absolute right to occupy his unit for as long as he owns the stock.

Deed A formal written instrument by which *title* to real property is transferred from one owner to another. The deed should contain an accurate description of the property being conveyed, should be signed and witnessed according to the laws of the state where the property is located, and should be delivered to the purchaser at closing day. There are two parties to a deed: the grantor and the grantee. See also *deed of trust; general warranty deed; quitclaim deed;* and *special warranty deed.*

Deed of trust Like a mortgage, a security instrument whereby real property is given as security for a debt. However, in a deed of trust there are three parties to the instrument: the borrower, the trustee, and the lender (or beneficiary). In such a transaction the borrower transfers the legal *title* for the property to the trustee who holds the property in trust as security for the payment of the debt to the lender or beneficiary. If the borrower pays the debt as agreed, the deed of trust becomes void. If, however, he defaults in the payment of the debt, the trustee may sell the property at a public sale, under the terms of the deed of trust. In most jurisdictions where the deed of trust is in force, the borrower is subject to having his property sold without benefit of legal proceedings. A few states have begun in recent years to treat the deed of trust like a mortgage.

Default   Failure to make mortgage payments as agreed to in a commitment based on the terms and at the designated time set forth in the *mortgage* or *deed of trust*. It is the mortgagor's responsibility to remember the due date and send the payment prior to the due date, not after. Thirty days after the due date if payment is not received, the mortgage is in default. In the event of default, the mortgage may give the lender the right to accelerate payments, take possession and receive rents, and start *foreclosure*. Defaults may also come about by the failure to observe other conditions in the mortgage or deed of trust.

Depreciation   Decline in value of a house due to wear and tear, adverse changes in the neighborhood, or any other reason.

Documentary stamps   A state tax, in the form of stamps, required on *deeds* and *mortgages* when real estate title passes from one owner to another. The amount of stamps required varies with each state.

Down payment   The amount of money to be paid by the purchaser to the seller upon the signing of the *agreement of sale*. The agreement of sale will refer to the down payment amount and will acknowledge receipt of the down payment. The down payment is usually a percentage of the total purchase price and varies according to market conditions, availability and type of financing, and the confidence the purchaser and seller have in each other's intent to close the sale. It may not be refundable if the purchaser fails to buy the property without good cause. If the purchaser wants the down payment to be refundable, he should insert a clause in the agreement of sale specifying the conditions under which the deposit will be refunded, if the agreement does not already contain such clause. If the seller cannot deliver good *title*, the agreement of sale usually requires the seller to return the down payment and to pay interest and expenses incurred by the purchaser.

Earnest money   The deposit money given to the seller or his agent by the potential buyer to show that he is serious about buying the house. If the sale goes through, the earnest money is applied against the *down payment*. If the sale does not go through, the earnest money will be forfeited or lost unless the binder or offer to purchase expressly provides that it is refundable.

Easement rights   A *right-of-way* granted to a person or company authorizing access to or over the owner's land. An electric company obtaining a right-of-way across private property is a common example.

Encroachment   An obstruction, building, or part of a building that intrudes beyond a legal boundary onto neighboring private or public land, or a building extending beyond the building line.

Encumbrance   A legal right or interest in land that affects a good or clear *title*, and diminishes the land's value. It can take numerous forms, such as zoning ordinances, easement rights, claims, mortgages, liens, charges, a pending legal action, unpaid taxes, or restrictive covenants. An encumbrance does not legally prevent transfer of the property to another. A title search is all that is usually done to reveal the existence of such encumbrances, and it is up to the buyer to determine whether he wants to purchase with the encumbrance, or what can be done to remove it.

Equity   The value of a homeowner's unencumbered interest in real estate. Equity is computed by subtracting from the property's fair market value the total of the unpaid mortgage balance and any outstanding liens or other debts against the property. A homeowner's equity increases as he pays off his mortgage or as the property appreciates in value. When the mortgage and all other debts against the property are paid in full, the homeowner has 100 percent equity in his property.

Escrow   Funds paid by one party to another (the *escrow agent*) to hold until the occurrence of a specified event, after which the funds are released to a designated individual. In FHA mortgage transactions an escrow account usually refers to the funds a mortgagor pays the lender at the time of the periodic mortgage payments. The money is held in a trust fund, provided by the lender for the buyer. Such funds should be adequate to cover yearly anticipated expenditures for mortgage insurance premiums, taxes, insurance premiums, and special assessments.

Foreclosure   A legal term applied to any of the various methods of enforcing payment of the debt secured by a mortgage or deed of trust, by taking and selling the mortgaged property, and depriving the mortgagor of possession.

General warranty deed   A deed which conveys not only all the grantor's interest in and title to the property of the grantee, but also warrants that if the title is defective or has a "cloud" on it (such as mortgage claims, tax liens, title claims, judgments, or mechanic's liens against it) the grantee may hold the grantor liable.

Grantee   That party in the deed who is the buyer or recipient.

Grantor   That party in the deed who is the seller or giver.

Hazard insurance   Protects against damages caused to property by fire, windstorms, and other common hazards.

HUD   U. S. Department of Housing and Urban Development. Housing Production and Mortgage Credit/Federal Housing Administration within HUD insures home mortgage loans made by lenders and sets minimum standards for such homes.

Interest   A charge paid for borrowing money. See *mortgage note.*

Lien   A claim by one person on the property of another as security for money owed. Such claims may include obligations not met or satisfied, judgments, unpaid taxes, materials, or labor. See also *special lien.*

Marketable title   A title that is free and clear of objectionable liens, clouds, or other title defects. A title which enables an owner to sell his property freely to others and which others will accept without objection.

Mortgage   A *lien* or claim against real property given by the buyer to the lender as security for money borrowed. Under government-insured or loan-guarantee provisions, the payments may include *escrow* amounts covering taxes, *hazard insurance*, water charges, and *special assessments*. Mortgages generally run from ten to thirty years, during which the loan is to be paid off.

Mortgage commitment   A written notice from the bank or other lending institution saying it will advance mortgage funds in a specified amount to enable a buyer to purchase a house.

Mortgagee   The lender in a mortgage agreement.

Mortgage insurance premium   The payment made by a borrower to the lender for transmittal to HUD to help defray the cost of the FHA mortgage insurance program and to provide a reserve fund to protect lenders against loss in insured mortgage transactions. In FHA-insured mortgages this represents an annual rate of one-half of one percent paid by the mortgagor on a monthly basis.

Mortgage note   A written agreement to repay a loan. The agreement is secured by a *mortgage*, serves as proof of an indebtedness, and states the manner in which it shall be paid. The note states the actual amount of the debt that the mortgage secures and renders the mortgagor personally responsible for repayment.

Mortgagor   The borrower in a mortgage agreement.

Open-end mortgage   A mortgage with a provision that permits borrowing additional money in the future without refinancing the loan or paying additional financing charges. Open-end provisions often limit such borrowing to no more than would raise the balance to the original loan figure.

Offer to purchase   See *binder.*

Particular lien   See *special lien.*

Plat   A map or chart of a lot, subdivision, or community drawn by a surveyor showing boundary lines, buildings, improvements on the land, and easements.

Points   Sometimes called "discount points." A point is one percent of the amount of the mortgage loan. For example, if a loan is for $25,000, one point is $250. Points are charged by a lender to raise the yield on his loan at a time when money is tight, interest rates are high, and there is a legal limit to the interest rate that can be charged on a mortgage. Buyers are prohibited from paying points on HUD or Veterans Administration guaranteed loans (sellers can pay, however). On a conventional mortgage points may be paid by either buyer or seller or split between them.

Prepayment   Payment of *mortgage* loan, or part of it, before due date. Mortgage agreements often restrict the right of prepayment either by limiting the amount that can be prepaid in any one year or charging a penalty for prepayment. The Federal Housing Administration does not permit such restrictions in FHA insured mortgages.

Principal The basic element of the loan as distinguished from *interest* and *mortgage insurance premium*. In other words, principal is the amount upon which interest is paid.

Purchase agreement See *agreement of sale*.

Quitclaim deed A deed which transfers whatever interest the maker of the deed may have in the particular parcel of land. A quitclaim deed is often given to clear the title when the grantor's interest in a property is questionable. By accepting such a deed the buyer assumes all the risks. Such a deed makes no warranties as to the title, but simply transfers to the buyer whatever interest the grantor has. See *deed; title*.

Real estate broker A middleman or agent who buys and sells real estate for a company, firm, or individual on a commission basis. The broker does not have title to the property but generally represents the owner.

Refinancing The process of paying off one loan with the proceeds from another loan.

Restrictive covenants Private restrictions limiting the use of real property. Restrictive covenants are created by deed and may "run with the land," binding all subsequent purchasers of the land, or may be "personal" and binding only between the original seller and buyer. The determination whether a covenant runs with the land or is personal is governed by the language of the covenant, the intent of the parties, and the law in the state where the land is situated. Restrictive covenants that run with the land are *encumbrances* and may affect the value and marketability of title. These covenants may limit the density of buildings per acre, regulate size, style or price range of buildings to be erected, or prevent particular businesses from operating or minority groups from owning or occupying homes in a given area. (This latter discriminatory covenant is unconstitutional and has been declared unenforceable by the U. S. Supreme Court.)

Sales agreement See *agreement of sale*.

Setback See *building line*.

Special lien A lien that binds a specified piece of property, unlike a general lien, which is levied against all one's assets. It creates a right to retain something of value belonging to another person as compensation for labor, material, or money expended in that person's behalf. In some localities it is called "particular" lien or "specific" lien. See *lien*.

Special warranty deed A deed in which the grantor conveys title to the grantee and agrees to protect the grantee against title defects or claims asserted by the grantor and those persons whose right to assert a claim against the title arose during the period the grantor held title to the property. In a special warranty deed the grantor guarantees to the grantee that he has done nothing during the time he held title to the property which has, or which might in the future, impair the grantee's title. See also *deed; title*.

State stamps See *documentary stamps*.

Survey A map or plat made by a licensed surveyor showing the results of measuring the land with its elevations, improvements, boundaries, and its relationship to surrounding tracts of land. A survey is often required by the lender to assure him that a building is actually sited on the land according to its legal description.

Tax As applied to real estate, an enforced charge imposed on persons, property, or income, to be used to support the state. The governing body in turn utilizes the funds in the best interest of the general public.

Title As generally used, the rights of ownership and possession of particular property. In real estate usage, title may refer to the instruments or documents by which a right of ownership is established (title documents), or it may refer to the ownership interest one has in the real estate.

Title insurance Protects lenders or homeowners against loss of their interest in property due to legal defects in title. Title insurance may be issued to either the mortgagor, as an "owner's title policy," or to the mortgagee, as a "mortgagee's title policy." Insurance benefits will be paid only to the "named insured" in the title policy, so it is important that an owner purchase an "owner's title policy" if he desires the protection of title insurance.

Title search or examination A check of the title records, generally at the local courthouse, to make sure the buyer is purchasing a house from the legal owner and there are no *liens*, overdue *special assessments*, or other claims or outstanding *restrictive covenants* filed in the record which would adversely affect the marketability or value of title.

Trustee A party who is given legal responsibility to hold property in the best interest of or "for the benefit of" another. The trustee is one placed in a position of responsibility for another, a responsibility enforceable in a court of law. See *deed of trust*.

Zoning ordinances The acts of an authorized local government establishing building codes and setting forth regulations for property land usage.

Appendix C
Amortized Loans

The high interest rates currently charged small businesses make it essential to determine interest costs before starting a company or going ahead with major capital improvements. Although interest is a business cost, a new firm may be at a competitive disadvantage if, for example, it has to pay too high a price for money to purchase a building or expensive machinery.

The following tables can be used to determine the amount of money one would pay to amortize a $100,000 loan at either 12 percent (Exhibit C-1) or 14 percent (Exhibit C-3) for thirty years. A look at the recapitulation pages indicates that at 12 percent the interest cost is $269,094.00 (Exhibit C-2) as compared with $325,544.00 at 14 percent (Exhibit C-4). Be sure to shop around for the lowest interest rate available from a reliable institution because even a quarter or an eighth of a percent can be a big savings over a long period of time.

In arriving at your loan decision, you should know that adjustable rate mortgages will be on the increase in the years ahead. In 1981, the comptroller of the currency (for national banks) and the Federal Home Loan Bank Board (for federally chartered savings and loan associations and federal mutual savings banks) gave thrift institutions almost unlimited freedom[1] to tie monthly mortgage payments to market interest rates. This action permitted these firms to increase or decrease the loan's monthly payments, principal, or duration[2] in accordance with a public index like treasury bill rates or average national mortgage rates. The index selected must be readily verifiable by the borrower and beyond the control of the lender.

Such adjustable rate mortgages make it more difficult for small businesses to estimate their costs. At this writing both fixed and adjustable mortgages are still available. Furthermore, existing mortgages were not

[1] The freedom is not total. For example, the comptroller of the currency will not permit national banks to modify loan rates by more than one percentage point every six months. Also a number of states impose more strict rate limits on their state chartered thrift institutions.

[2] In lieu of raising monthly interest payments, as S & L could, for instance, increase the loan's principal or spread out payments from say 30 to 35 years.

affected by the 1981 rules, so it may be desirable, in some cases, to take over a fixed mortgage.

Exhibit C-1   Monthly Payments on a $100,000 loan at 12 percent interest over thirty years

Monthly payment	Interest paid	Prin- cipal paid	Total pay- ment	Total princi- pal due (bal- ance)
1	$ 1,000	$ 29	$ 1,029[a]	$99,971
2	1,000	29	1,029	99,942
3	999	30	1,029	99,912
4	999	30	1,029	99,882
5	999	30	1,029	99,852
6	999	30	1,029	99,822
7	998	31	1,029	99,791
8	998	31	1,029	99,760
9	998	31	1,029	99,729
10	997	32	1,029	99,697
11	997	32	1,029	99,665
12	997	32	1,029	99,633
1st year total	$11,981	$ 367	$12,348	
13	$ 996	$ 33	$ 1,029	$99,600
14	996	33	1,029	99,567
15	996	33	1,029	99,534
16	995	34	1,029	99,500
17	995	34	1,029	99,466
18	995	34	1,029	99,432
19	994	35	1,029	99,397
20	994	35	1,029	99,362
21	994	35	1,029	99,327
22	993	36	1,029	99,291
23	993	36	1,029	99,255
24	993	36	1,029	99,219
2nd year total	$11,934	$ 414	$12,348	
25	$ 992	$ 37	$ 1,029	$99,182
26	992	37	1,029	99,145
27	991	38	1,029	99,107
28	991	38	1,029	99,069
29	991	38	1,029	99,031

[a] Monthly payment per $1,000 = $10.29

Exhibit C-1 Continued

Monthly payment	Interest paid	Prin- cipal paid	Total pay- ment	Total princi- pal due (bal- ance)
30	990	39	1,029	98,992
31	990	39	1,029	98,953
32	990	39	1,029	98,914
33	989	40	1,029	98,874
34	989	40	1,029	98,834
35	988	41	1,029	98,793
36	988	41	1,029	98,752
3rd year total	$11,881	$ 467	$12,348	
37	$ 988	$ 41	$ 1,029	$98,711
38	987	42	1,029	98,669
39	987	42	1,029	98,627
40	986	43	1,029	98,584
41	986	43	1,029	98,541
42	985	44	1,029	98,497
43	985	44	1,029	98,453
44	985	44	1,029	98,409
45	984	45	1,029	98,364
46	984	45	1,029	98,319
47	983	46	1,029	98,273
48	983	46	1.029	98,227
4th year total	$11,823	$ 525	$12,348	
49	$ 982	$ 47	$ 1,029	$98,180
50	982	47	1,029	98,133
51	981	48	1,029	98,085
52	981	48	1,029	98,037
53	980	49	1,029	97,988
54	980	49	1,029	97,939
55	979	50	1,029	97,889
56	979	50	1,029	97,839
57	978	51	1,029	97,788
58	978	51	1,029	97,737
59	977	52	1,029	97,685
60	977	52	1,029	97,633
5th year total	$11,754	$ 594	$12,348	
61	$ 976	$ 53	$ 1,029	$97,580
62	976	53	1,029	97,527
63	975	54	1,029	97,473

Exhibit C-1 Continued

Monthly payment	Interest paid	Principal paid	Total payment	Total principal due (balance)
64	975	54	1,029	97,419
65	974	55	1,029	97,364
66	974	55	1,029	97,309
67	973	56	1,029	97,253
68	973	56	1,029	97,197
69	972	57	1,029	97,140
70	971	58	1,029	97,082
71	971	58	1,029	97,024
72	970	59	1,029	96,965
6th year total	$11,680	$ 668	$12,348	
73	$ 970	$ 59	$ 1,029	$96,906
74	969	60	1,029	96,846
75	968	61	1,029	96,785
76	968	61	1,029	96,724
77	967	62	1,029	96,662
78	967	62	1,029	96,600
79	966	63	1,029	96,537
80	965	64	1,029	96,473
81	965	64	1,029	96,409
82	964	65	1,029	96,344
83	963	66	1,029	96,278
84	963	66	1,029	96,212
7th year total	$11,595	$ 753	$12,348	
85	$ 962	$ 67	$ 1,029	$96,145
86	961	68	1,029	96,077
87	961	68	1,029	96,009
88	960	69	1,029	95,940
89	959	70	1,029	95,870
90	959	70	1,029	95,800
91	958	71	1,029	95,729
92	957	72	1,029	95,657
93	957	72	1,029	95,585
94	956	73	1,029	95,512
95	955	74	1,029	95,438
96	954	75	1,029	95,363
8th year total	$11,499	$ 849	$12,348	

Exhibit C-1 Continued

Monthly payment	Interest paid	Prin- cipal paid	Total pay- ment	Total princi- pal due (bal- ance)
97	$ 954	$ 75	$ 1,029	$95,288
98	953	76	1,029	95,212
99	952	77	1,029	95,135
100	951	78	1,029	95,057
101	951	78	1,029	94,979
102	950	79	1,029	94,900
103	949	80	1,029	94,820
104	948	81	1,029	94,739
105	947	82	1,029	94,657
106	947	82	1,029	94,575
107	946	83	1,029	94,492
108	945	84	1,029	94,408
9th year total	$11,393	$ 955	$12,348	
109	$ 944	$ 85	$ 1,029	$94,323
110	943	86	1,029	94,237
111	942	87	1,029	94,150
112	942	87	1,029	94,063
113	941	88	1,029	93,975
114	940	89	1,029	93,886
115	939	90	1,029	93,796
116	938	91	1,029	93,705
117	937	92	1,029	93,613
118	936	93	1,029	93,520
119	935	94	1,029	93,426
120	934	95	1,029	93,331
10th year total	$11,271	$ 1,077	$12,348	
121	$ 933	$ 96	$ 1,029	$93,235
122	932	97	1,029	93,138
123	931	98	1,029	93,040
124	930	99	1,029	92,941
125	929	100	1,029	92,841
126	928	101	1,029	92,740
127	927	102	1,029	92,638
128	926	103	1,029	92,535
129	925	104	1,029	92,431
130	924	105	1,029	92,326

Exhibit C-1 Continued

Monthly payment	Interest paid	Prin- cipal paid	Total pay- ment	Total princi- pal due (bal- ance)
131	923	106	1,029	92,220
132	922	107	1,029	92,113
11th year total	$11,130	$ 1,218	$12,348	
133	$ 921	$ 108	$ 1,029	$92,005
134	920	109	1,029	91,896
135	919	110	1,029	91,786
136	918	111	1,029	91,675
137	917	112	1,029	91,563
138	916	113	1,029	91,450
139	915	114	1,029	91,336
140	913	116	1,029	91,220
141	912	117	1,029	91,103
142	911	118	1,029	90,985
143	910	119	1,029	90,866
144	909	120	1,029	90,746
12th year total	$10,981	$ 1,367	$12,348	
145	$ 907	$ 122	$ 1,029	$90,624
146	906	123	1,029	90,501
147	905	124	1,029	90,377
148	904	125	1,029	90,252
149	903	126	1,029	90,126
150	901	128	1,029	89,998
151	900	129	1,029	89,869
152	899	130	1,029	89,739
153	897	132	1,029	89,607
154	896	133	1,029	89,474
155	895	134	1,029	89,340
156	893	136	1,029	89,204
13th year total	$10,806	$ 1,542	$12,348	
157	$ 892	$ 137	$ 1,029	$89,067
158	891	138	1,029	88,929
159	889	140	1,029	88,789
160	888	141	1,029	88,648
161	886	143	1,029	88,505
162	885	144	1,029	88,361
163	884	145	1,029	88,216

Exhibit C-1 Continued

Monthly payment	Interest paid	Principal paid	Total payment	Total principal due (balance)
164	882	147	1,029	88,069
165	881	148	1,029	87,921
166	879	150	1,029	87,771
167	878	151	1,029	87,620
168	876	153	1,029	87,467
14th year total	$10,611	$ 1,737	$12,348	
169	$ 875	$ 154	$ 1,029	$87,313
170	873	156	1,029	87,157
171	872	157	1,029	87,000
172	870	159	1,029	86,841
173	868	161	1,029	86,680
174	867	162	1,029	86,518
175	865	164	1,029	86,354
176	864	165	1,029	86,189
177	862	167	1,029	86,022
178	860	169	1,029	85,853
179	859	170	1,029	85,683
180	857	172	1,029	85,511
15th year total	$10,392	$ 1,956	$12,348	
181	$ 855	$ 174	$ 1,029	$85,337
182	853	176	1,029	85,161
183	852	177	1,029	84,984
184	850	179	1,029	84,805
185	848	181	1,029	84,624
186	846	183	1,029	84,441
187	844	185	1,029	84,256
188	843	186	1,029	84,070
189	841	188	1,029	83,882
190	839	190	1,029	83,692
191	837	192	1,029	83,500
192	835	194	1,029	83,306
16th year total	$10,143	$ 2,205	$12,348	
193	$ 833	$ 196	$ 1,029	$83,110
194	831	198	1,029	82,912
195	829	200	1,029	82,712
196	827	202	1,029	82,510
197	825	204	1,029	82,306

Exhibit C-1 Continued

Monthly payment	Interest paid	Principal paid	Total payment	Total principal due (balance)
198	823	206	1,029	82,100
199	821	208	1,029	81,892
200	819	210	1,029	81,682
201	817	212	1,029	81,470
202	815	214	1,029	81,256
203	813	216	1,029	81,040
204	810	219	1,029	80,821
17th year total	$ 9,863	$ 2,485	$12,348	
205	$ 808	$ 221	$ 1,029	$80,600
206	806	223	1,029	80,377
207	804	225	1,029	80,152
208	802	227	1,029	79,925
209	799	230	1,029	79,695
210	797	232	1,029	79,463
211	795	234	1,029	79,229
212	792	237	1,029	78,992
213	790	239	1,029	78,753
214	788	241	1,029	78,512
215	785	244	1,029	78,268
216	783	246	1,029	78,022
18th year total	$ 9,549	$ 2,799	$12,348	
217	$ 780	$ 249	$ 1,029	$77,773
218	778	251	1,029	77,522
219	775	254	1,029	77,268
220	773	256	1,029	77,012
221	770	259	1,029	76,753
222	768	261	1,029	76,492
223	765	264	1,029	76,228
224	762	267	1,029	75,961
225	760	269	1,029	75,692
226	757	272	1,029	75,420
227	754	275	1,029	75,145
228	751	278	1,029	74,867
19th year total	$ 9,193	$ 3,155	$12,348	
229	$ 749	$ 280	$ 1,029	$74,587
230	746	283	1,029	74,304
231	743	286	1,029	74,018

Exhibit C-1   Continued

Monthly payment	Interest paid	Principal paid	Total payment	Total principal due (balance)
232	740	289	1,029	73,729
233	737	292	1,029	73,437
234	734	295	1,029	73,142
235	731	298	1,029	72,844
236	728	301	1,029	72,543
237	725	304	1,029	72,239
238	722	307	1,029	71,932
239	719	310	1,029	71,622
240	716	313	1,029	71,309
20th year total	$ 8,790	$ 3,558	$12,348	
241	$ 713	$ 316	$ 1,029	$70,993
242	710	319	1,029	70,674
243	707	322	1,029	70,352
244	704	325	1,029	70,027
245	700	329	1,029	69,698
246	697	332	1,029	69,366
247	694	335	1,029	69,031
248	690	339	1,029	68,692
249	687	342	1,029	68,350
250	684	345	1,029	68,005
251	680	349	1,029	67,656
252	677	352	1,029	67,304
21st year total	$ 8,343	$ 4,005	$12,348	
253	$ 673	$ 356	$ 1,029	$66,948
254	669	360	1,029	66,588
255	666	363	1,029	66,225
256	662	367	1,029	65,858
257	659	370	1,029	65,488
258	655	374	1,029	65,114
259	651	378	1,029	64,736
260	647	382	1,029	64,354
261	644	385	1,029	63,969
262	640	389	1,029	63,580
263	636	393	1,029	63,187
264	632	397	1,029	62,790
22nd year total	$ 7,834	$ 4,514	$12,348	

Exhibit C-1 Continued

Monthly payment	Interest paid	Principal paid	Total payment	Total principal due (balance)
265	$ 628	$ 401	$ 1,029	$62,389
266	624	405	1,029	61,984
267	620	409	1,029	61,575
268	616	413	1,029	61,162
269	612	417	1,029	60,745
270	607	422	1,029	60,323
271	603	426	1,029	59,897
272	599	430	1,029	59,467
273	595	434	1,029	59,033
274	590	439	1,029	58,594
275	586	443	1,029	58,151
276	582	447	1,029	57,704
23rd year total	$ 7,262	$ 5,086	$12,348	
277	$ 577	$ 452	$ 1,029	$57,252
278	573	456	1,029	56,796
279	568	461	1,029	56,335
280	563	466	1,029	55,869
281	559	470	1,029	55,399
282	554	475	1,029	54,924
283	549	480	1,029	54,444
284	544	485	1,029	53,959
285	540	489	1,029	53,470
286	535	494	1,029	52,976
287	530	499	1,029	52,477
288	525	504	1,029	51,973
24th year total	$ 6,617	$ 5,731	$12,348	
289	$ 520	$ 509	$ 1,029	$51,464
290	515	514	1,029	50,950
291	510	519	1,029	50,431
292	504	525	1,029	49,906
293	499	530	1,029	49,376
294	494	535	1,029	48,841
295	488	541	1,029	48,300
296	483	546	1,029	47,754
297	478	551	1,029	47,203
298	472	557	1,029	46,646

Exhibit C-1 Continued

Monthly payment	Interest paid	Principal paid	Total payment	Total principal due (balance)
299	466	563	1,029	46,083
300	461	568	1,029	45,515
25th year total	$ 5,890	$ 6,458	$12,348	
301	$ 455	$ 574	$ 1,029	$44,941
302	449	580	1,029	44,361
303	444	585	1,029	43,776
304	438	591	1,029	43,185
305	432	597	1,029	42,588
306	426	603	1,029	41,985
307	420	609	1,029	41,376
308	414	615	1,029	40,761
309	408	621	1,029	40,140
310	401	628	1,029	39,512
311	395	634	1,029	38,878
312	389	640	1,029	38,238
26th year total	$ 5,071	$ 7,277	$12,348	
313	$ 382	$ 647	$ 1,029	$37,591
314	376	653	1,029	36,938
315	369	660	1,029	36,278
316	363	666	1,029	35,612
317	356	673	1,029	34,939
318	349	680	1,029	34,259
319	343	686	1,029	33,573
320	336	693	1,029	32,880
321	329	700	1,029	32,180
322	322	707	1,029	31,473
323	315	714	1,029	30,759
324	308	721	1,029	30,038
27th year total	$ 4,148	$ 8,200	$12,348	
325	$ 300	$ 729	$ 1,029	$29,309
326	293	736	1,029	28,573
327	286	743	1,029	27,830
328	278	751	1,029	27,079
329	271	758	1,029	26,321
330	263	766	1,029	25,555
331	256	773	1,029	24,782

Exhibit C-1 Continued

Monthly payment	Interest paid	Principal paid	Total payment	Total principal due (balance)
332	248	781	1,029	24,001
333	240	789	1,029	23,212
334	232	797	1,029	22,415
335	224	805	1,029	21,610
336	216	813	1,029	20,797
28th year total	$ 3,107	$ 9,241	$12,348	
337	$ 208	$ 821	$ 1,029	$19,976
338	200	829	1,029	19,147
339	191	838	1,029	18,309
340	183	846	1,029	17,463
341	175	854	1,029	16,609
342	166	863	1,029	15,746
343	157	872	1,029	14,874
344	149	880	1,029	13,994
345	140	889	1,029	13,105
346	131	898	1,029	12,207
347	122	907	1,029	11,300
348	113	916	1,029	10,384
29th year total	$ 1,935	$10,413	$12,348	
349	$ 104	$ 925	$ 1,029	$ 9,459
350	95	934	1,029	8,525
351	85	944	1,029	7,581
352	76	953	1,029	6,628
353	66	963	1,029	5,665
354	57	972	1,029	4,693
355	47	982	1,029	3,711
356	37	992	1,029	2,719
357	27	1,002	1,029	1,717
358	17	1,012	1,029	705
359	7	705	712[b]	—
360	—	—	—[b]	—
30th year total	$ 618	$10,384	$11,002	

[b] The total monthly payments for the 359th and 360th months are short because the earlier payments were rounded off upward.

Exhibit C-2 Recapitulation — Annual payments on a $100,000 loan at 12 percent interest over thirty years

Yearly payment	Interest paid	Principal paid	Total payment
1	$ 11,981	$ 367	$ 12,348
2	11,934	414	12,348
3	11,881	467	12,348
4	11,823	525	12,348
5	11,754	594	12,348
6	11,680	668	12,348
7	11,595	753	12,348
8	11,499	849	12,348
9	11,393	955	12,348
10	11,271	1,077	12,348
11	11,130	1,218	12,348
12	10,981	1,367	12,348
13	10,806	1,542	12,348
14	10,611	1,737	12,348
15	10,392	1,956	12,348
16	10,143	2,205	12,348
17	9,863	2,485	12,348
18	9,549	2,799	12,348
19	9,193	3,155	12,348
20	8,790	3,558	12,348
21	8,343	4,005	12,348
22	7,834	4,514	12,348
23	7,262	5,086	12,348
24	6,617	5,731	12,348
25	5,890	6,458	12,348
26	5,071	7,277	12,348
27	4,148	8,200	12,348
28	3,107	9,241	12,348
29	1,935	10,413	12,348
30	618	10,384	11,002
Total	$269,094	$100,000	$369,094

Exhibit C-3 Monthly payments on a $100,000 loan at 14 percent interest over thirty years

Monthly payment	Interest paid	Principal paid	Total payment	Total principal due (balance)
1	$ 1,167	$ 18	$ 1,185[a]	$99,982
2	1,166	19	1,185	99,963
3	1,166	19	1,185	99,944
4	1,166	19	1,185	99,925
5	1,166	19	1,185	99,906
6	1,166	19	1,185	99,887
7	1,165	20	1,185	99,867
8	1,165	20	1,185	99,847
9	1,165	20	1,185	99,827
10	1,165	20	1,185	99,807
11	1,164	21	1,185	99,786
12	1,164	21	1,185	99,765
1st year total	$13,985	$ 235	$14,220	
13	$ 1,164	$ 21	$ 1,185	$99,740
14	1,164	21	1,185	99,719
15	1,163	22	1,185	99,697
16	1,163	22	1,185	99,675
17	1,163	22	1,185	99,653
18	1,163	22	1,185	99,631
19	1,162	23	1,185	99,608
20	1,162	23	1,185	99,585
21	1,162	23	1,185	99,562
22	1,162	23	1,185	99,539
23	1,161	24	1,185	99,515
24	1,161	24	1,185	99,491
2nd year total	$13,950	$ 270	$14,220	
25	$ 1,161	$ 24	$ 1,185	$99,467
26	1,160	25	1,185	99,442
27	1,160	25	1,185	99,417
28	1,160	25	1,185	99,392
29	1,160	25	1,185	99,367
30	1,159	26	1,185	99,341
31	1,159	26	1,185	99,315
32	1,159	26	1,185	99,289

[a] Monthly payment per $1,000 = $11.85.

Exhibit C-3 Continued

Monthly payment	Interest paid	Prin-cipal paid	Total pay-ment	Total princi-pal due (bal-ance)
33	1,158	27	1,185	99,262
34	1,158	27	1,185	99,235
35	1,158	27	1,185	99,208
36	1,157	28	1,185	99,180
3rd year total	$13,909	$ 311	$14,220	
37	$ 1,157	$ 28	$ 1,185	$99,152
38	1,157	28	1,185	99,124
39	1,156	29	1,185	99,095
40	1,156	29	1,185	99,066
41	1,156	29	1,185	99,037
42	1,155	30	1,185	99,007
43	1,155	30	1,185	98,977
44	1,155	30	1,185	98,947
45	1,154	31	1,185	98,916
46	1,154	31	1,185	98,885
47	1,154	31	1,185	98,854
48	1,153	32	1,185	98,822
4th year total	$13,862	$ 358	$14,220	
49	$ 1,153	$ 32	$ 1,185	$98,790
50	1,153	32	1,185	98,758
51	1,152	33	1,185	98,725
52	1,152	33	1,185	98,691
53	1,151	34	1,185	98,657
54	1,151	34	1,185	98,623
55	1,151	34	1,185	98,589
56	1,150	35	1,185	98,554
57	1,150	35	1,185	98,519
58	1,149	36	1,185	98,483
59	1,149	36	1,185	98,447
60	1,149	36	1,185	98,411
5th year total	$13,810	$ 410	$14,220	
61	$ 1,148	$ 37	$ 1,185	$98,374
62	1,148	37	1,185	98,337
63	1,147	38	1,185	98,299
64	1,147	38	1,185	98,261
65	1,146	39	1,185	98,222
66	1,146	39	1,185	98,183

Exhibit C-3 Continued

Monthly payment	Interest paid	Prin- cipal paid	Total pay- ment	Total princi- pal due (bal- ance)
67	1,145	40	1,185	98,143
68	1,145	40	1,185	98,103
69	1,145	40	1,185	98,063
70	1,144	41	1,185	98,022
71	1,144	41	1,185	97,981
72	1,143	42	1,185	97,939
6th year total	$13,748	$ 472	$14,220	
73	$ 1,143	$ 42	$ 1,185	$97,897
74	1,142	43	1,185	97,854
75	1,142	43	1,185	97,811
76	1,141	44	1,185	97,767
77	1,141	44	1,185	97,723
78	1,140	45	1,185	97,678
79	1,140	45	1,185	97,633
80	1,139	46	1,185	97,587
81	1,139	46	1,185	97,541
82	1,138	47	1,185	97,494
83	1,137	48	1,185	97,446
84	1,137	48	1,185	97,398
7th year total	$13,679	$ 541	$14,220	
85	$ 1,136	$ 49	$ 1,185	$97,349
86	1,136	49	1,185	97,300
87	1,135	50	1,185	97,250
88	1,135	50	1,185	97,200
89	1,134	51	1,185	97,149
90	1,133	52	1,185	97,097
91	1,133	52	1,185	97,045
92	1,132	53	1,185	96,989
93	1,132	53	1,185	96,936
94	1,131	54	1,185	96,882
95	1,130	55	1,185	96,827
96	1,130	55	1,185	96,772
8th year total	$13,597	$ 623	$14,220	
97	$ 1,129	$ 56	$ 1,185	$96,716
98	1,128	57	1,185	96,659
99	1,128	57	1,185	96,602
100	1,127	58	1,185	96,544

Exhibit C-3 Continued

Monthly payment	Interest paid	Principal paid	Total payment	Total principal due (balance)
101	1,126	59	1,185	96,485
102	1,126	59	1,185	96,426
103	1,125	60	1,185	96,366
104	1,124	61	1,185	96,305
105	1,124	61	1,185	96,244
106	1,123	62	1,185	96,182
107	1,122	63	1,185	96,119
108	1,121	64	1,185	96,055
9th year total	$13,503	$ 717	$14,220	
109	$ 1,121	$ 64	$ 1,185	$95,991
110	1,120	65	1,185	95,926
111	1,119	66	1,185	95,860
112	1,118	67	1,185	95,793
113	1,118	67	1,185	95,726
114	1,117	68	1,185	95,658
115	1,116	69	1,185	95,589
116	1,115	70	1,185	95,519
117	1,114	71	1,185	95,448
118	1,114	71	1,185	95,377
119	1,113	72	1,185	95,305
120	1,112	73	1,185	95,232
10th year total	$13,397	$ 823	$14,220	
121	$ 1,111	$ 74	$ 1,185	$95,158
122	1,110	75	1,185	95,083
123	1,109	76	1,185	95,007
124	1,108	77	1,185	94,930
125	1,108	77	1,185	94,853
126	1,107	78	1,185	94,775
127	1,106	79	1,185	94,696
128	1,105	80	1,185	94,616
129	1,104	81	1,185	94,535
130	1,103	82	1,185	94,453
131	1,102	83	1,185	94,370
132	1,101	84	1,185	94,286
11th year total	$13,274	$ 946	$14,220	
133	$ 1,100	$ 85	$ 1,185	$94,201
134	1,099	86	1,185	94,115

Exhibit C-3 Continued

Monthly payment	Interest paid	Principal paid	Total payment	Total principal due (balance)
135	1,098	87	1,185	94,028
136	1,097	88	1,185	93,940
137	1,096	89	1,185	93,851
138	1,095	90	1,185	93,761
139	1,094	91	1,185	93,670
140	1,093	92	1,185	93,578
141	1,092	93	1,185	93,485
142	1,091	94	1,185	93,391
143	1,090	95	1,185	93,296
144	1,088	97	1,185	93,199
12th year total	$13,133	$ 1,087	$14,220	
145	$ 1,087	$ 98	$ 1,185	$93,101
146	1,086	99	1,185	93,002
147	1,085	100	1,185	92,902
148	1,084	101	1,185	92,801
149	1,083	102	1,185	92,699
150	1,081	104	1,185	92,595
151	1,080	105	1,185	92,490
152	1,079	106	1,185	92,384
153	1,078	107	1,185	92,277
154	1,077	108	1,185	92,169
155	1,075	110	1,185	92,059
156	1,074	111	1,185	91,948
13th year total	$12,969	$ 1,251	$14,220	
157	$ 1,073	$ 112	$ 1,185	$91,836
158	1,071	114	1,185	91,722
159	1,070	115	1,185	91,607
160	1,069	116	1,185	91,491
161	1,067	118	1,185	91,373
162	1,066	119	1,185	91,254
163	1,065	120	1,185	91,134
164	1,063	122	1,185	91,012
165	1,062	123	1,185	90,889
166	1,060	125	1,185	90,764
167	1,059	126	1,185	90,638
168	1,057	128	1,185	90,510
14th year total	$12,782	$ 1,432	$14,220	

Exhibit C-3 Continued

Monthly payment	Interest paid	Principal paid	Total payment	Total principal due (balance)
169	$ 1,056	$ 129	$ 1,185	$90,381
170	1,054	131	1,185	90,250
171	1,053	132	1,185	90,118
172	1,051	134	1,185	89,984
173	1,050	135	1,185	89,849
174	1,048	137	1,185	89,712
175	1,047	138	1,185	89,574
176	1,045	140	1,185	89,434
177	1,043	142	1,185	89,292
178	1,042	143	1,185	89,129
179	1,040	145	1,185	88,984
180	1,038	147	1,185	88,837
15th year total	$12,567	$ 1,653	$14,220	
181	$ 1,036	$ 149	$ 1,185	$88,690
182	1,035	150	1,185	88,540
183	1,033	152	1,185	88,388
184	1,031	154	1,185	88,234
185	1,029	156	1,185	88,078
186	1,028	157	1,185	87,921
187	1,026	159	1,185	87,762
188	1,024	161	1,185	87,601
189	1,022	163	1,185	87,438
190	1,020	165	1,185	87,273
191	1,018	167	1,185	87,106
192	1,016	169	1,185	86,937
16th year total	$12,318	$ 1,902	$14,220	
193	$ 1,014	$ 171	$ 1,185	$86,766
194	1,012	173	1,185	86,593
195	1,010	175	1,185	86,418
196	1,008	177	1,185	86,241
197	1,006	179	1,185	86,062
198	1,004	181	1,185	85,881
199	1,002	183	1,185	85,698
200	1,000	185	1,185	85,513
201	998	187	1,185	85,326
202	995	190	1,185	85,136

Exhibit C-3   Continued

Monthly payment	Interest paid	Prin- cipal paid	Total pay- ment	Total princi- pal due (bal- ance)
203	993	192	1,185	84,944
204	991	194	1,185	84,750
17th year total	$12,033	$ 2,187	$14,220	
205	$ 989	$ 196	$ 1,185	$84,554
206	986	199	1,185	84,355
207	984	201	1,185	84,154
208	982	203	1,185	83,951
209	979	206	1,185	83,745
210	977	208	1,185	83,537
211	975	210	1,185	83,327
212	972	213	1,185	83,114
213	970	215	1,185	82,899
214	967	218	1,185	82,681
215	965	220	1,185	82,461
216	962	223	1,185	82,238
18th year total	$11,708	$ 2,512	$14,220	
217	$ 959	$ 226	$ 1,185	$82,012
218	957	228	1,185	81,784
219	954	231	1,185	81,553
220	951	234	1,185	81,319
221	947	238	1,185	81,081
222	946	239	1,185	80,842
223	943	242	1,185	80,600
224	940	245	1,185	80,359
225	937	248	1,185	80,107
226	935	250	1,185	79,857
227	932	253	1,185	79,604
228	929	256	1,185	79,348
19th year total	$11,330	$ 2,890	$14,220	
229	$ 926	$ 259	$ 1,185	$79,089
230	923	262	1,185	78,827
231	920	265	1,185	78,562
232	917	268	1,185	78,294
233	913	272	1,185	78,022
234	910	275	1,185	77,747
235	907	278	1,185	77,469

Exhibit C-3 Continued

Monthly payment	Interest paid	Principal paid	Total payment	Total principal due (balance)
236	904	281	1,185	77,188
237	901	284	1,185	76,904
238	897	288	1,185	76,616
239	894	291	1,185	76,325
240	890	295	1,185	76,030
20th year total	$10,902	$ 3,318	$14,220	
241	$ 887	$ 298	$ 1,185	$75,732
242	884	301	1,185	75,431
243	880	305	1,185	75,126
244	876	309	1,185	74,817
245	873	312	1,185	74,505
246	869	316	1,185	74,189
247	866	319	1,185	73,870
248	862	323	1,185	73,547
249	858	327	1,185	73,220
250	854	331	1,185	72,889
251	850	335	1,185	72,554
252	846	339	1,185	72,215
21st year total	$10,405	$ 3,815	$14,220	
253	$ 843	$ 342	$ 1,185	$71,873
254	839	346	1,185	71,527
255	834	351	1,185	71,176
256	830	355	1,185	70,821
257	826	359	1,185	70,462
258	822	363	1,185	70,099
259	818	367	1,185	69,732
260	814	371	1,185	69,361
261	809	376	1,185	68,985
262	805	380	1,185	68,605
263	800	385	1,185	68,220
264	796	389	1,185	67,831
22nd year total	$ 9,836	$ 4,384	$14,220	
265	$ 791	$ 394	$ 1,185	$67,437
266	787	398	1,185	67,039
267	782	403	1,185	66,636
268	777	408	1,185	66,228
269	773	412	1,185	65,816

Exhibit C-3 Continued

Monthly payment	Interest paid	Principal paid	Total payment	Total principal due (balance)
270	768	417	1,185	65,399
271	763	422	1,185	64,977
272	758	427	1,185	64,550
273	753	432	1,185	64,118
274	748	437	1,185	63,681
275	743	442	1,185	63,239
276	738	447	1,185	62,792
23rd year total	$ 9,181	$ 5,039	$14,220	
277	$ 733	$ 452	$ 1,185	$62,340
278	727	458	1,185	61,882
279	722	463	1,185	61,419
280	717	468	1,185	60,951
281	711	474	1,185	60,477
282	706	479	1,185	59,998
283	700	485	1,185	59,513
284	694	491	1,185	59,022
285	689	496	1,185	58,526
286	683	502	1,185	58,024
287	677	508	1,185	57,516
288	671	514	1,185	57,002
24th year total	$ 8,430	$ 5,790	$14,220	
289	$ 665	$ 520	$ 1,185	$56,482
290	659	526	1,185	55,956
291	653	532	1,185	55,424
292	647	538	1,185	54,886
293	640	545	1,185	54,341
294	634	551	1,185	53,790
295	628	557	1,185	53,233
296	621	564	1,185	52,669
297	614	571	1,185	52,098
298	608	577	1,185	51,521
299	601	584	1,185	50,937
300	594	591	1,185	50,346
25th year total	$ 7,564	$ 6,656	$14,220	
301	$ 587	$ 598	$ 1,185	$49,838
302	581	604	1,185	49,234
303	574	611	1,185	48,623

Exhibit C-3   Continued

Monthly payment	Interest paid	Principal paid	Total payment	Total principal due (balance)
304	567	618	1,185	48,005
305	560	625	1,185	47,380
306	553	632	1,185	46,748
307	545	640	1,185	46,108
308	538	647	1,185	45,461
309	530	655	1,185	44,806
310	523	662	1,185	44,144
311	515	670	1,185	43,474
312	507	678	1,185	42,796
26th year total	$ 6,580	$ 7,640	$14,220	
313	$ 499	$ 686	$ 1,185	$42,110
314	491	694	1,185	41,416
315	483	702	1,185	40,714
316	475	710	1,185	40,004
317	467	718	1,185	39,286
318	458	727	1,185	38,559
319	450	735	1,185	37,824
320	441	744	1,185	37,080
321	433	752	1,185	36,328
322	424	761	1,185	35,567
323	415	770	1,185	34,797
324	406	779	1,185	34,018
27th year total	$ 5,442	$ 8,778	$14,220	
325	$ 397	$ 788	$ 1,185	$33,230
326	388	797	1,185	32,433
327	378	807	1,185	31,626
328	369	816	1,185	30,810
329	359	826	1,185	29,984
330	350	835	1,185	29,149
331	340	845	1,185	28,304
332	330	855	1,185	27,449
333	320	865	1,185	26,584
334	310	875	1,185	25,709
335	300	885	1,185	24,824
336	290	895	1,185	23,929
28th year total	$ 4,131	$10,089	$14,220	

Exhibit C-3 Continued

Monthly payment	Interest paid	Prin-cipal paid	Total pay-ment	Total princi-pal due (bal-ance)
337	$ 279	$ 906	$ 1,185	$23,023
338	269	916	1,185	22,107
339	258	927	1,185	21,180
340	247	938	1,185	20,242
341	236	949	1,185	19,293
342	225	960	1,185	18,333
343	214	971	1,185	17,362
344	203	982	1,185	16,380
345	191	994	1,185	15,386
346	180	1,005	1,185	14,381
347	168	1,017	1,185	13,364
348	156	1,029	1,185	12,335
29th year total	$ 2,626	$11,594	$14,220	
349	$ 144	$ 1,041	$ 1,185	$11,294
350	132	1,053	1,185	10,241
351	119	1,066	1,185	9,175
352	107	1,078	1,185	8,097
353	94	1,091	1,185	7,006
354	82	1,103	1,185	5,903
355	69	1,116	1,185	4,787
356	56	1,129	1,185	3,658
357	43	1,142	1,185	2,516
358	29	1,156	1,185	1,360
359	16	1,169	1,185	191
360	2	127	193[b]	
30th year total	$ 893	$12,271	$13,164	

[b] The total monthly payment for the 360th month is short because the earlier payments were rounded off upward.

Exhibit C-4 Recapitulation — Annual payments on a $100,000 loan at 14 percent interest over thirty years

Yearly payment	Interest paid	Principal paid	Total payment
1	$ 13,985	$ 235	$ 14,220
2	13,950	270	14,220
3	13,909	311	14,220
4	13,862	358	14,220
5	13,810	410	14,220
6	13,748	472	14,220
7	13,679	541	14,200
8	13,597	623	14,220
9	13,503	717	14,220
10	13,397	823	14,220
11	13,274	946	14,220
12	13,133	1,087	14,220
13	12,969	1,251	14,220
14	12,782	1,438	14,220
15	12,567	1,653	14,220
16	12,318	1,902	14,220
17	12,033	2,187	14,220
18	11,708	2,512	14,220
19	11,330	2,890	14,220
20	10,902	3,318	14,220
21	10,405	3,815	14,220
22	9,836	4,384	14,220
23	9,181	5,039	14,220
24	8,430	5,790	14,220
25	7,564	6,656	14,220
26	6,580	7,640	14,220
27	5,442	8,778	14,220
28	4,131	10,089	14,220
29	2,626	11,594	14,220
30	893	12,271	13,164
Total	$325,544	$100,000	$425,544

Bibliography

The publications listed here will be of interest to those who desire additional background on small business management. The bibliography is divided into ten parts to correspond with the chapters. Much of the material can be found in the larger libraries.

PART I OVERVIEW OF MANAGEMENT

Chapter 1 Understanding Your Management Responsibilities

Archer M., and White, J., "Starting and managing your own business." *Cost and Management*, January/February 1979, p. 40.

Burack, Elmer H., and Calero, Thomas, "Seven perils of the family firm." *Nation's Business,* January 1981, p. 62.

"Checklist for going into business." *Occupational Outlook*, Winter 1979, p. 27.

Davidson, J. P., "Small business survival tips." *Journal of Applied Management,* January/February 1980, p. 6.

Fowler, Elizabeth M., "Getting aid on starting a business." *The New York Times,* September 26, 1979, p. 19.

Graham, Roberta, "Free advice pays off for small business." *Nation's Business,* February 1979, p. 50.

Graham, Roberta, "Small business — Fighting to stay alive." *Nation's Business,* July 1980, p. 33.

Greenwood, Ronald G., "Management by objectives: As developed by Peter Drucker, assisted by Harold Smiddy." *Academy of Management Review*, April 1981, p. 225.

Gumpert, David E., "Future of small business may be brighter than portrayed." *Harvard Business Review*, July/August 1979, p. 170.

"Heaven help small business." *Nation's Business*, June 1979, p. 30.

"How small companies can survive hard times." *U. S. News and World Report*, May 19, 1980, p. 76.

"How to start a sideline business." *Business Week*, August 6, 1979, p. 94.

Immel, Richard A., "Small business innovators feel stymied by bureaucracy, big-business timidity." *Wall Street Journal*, March 25, 1980, p. 17.

Ingle, K. D. "New lures for new business." *Venture*, April 1980, p. 46.

Jacobs, Sanford L., "Being small can be a big advantage for business coping with bad times." *Wall Street Journal*, March 13, 1980, p. 18.

Jacobs, Sanford L., "Getting outside management can be difficult — but rewarding." *Wall Street Journal*, January 19, 1981, p. 21.

Jacobs, Sanford L., "Operating a franchise often pays, but demands on buyer are great." *Wall Street Journal*, November 3, 1980, p. 33.

Lundborg, Louis B., "Survival of women-owned businesses." *Industry Week*, October 27, 1980, p. 136.
Scharff, Edward E., "Starting a business the easy way." *Money*, November 1979, p. 58.
Weaver, V. "How government helps small business in the U. S. A.," *Director*, February 1980, p. 47.

Chapter 2 Functions of a Manager

Fowler, Elizabeth M., "Learning to start a business." *The New York Times*, September 5, 1979, p. 17.
Harris, Marlys, "Working hard to make fortune smile." *Money,* May 1979, p. 98.
Levine, Bonnye, "How to investigate a franchise investment opportunity as a woman," *Barrons*, July 28, 1980, p. 52.
Schiro, Anne M., "Learning the basics of the boutique business." *The New York Times*, February 4, 1980, p. 17.
"SEC help for small companies." *Business Week*, May 7, 1979, p. 119.

PART II AREAS OF RESPONSIBILITY

Chapter 3 Legal Requirements

Daugherty, W. K., "The limited partnership — A financing vehicle." *Journal of Small Business Management*, April 1980, p. 55.
Reich, P., "Staying ahead of the regulation game." *Inc.*, April 1980, p. 92.
Seixas, Suzanne, "Singin' the bankruptcy blues." *Money*, November 1980, p. 150.

Chapter 4 Production

Buckley, William M., "In buying that first computer, some homework can be crucial." *Wall Street Journal*, October 6, 1980, p. 37.
"Computer trims costs, boosts efficiency: Transland Inc." *Modern Office Procedures*, November 1979, p. 63.
Edmunds, Stahrl W., "Performance measures for small businesses." *Harvard Business Review*, January/February 1979, p. 173.
Maloney, W. J., "Fighting off the import threat." *Inc.*, July 1980, p. 51.
Mark, Kindley, "The computerization of small business." *Colorado Business*, January 1981, p. 38.
"Small business computers." *Modern Office Procedures*, September 1980, p. 108.

Chapter 5 Marketing

Chapin, H., "Why my bike shop sees 20 percent rise in profits this year." *Marketing Times*, May/June 1980, p. 35.
Hodges, L. H., "The challenge to small business — Export your products." *Vital Speeches*, February 15, 1980, p. 282.
Pezeshkpur, Changiz, "Growing concerns — Systematic approach to finding export opportunities." *Harvard Business Review*, September/October 1979, p. 182.

"Profits made to measure." *Time*, January 25, 1981, p. 53.

Runde, Robert, "Nothing succeeds like selling success." *Money*, December 1979, p. 72.

Taylor, Thayer C., "Marketing in small companies: A fine time for Timeplex." *Sales and Marketing Management*, February 5, 1979, p. 33.

Chapter 6 Financial Requirements

Arenson, Karen W., "New Merrill-Lynch aims: Small business lending." *The New York Times*, November 14, 1980, p. 25.

Belt, Brian, "Working capital policy and liquidity for small business." *Journal of Small Business Management*, July 1979, p. 43.

Binks, M., "Expansion in the small firm: Some problems of finance." *Planned Innovation*, January/February 1980, p. 27.

Brandenberg, M., "Can your client make good on franchising?" *Accountancy*, April 1980, p. 32.

"Cheap money for small business." *Business Week*, November 1, 1980, p. 33.

Crittenden, Ann, "Ways to insure flow of funds (Interview with Morton Collins of Venture Capital Association)." *The New York Times*, December 9, 1980, p. 28.

Dallow, R. P., "Audit requirements of small companies." *The Accountant*, January 31, 1980, p. 142.

Davison, I. H., "The new auditing standards and the smaller company." *Accountancy*, April 1979, p. 60.

Doctors, Samuel I., and Wokutch, Richard, "SBA lending patterns in nine metropolitan areas." *Journal of Small Business Management*, July 1979, p. 53.

English, J., "Audit exemptions for small companies." *Accountancy*, September 1979, p. 129.

"Financial vise grips small business." *Business Week*, March 3, 1980, p. 22.

Fitch, J. H., "SBA's proposed size standards — A new light in the darkness." *National Public Accountant*, May 1980, p. 14.

Gilman, D., "How five new business owners solved their credit problems." *Professional Report*, March 1979, p. 17.

Grablowsky, Bernie J., and Burns, William L., "The application of capital allocation techniques by small business." *Journal of Small Business Management*, July 1980, p. 50.

Halverson, Guy, "High interest rates, inflation hit small business extra hard." *Christian Science Monitor*, February 27, 1980, p. 11.

Hewitt, G., "The interest rate crunch." *International Management*, May 1980, p. 41.

Jacobs, Sanford L., "Where entrepreneurs get start-up cash." *Wall Street Journal*, November 24, 1980, p. 29.

Jacobs, Sanford L., "Where new venture capital is likely to go." *Wall Street Journal*, January 12, 1981, p. 21.

"Maximum interest fee on guaranteed loans is boosted by the SBA." *Wall Street Journal*, September 24, 1979, p. 17.

"More banks give small firms a break." *Industry Week*, January 26, 1981, p. 92.

Mottershead, A., "Smaller company audits — The case for retention." *Accountancy*, November 1979, p. 61.

Nelson, Susan, "SBA investigates loans to bookstores, publishers." *Publishers Weekly*, November 7, 1980, p. 13.

Popell, Steven D., "Effectively manager receivables to cut costs." *Harvard Business Review*, January/February 1981, p. 58.

Rankin, Deborah, "Small business capital search." *The New York Times*, April 8, 1980, p. 62.

Roberts, Guy C., "Seven ways to land a loan." *Nation's Business*, June 1980, p. 62.

Scharff, Edward E., "Worry that enough is not enough." *Money*, December 1979, p. 96.

Seixas, Suzanne, "Investing money but no time." *Money*, November 1979, p. 64.

Sherwood, K., "Why the small company needs the auditor." *Accountancy*, July 1979, pp. 55 – 56.

Simon, E., "Standardized audit procedures in the smaller practice." *Accountancy*, January 1979, p. 73.

"Small business aid is urged." *The New York Times*, May 16, 1980, p. 5.

Sloan, Don, "Collecting bad debts." *Dallas Magazine*, April 1980, p. 82.

"Those small business blues." *Time*, May 5, 1980, p. 84.

Tuhy, Carrie, "Out of the frying pan into the black." *Money*, November 1979, p. 74.

"What it takes to get a loan from the Small Business Administration." *Professional Report*, January 1980, p. 12.

Wichtman, Henry Jr., "Guidelines for obtaining an SBA business loan." *Journal of Small Business Management*, April 1979, p. 36.

Wucinich, W., "How to finance a small business." *Management Accounting*, November 1979, p. 16.

Chapter 7 Personnel

Dailey, R. C., and Reuschling, T. E., "Human resource management in the family-owned company." *Journal of General Management*, Spring 1980, p. 49.

Lohr, Steve, "Small business job role highlighted." *The New York Times*, January 18, 1980, p. 21.

Patrick, Thomas, "Employees as a source of funds." *Journal of Small Business Management*, October 1980, p. 55.

Chapter 8 Insurance

Gristmacher, Wendy, "Small insurance agencies may be going the way of the corner grocery." *Christian Science Monitor*, July 11, 1980, p. 11.

PART III THE PERSONAL FACTOR — YOU

Chapter 9 Leadership

Frohman, A. L., and Ober, S. P., "Establishing leadership — How to analyze and deal with the basic issues." *Management Review*, April 1980, p. 46.

Hayes, T. L., "Operation enterprise — Business leadership by example." *Management Review*, September 1979, p. 2.

Holt, Donald D., "The hall of fame for business leadership." *Fortune*, March 23, 1981, p. 105.

"Leadership development — step by step." *Association Management*, October 1979, p. 53.

Mowday, R. T., "Leader characteristics, self-confidence, and methods of upward influence in organizational decision situations." *Academy of Management Journal*, December 1979, p. 709.

Scanlan, B. K., "Managerial leadership in perspective: Getting back to basics." *Personnel Journal*, March 1979, p. 168.

Schlueter, J. F., "The 1980s: Leadership on trial." *Vital Speeches*, June 15, 1980, p. 537.

Stratton, D. J., "How to be a successful leader." *Association Management*, November 1979, p. 26.

Stratton, D. J., "The leader sets the tone." *Association Management*, June 1980, p. 9.

Weihrich, H., "How to change a leadership pattern." *Management Review*, April 1979, p. 26.

Zierden, W. E., "Leading through the follower's point of view." *Organizational Dynamics*, Spring 1980, p. 27.

Chapter 10 Managing Your Business Time Wisely

Barrett, F. D., "Tilting at time." *Business Quarterly*, Spring 1979, p. 54.

Bensahel, J. G., "Getting the best out of your time." *International Management*, June 1979, p. 67.

Bobys, Harold J., "How well you plan your time can be one of the most important aspects of your ability to be a manager." *Administrative Management*, February 1979, p. 100.

Bond, B., "Getting more for your time." *National Public Accountant*, March 1980, p. 7.

Harbaugh, N. R., and Rue, L. W., "Do you have time to manage your time?" *Business*, March/April 1980, p. 19.

Hill, W. D., "Planning's voyage through time." *Managerial Planning*, July/August 1980, p. 27.

Lane, C., "Beating time to meet objectives." *Personnel Management*, March 1980, p. 36.

Lundborg, Louis B., "Manage thyself." *Industry Week*, December 8, 1980, p. 128.

MacColl, T. A., "How to use your time more efficiently." *Practical Accountant*, August 1980, p. 58.

Meyer, Paul J., "Make every moment count." *Sales and Marketing Management*, March 17, 1980, p. 48.

Index